Praise for *Fat*

"Sort of reminds me of *The Wealthy Barber,* by Chilton. Ireland does a good job of creating an enjoyable, readable story that teaches at the same time. The reader engages with the hero, lives a bit of his life, and starts to understand what existence can be like for those afflicted with morbid obesity. More than this, someone struggling can find a personal path towards better health. I loved his writing style, and his message."

—Chris Cobourn, MD, CEO and Medical Director, SmartShape, Mississauga, Ontario, Canada.

"Fat" is a great story providing clarity to a complex issue. Overweight and obesity is a worldwide phenomenon, striking areas even traditionally felt to be isolated from the hub of urban life, areas in remote little corners. Ireland sheds light on factors influencing the obesity epidemic. The medical information in "Fat" is interesting and presented well but there's more to this read: the struggles in the life of a morbidly obese person we get to know. The stigma. His fight to change and assume a better life. Barriers to change can be surmounted more effectively when clearly understood, and Ireland helps the reader do just that!"

—Paul Hardy, MD, General Surgeon, Red Deer, Alberta, Canada.

Obesity and overweight is not a North American problem. I've been fortunate enough to see a lot of the world. During my work in different capacities in the US and Canada, to Brazil, to even the Amazon, and across four different continents, obesity has been a constant. A constant factor in my consulting work in disease prevention and health economics, in risk analysis, in my one on one patient work, in the ICU, in pain management, just simply in life.

No country gets a badge, an award of merit. There is no shining example of how to tackle this societal affliction. "Fat," Ron Ireland's book, tackles the tough stuff. Yes, there is medical information. Good information that can help one afflicted. But more than that, this is a story. A story about prejudice. About routine. About pulling one's self out of old regimes, and starting anew.

I've known Ron from medical school. His dedication and caring for others is admirable and makes him superbly qualified as an author on the subject. More than a book, he has written for all of us a call to courage and action.

—Dariush Akhavan, MD, M. Public Health,
Brasilia, Brazil.

Medicine, in N. America, is basically dealing with excess. Too much tobacco, too much alcohol, too much leisure time, too much rest, too much...food. Just too much. These factors, taken together, produce a deadly, toxic brew. And we're all just reeking of it.

Perhaps that's an oversimplification. Or is it? Take away the toxins, take away our proclivity to sit and stare at video screens, take away the excess food and alcohol...just think. What would we have?

Utopia?

Certainly less hospitals. Clinics. Doctors. Taxes. And less grief, less tears.

Fat tackles obesity and overweight. And a lot of its ripple effect. Stigma. Prejudice. And the simple loss of life. Too many of us, consumed with consuming, desperate to just rest our weary bones after a day glued to the video screen, are slowly dying.

Diabetes. Heart disease. Stroke. Osteoarthritis. Cancer. All nails in our collective coffins...

Read how one man found his way out. Discovered living again.

Read "Fat." I think it just may make a difference.

—A. S. C. Lam, MD, internal medicine, Grimsby, Ontario, Canada.

In 1986, the prevalence of obesity in the USA was 10%. By 2010, this had risen to over 35% while an additional 33% were overweight. More than 2/3 of us are now overweight or obese with serious complications that we all know about. How is it that being overweight or obese is now so common and has become normalized in our society?

"Fat" is not just another book about the obesity epidemic. This is the story of Desmond whose onset of obesity was in childhood. As we accompany him to young adulthood, we glean a deeper understanding of the day-to-day struggles and the stigma faced by an obese individual. The doctor-patient relationship between Des and his family physician over two decades allows Dr. Ireland to translate much of the existing theory and science related to obesity in an easily digestible manner. The story of Des artfully shifts and enhances our understanding of why successful weight loss and reduction of related risks is so much more than "eat less, move more." As Des finds some answers, a path towards better health is illuminated. Novice or expert will appreciate the insights offered in this book.

—Connie Deline, MD, integrative medicine, Camp Hill, Pennsylvania, USA.

FAT

FAT

RONALD M. IRELAND, MD

ISBN: 978-0-692-90016-1 (pbk)
ISBN: 978-0-692-90017-8 (hbk)

Library of Congress Control Number: 2017945896

Cut to the Chase Publishing
P.O. Box 43
Powell, OH, 43035

For my father: the consummate family man, who by leaving us too early left big shoes to fill and a hole in our lives.

And for my mother, who at eighty-six is still walking that tissue box she calls a dog...

And of course for Shelley, Brenna, Kevin and Craig... Gasp...and for Hershey!

...no suggestion is worth a damn until someone takes it...

Yapko, M.

CONTENTS

NOTE TO THE READER

Authors could call the format of this book a *Trojan Horse.* It is a work of fiction, written around a semi-academic treatise on overweight and obesity. Why go to all the trouble? The story is meant to make the information go down easier... Multiple references can be found throughout the book and are listed at the back by author in alphabetical order. The story here however serves to answer the question, *"Why does the suggestion to eat less, and move more not work?"* All the characters, organizations and events in this book are either used fictitiously, or are the products of my imagination.

The scientific, health related materials presented here are as accurate as I can make them at the time of writing, to my level of understanding as a family physician in practice now for almost 30 years. Medicine changes and evolves, at times with an incredible speed. As this book goes to print, some of the information will already be antiquated. Medical colleagues, please forgive any incompleteness, or shortcoming in understanding. I have done my best to address a topic with a burgeoning literature. Thanks to those physicians and researchers that have given me pithy feedback on the science and have improved the product.

Science changes, opinions evolve, yet the basics, the bones and the essence, will remain the same.

Readers take careful note: I'm a family physician. That does NOT mean in any way that I am *your* physician, nor that anything within these pages is *even implying* personal medical advice. I hope that this book makes you think and see things differently. I pray that with reading this, a spark is struck deep inside you, that things in the shadow have more form, that a light has been turned on.

With these new, blossoming ideas, go *straight to your doctor.* If you are morbidly obese, suffering from obesity, or overweight, you need personal medical advice. By all means, challenge your physician. With knowledge gained here, you can achieve a new vantage point, a perspective on the problem that will allow you a fibrous, meaningful interaction *with your doctor.*

Because it's NOT just diet. Or exercise. Or where you're living. Or your genetics. Or your stress level. Or your family habits, your concept of health, or beauty.

It's all of it. And more. Helping someone tackle their weight problem involves rendering assistance in *living life.* Only with help in *perception,* and *performance,* will one *prevail.* Not by carrying a tote of parts, pieces, nuts and bolts.

There's simply too much *thread analysis* going on. When the problem is in *the fabric.*

Eat less, and move more. It falls off the lips of every physician. You'll hear it. Be prepared, engage and ask for some specific direction, for you. People are unique; good health care requires an individualized approach, from a personal physician.

WHICH, unless you are one of my patients, IS NOT ME. If you are one of my patients, you still need an *individualized approach. See me in clinic!*

This text is merely informational. It does NOT purport to suggest treatment, or treat anyone or anything, but endeavours to TEACH.

I hope you like Desmond. The website he suggests, Defy-the-Lie.com, will bring you to ronireland.com. You can follow him on Instagram, obrien.desmond.

Connect at ronireland.com, where you can find his artwork, a link for email and details about upcoming courses on Teachable, like The Emergence Procol: Adipose.

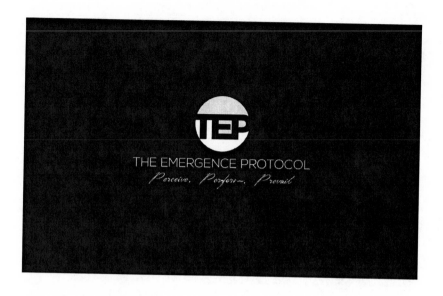

THE INFORMATION IN THIS VOLUME IS NOT IN-
TENDED AS A SUBSTITUTE FOR CONSULTATION WITH
HEALTHCARE PROFESSIONALS.

EACH INDIVIDUAL'S HEALTH CONCERNS SHOULD
BE EVALUATED BY A QUALIFIED PROFESSIONAL. See
your physician!

Life seems to just...catch.

Not unlike the ember, dull red, glowing brighter with a gust, touching dry tinder.

Or like streptococcus, floating in its aerosol, encountering some moist nasal mucosa. One becomes two. Then 4, 8, 16, 32, 64, 128, 256, 512, 1024...

It occurs in almost every aspect, from dress, to mood, to even ideas. Bell bottom pants and platform shoes have given way to tattoos, waves of style that affect every societal niche. Ink that was once a diagnostic sign of antisocial personality disorder is now commonplace, and on the back of your pastor's neck.

One person in a family, through biology or lack of adaptive life skills becomes depressed. Perspective on circumstance blurs, warps, and morphs into a pair of spectacles that misinforms. Interaction with other family members warps their view of reality, and mental top sheets become distorted.

Depression catches. Just like mood in a party, when that certain someone shows up.

Habits. One cigarette is taken to be cool in front of some friends. Noxious fumes! A stupid mistake. Then it comes with coffee. After meals. Turning the key in the ignition. One after the other. Soon it's yellow teeth, fingers and sputum. And the ER.

Tea gets thrown into the harbour. Ideas. New cognitions can spread on the wind like absolute wildfire. Suddenly farmers, armed with hoes and picks take on and beat the world's most advanced armed forces.

How long did the wheel take to spread? From that first person, recognizing their sledge could roll on logs...

Nothing looks more inviting than maneuvers to save exertion. Except a bed, of course. And a sandwich that's triple-stuffed, held together with a toothpick?

What looks better than that?

Overweight and obesity has been identified as one of the most pressing health care issues, and termed an epidemic.

Life... catches.

CHAPTER ONE

The schoolyard dirt bit into Desmond's head.

Early September sun, still hot, seared his bare skin.

The preceding tussle had left his shirt yanked half over his head, now chafing under his arms.

The sweat made it worse. Sweat trickled down his sides, into his eyes, his pits, stung, off his nose. Damp underwear, rolled right up between his glutes like usual, like what else is new, was merely distant background noise. Seemed to fit right in with the hoots, chants, cheers and jeers...

...the abrasions, and probable contusions. They were trying, gotta give them that.

Hoarse screams, but not his. From not just bystanders, but participants, egging them on, hollering at the top of their lungs, bloodlust. Typical. Not one had stood up, or likely would. Was the teacher absolutely stone deaf? Sheep. Lemmings? But then, you could lead them off a cliff or something. Nice.

Brains of s—t. S—t for brains. There was just too many of them, thugs and S—t-heads. Not that the thugs weren't S—t-heads.

Ugh.

As if you could pick where. This time, gravel. Not the best surface. And his head was taking the brunt of it, with this stupid turtle maneuver.

Well, forehead. Teachers, parents and PTA committees. Really. Like they really knew the score, what it was like, out in the yard.

But he had had it. The meetings, the grilling, the accusations. His fault. Always seems he started it, or had something to do with it. Once on the label stuck, riveted on his record, tattooed on his ass, from primary to elementary school and now district to district. Worse, pinned smack on his chest with big blinking neon lights. So, he was determined to turtle like they taught him until it was over.

At least they wore Nike Airs.

Physics. Idiots. What did they think they were going to accomplish?

Oof. Where was that stupid teacher? It was always like this. Things might look different at different schools. Layout, baseball diamonds. Superficialities. But always the same thing. Him, on this side of the schoolyard. Teacher on the f—ing other.

Oof. Bastards.

Oof. Airs were going to stick in his head. *Just do it.* Right.

Oof. Not a word. Wouldn't give them that. But the air, the air always found a way out.

"Turtle, will you? Just drop on your knees and f—ing turtle, will you? Get UP, FAT BOY!!"

Keebler, then DEE-kew. One side, then the other. Left. Right. Beating their brand new kicks into his flanks, one side, then the other, then the other. And another.

He wondered if he was going to grace YouTube again tonight, and how long it would take to get removed. Violence, you see. Kids are innocent. Right. Puppy dogs and kittens. Can't show the world how it is, you know, gotta clean up those downloads. Probably even got it from different angles. Maybe some zoom shots. Maybe some special editing. A video collage, even. And the title: *Fat Boy gets his? Summer fun? How to Flip a Turtle?* Brief YouTube glory. He could have had his own channel, an underground star.

"You just come to our town, come into our class, and think you can laugh at our names? Desmond? What kind of name is Desmond?"

Oof. Maybe, *Desmond Gets His.*

He could just see them in his mind's eye. The mad glint in theirs. Sunlight holding one in garish silhouette. The other in Hi Def, face contorted, sneer, flushed. T-shirts emblazoned with skulls, motorbikes, surfboards, toughie wannabes.

Keebler and DEE-kew. Like he was able to stop from laughing at those names. Keebler, sure, cookies, but weren't they supposed to be elves? Little people? Like who's he calling fat boy?

"ROLL! Roll, FAT BOY! ROLL!"

Oof. New strategy. Both on one side. Showing they had three, instead of two neurons. Where was that goddamn teacher? One more minute, he was going to just go nuclear, and then they'd be sorry.

OOF. Ok, that's it. Must have looked like...a bruised, beached whale.

No, a sub run aground. Could just visualize the two keys turning, could just feel the grim, steely determination on the bridge. Resolve built. Teeth grit. Strategy laid.

Enough.

Sometimes. Sometimes it just had to be. And hey, everyone was expecting it, right? What use is a label if you just ignore it and act otherwise?

OOOF. This time, one Nike shoe, and its foot, was HIS.

* * *

"Desmond. DESMOND! What did we talk about? DESMOND!!"

Everything hurt. Forehead, knees, elbows, kidneys, intercostals, testicles. The fluorescents grabbed his eyelids and pierced the frontal lobes, ice picks. The voice roared, moaned, warped.

He spat out a tooth. Chin spittle. Things seemed to stabilize, a bit. Distorted wails became discernible words.

"We can't keep moving, Desmond! Braden is just starting to get some nice friends! Moving, because of you? YOU! Couldn't you control yourself, just keep your head down until the teacher came?"

Guessed that was mom. Of course. Good old mom.

Seemed there was a matching hole on both sides of his upper gums. His tongue snaked from one, to the other. One, then the other. Just like DEE-kew and Keebler. Maybe he'd name them.

Name the sockets. Which one was the bleeder? DEE-kew. He bled more. The new hole was DEE-kew.

He started to laugh, remembering his thought that Nike Airs were going to stick in his head…

They did, didn't they?

Names. This time, it was names that did it. It was supposed to be just sticks and stones. Laugh? Humph. There was the real joke. It was always the names. Sticks, stones, any day.

Names always really bit hard.

Desmond. They didn't like his name. Everyone there had names. There were Stilts, Bubbles, "The Groove." Dudster, Roadster, Wench. Cool names. All of them.

2-Gulp. He was the biggest. Used to be called Big. Until he did two of them and became an instant celebrity. Keebler and DEE-kew were his henchmen, despite the different leanings. Gulp was the class boss. He figured out the names.

And Desmond was going to be called, wait for it, "The ROLL."

The flashback rolled in quickly.

He had actually thought he could sit in the desk, one of those with the seat attached. It was one of the old style ones. Lift up the hinged, inked up, defaced working surface to look inside. Bigger than most, he was sure he could do it. Sure he could fit. But he couldn't, even with the added velocity. And the desk tipped over. 2-Gulp must have made a big splash by downing two of them. Desmond? He did it, literally. ROLLED it. The really big, splashy class entrance.

Tidal wave.

"DESMOND!!!"

"Mom, you're really upset. I'm sure seeing your son bleeding isn't helping. I've got to start plucking out all these little stones, then he'll need some sutures. Not pleasant to watch. Why don't you go get a coffee, and come back in 30? Des and I will do just fine. Nurse, could you please take mom out in the hall, or the waiting room? This isn't helping."

He seemed like a nice enough guy. Sure enough, greens. White coats were for TV. Salt and pepper hair, with a kid primed to do the work. Seemed kind of nervous, that one. Hoped his goddamned hands wouldn't shake.

"2% without?" Pimples, give a guy a break. How old was this plebe?

He nodded, "5-0 for the face, he's a guy. Right, guy?"

Yes. Of course he was a guy. Prick.

"Use some xylocaine viscous for the road burn. We should try to stick that tooth in until he can get to a dentist, hopefully today. That cut there, will need some chromic, right?" Felt fingers demonstrate on his face.

"Think it's metabolic? Endocrine?"

"Nah, chip off the old block."

Mom. He was talking about his mom.

Bastard.

* * *

Birthdays were always at Ronnie's place, with the big golden arches out front. In those days, Ronnie was the big deal with all his buds, and he was actually there, not just on the tube. Almost life size, sitting his synthetic self on a bench right there by the cash. Expression kinda plastic. Well, fibreglass. There was the burger masked dude and some other characters that fade from memory. Neat little kits of food, complete with a pretty cool prize. Lots of ketchup and free refills from the fountain.

All the kids met at the house, then got tucked into the family station wagon. Big round headlights, enormous wing taillights, a virtual ocean liner that rocked from side to side on sloppy shocks, as if regularly hit broadside by waves. He would usually sit up front with his favourite bud of the day, bench seats, no belts worn. Ashtrays actually used, a butt hanging out of Dad's mouth, billows of smoke out the stack. Well, most of it. Gag. Bygone days. Yell and scream at passers-by, hang over the bow to just get some air, tongues protruded.

Mom learned to pre-order. What sensible adult would want to deal with a flocking gaggle of gigglers hovering over the counter, with puzzled fingers stuck up their noses? She would go around to each kid before we boarded the land cruiser, pencil with well used eraser in hand. Little private talks. Knew the menu by heart, of course, what mom didn't? Not much choice though, basically burger, with or without toppings, or chunks of chicken, or whatever. He started to get mad about that, these little private tête-à-têtes, probably jealousy, but, hey, Mom knew Des. No need for a private one on one.

Mom would march up to the counter, talk right over Mr. Acne at the cash and get the manager herself. Rapid nods of under-standing, the whole thing pre planned. Somehow we usually got an entire corner of the place to ourselves. One year there was an actual janitorial cleaning cart floating beside the table before we even got to it, a barricade to navigate other people away.

Or...maybe it was there for more obvious reasons...

I remembered the little paper bag of fries, the burger with little dabs of ketchup, mustard, relish, sitting on a slice of processed cheese. Filling up tiny tubs with little red gobs of paint, reaching up, pumping the machine once too often, and then tables all to ourselves, with mom down on the far end. And knowing that this was the place. The cool place. Just ours. Our place was just neat, all in itself.

Why would you go anywhere else for a birthday?

Part of that pre-party connection with the manager was to get the okay, so Mom could bring the double chocolate triple layer cake. It was sort of frowned upon. Guess they wanted all the kids to eat apple pies. Kids, eat apple pies? Come on.

Birthdays would always bring back the fond images. Sunbeams slanting through the glass, Styrofoam and paper bags. The sugar high, grease slide, swamp water. Half orange, quarter coke and splash of pepper. Next time Canada Dry, Fanta and whatever, the grosser the better.

And Schwartz spewing it all over his sister.

Those were the days. Can't get better than that.

* * *

"Desy, please just hold still. It's only one, just one!" Mom's eyes could really bug out. That left one had a little fleshy bulgy red thing, right next to that central coloured part...the iris. It seemed bigger now...

And Des. Des was planted on the exam table, an obstinate monolith. Could say he wasn't moving. Wasn't moved. Pretty stuck.

"Actually mom, it's two vaccines; we reviewed this. He's really behind. Sorry. Remember?" Oh yes, the voice from above. Right.

"Two? My poor Desy! Can't you mix 'em up? Just get a bigger needle, shake it up?"

"No, sorry. Good idea, though, eh, Desmond?" Smooth. Very smooth. Smooth as glass.

He was big. Fake smile. Big Fake Smile.

Had him worried. Not that big, not big enough. This was Desmond, after all. Physics. It struck him that usually doctors don't do this. Vaccines? Nursing business. Said nurse was right behind the doc, peering over his shoulder.

"DESMOND!!!"

They were his first squash. Wasn't that hard, just tip, aim and plant.

Ugh. Double ugh.

"He fell! He just fell! I'm so sorry! You 'K? Doc? Maisy?"

Ragged breath, stiff face, and Doc walked right out. Victory. He probably knew it. Monoliths don't tip easy. Maisy was tougher. She stood there with hands on her hips, hair mussed. And glared.

"Desy. That man is trying to help you. Maisy is trying to help you! Apologize!"

Well, two can glare. Little sterile glass bottles glinted on the counter. They were glaring, too.

Little wooden paddles, cotton balls, tongue depressors. A little kid scale. The black blood pressure thing on the wall. Even a fridge, lots of ammo if he decided to go postal.

Mom must have seen those eyes pick up potential targets.

"Desmond! A chocolate shake and some Timbits! Right after this! I promise!" Well, look at that chin quiver. Had her.

OK. Well, it was close…

"Harvey's, it's a burger, a big one, and one of their shakes. And Timbits? Give me a break. That was five years ago…"

"Desmond?" Mom looked a bit…nonplussed. Come on. Where did she live?

"What are you waiting for? You've got your deal… do it."

* * *

Mom so carefully opened the envelope from school, winking. Quite official, 8 x 10 brown, *to the parents of Desmond O'Brien…*

The paring knife surgically worked its way down, the slender edge allowing access without damaging either the precious contents, or the official scotch tape, or the official stamps. It was all to be kept together for posterity, likely in some high tech time capsule, knowing mom. They were all seated at the dining room table, that table used only for Easter, Christmas or some huge occasion. Which is what this was.

It had become a tradition. The long drawn out drama. There were term events, but the end of the year, that was a big deal. Or rather, the big deal. Drawing the paper out with apparent trepidation, the deliberate unfolding, the indrawn breath. A weighty pause, the due consideration, the mulling over.

Oh, come on, GIVE A GUY A BREAK. A big, great big, BIG FREAKING BREAK.

Des shifted a bit in his chair, rested his feet on the floor, and took a deep breath. He kept his eyes focused on a particle of dust, turning and sparkling in a sunbeam, and let the little drama play out.

As if everyone didn't know the score. Sure, there was, "THE DIET." Measured portions, small plates, and all the good stuff hidden at the back of the fruit cellar, in the old dinged cookie tin on the bottom shelf. Somehow it always got filled back up again. And also somehow, no one seemed to mention anything about it missing contents. So there was also, "THE GAME."

That's what Desmond called it. "THE DIET" and "THE GAME." He played ball. Ate his niggardly portion and took action afterwards. Sometimes he got legitimate dessert, especially if he choked down kale, awful despite the bacon lardons.

Open rule-smashing occurred only rarely, at certain defined moments. It was always a reward. If he came home with a shiner, and no abrasions on his knuckles that was good for real smash. DQ, or barbecued hotdogs, or pizza for dinner. Holding a door open for Mrs. Kinsey-Smith, the disabled lady next door, that was another, but not so big. Maybe a gum ball or something. But tests, that's where the real meat was. Report cards. The cream of the crop. The flippin' candy floss.

Of course it was good. The response seemed honest. Mom truly loved that Desi was smart.

Yes, he was smart. Gotta be in this world. Gotta be when you're like him, peg-holed. You know, like everyone hates. Everyone was, but everybody hated it. Gotta be to make it, gotta be to just be, to survive.

"What's it tonight, big boy? Eh, Des? You know how good this is? You've been put in advanced classes! You've won the English award!!! This is way more than Ronnie's place, this time. What is it tonight, huh?"

It's what he'd been working for all year. It was a drive, but oh so worth it. The whole family liked this place, but Des felt his soul here. He fit. Gravel parking lot with pot holes, smoker out back. Picnic tables out front for overflow. Jukebox. Cheap neon. Old style shake blenders, real hard ice cream, and malt if you can believe it. White table cloths over laminate. Elvis, Sammy Davis Jr. and Sinatra on the walls. A surfboard on the ceiling.

Real, honest to God, chocolate malts. Made with hard ice cream, in a mint green 1940's blender. So big they filled up the glass, put whipped cream on top and cherry, and gave you the metal cup they whipped it up in. Half full itself! Like two shakes!

Brisket, pulled pork, ribs, fried chicken. And all of it on an *around the world plate*, where you could try it all. Baked beans, fresh biscuits as big as your fist and homemade pie for dessert. Pies he'd never heard of, like Mississippi mud, Derby, flapper, or even peanut butter!

And servings so big most people took home doggie boxes. Crates. On wagons.

Most people.

Yes, gotta be smart. Gotta read that thesaurus, read the dictionary, do your homework. Gotta stay on top, gotta watch over your shoulder. When you were like Desmond.

Fat. It was more than a thing, more than an adjective, even more than an expletive. A label.

It was Desmond.

Desmond was.

Fat.

* * *

If Grandma told the story one more time, so help him. One more story about the fake Easter Bunny and how stupid it all is over here, like, Kill me now!

Yes, she used to boil eggs. Back in the old country. Yes, she'd paint them, then they'd roll them down the hill, until they cracked at the bottom. Then eat them, a picnic for heaven's sake, a goddamn picnic. In the middle of a field. Picnic basket, pack it, walk all that way, then climb the hill. Come on. Symbolic, point taken. Got it. Rolling the stone.

All this rolling stuff was getting under the skin. The nickname had stuck. For his family, he was Desmond. Desy. Des. To everyone else, the fat guy was, "The ROLL." So, he didn't appreciate all the rolling stuff. Kept thinking of himself, rolling down the hill. As if he could get his great freaking body up the hill in the first place.

No, Easter traditions had gotten better. No trekking about with wicker baskets, or hard boiled eggs for lunch. Modern eggs galore were chocolate, sometimes gooey, and not hidden real well. Then there was what came after church.

Yes, Des went to church. You see, there was THE DIET, THE GAME, and also, but of course, THE CODE. You could think of it as rules of the game, or side rules at least, versus the basic principles. THE CODE was sort of the way you just did things, the way things worked. The underlying structural underpinnings of the entire universe and galaxy. Piss mom off and GAME OVER. For God knows how long.

And anyway, there was always after Easter Sunday.

"Mrs. O'Brien, it's such a pleasure to see you here on Easter Sunday. And your family. Little Des was such a delight! I wish all the children could behave as well!"

Deacon Dick absolutely glowed. Little bow tie, hair starting at the back of his head carefully combed forward, sparsely covering his dome. Actually a checked sports coat. Des heard he sold cars downtown, busted up jalopies with a bit of new paint, sporting seriously inflated price tags. Funny what kids hear. Kids hear it all. Heard him talk once to Dad, something like, "Sunday is the Lord's day. Sunday, you play by the rules, you go to church. But Monday comes and a man has to make a living…"

Mom's chest puffed up, a bit of a flush to her cheeks. She smiled, shook the Deacon's hand. Des felt one of hers touch him behind his back.

"Desy is a good boy. Always has been. Heart of gold. This is the Lord's Day, and he's come to celebrate with us."

You mean put in dues. Ran the gauntlet outside the church doors. Cousins from the other side of the tracks, whatever that meant. Auxiliary. Handshake, handshake, kiss.

Done. Again.

Back in the ocean liner to ride the waves home. Dad and Des, two peas in a pod, monkeys two, manning the oars. Dad drove,

Des was dutiful. Daffodils were duly counted. Dad drove, so Des spotted them, little islands of yellow in the sandy sea. With every one mom became more delighted.

Last year, "Bunny" gave him a nineteen-inch masterpiece driven in all the way from Pennsylvania on the back seat of dad's car. Some perks to this salesman gig...

This year, Bunny went all out.

"Desy, I'm so proud of you. Straight A's on your spring report card, and you were an absolute angel in church! And I know you don't care about daffodils. Thank you!"

There were actual tears in mom's eyes. Oh, brother.

This year there was serious heft. Two and a half feet tall, a handmade serious masterpiece.

Now, you're talking.

Now it was just making it through the mashed potatoes, stuffing, corn, dinner rolls, meat on a stick, devilled eggs, ham, turkey and gravy. Oh, and peas. Things they didn't have in Africa. So we were determined to eat it all.

CHAPTER TWO

Dad said when he was a kid the girls did, "home ec" and the guys did, "industrial arts," or, "shop class." They went one way, the guys the other. Not anymore. "Human ecology. Family and consumer science. Skills for everyday living." Every year they called it something else. Last year you had to carry a specially marked egg around for a week to see if you could do it without smashing. Desmond's egg lasted about sixty minutes.

This year, it was a speech. Dread didn't quite cover it. Des imagined himself standing up there in front of the class, in all his enormity.

At least he could pick a topic. It had to be food related.

You learned a few things along the way, in that quest for an "A". Stick your hand up fast and volunteer first. Serious brownie points. Teachers noticed.

"Sugar!" The class laughed. Score one. Teacher was pleased at the enthusiastic volunteerism. Score two.

So, it was sugar. Thank God for the Internet. No pedalling around to the library, walking up and down the stupid aisles wasting energy trying to find outdated sources. You could just sit, concentrate, read and type. No running around. Focused. He was going to do a bang up job. Parents were going to be invited, all the schoolteachers. The actual speeches being heard in the gym, if you could believe it.

"Mom, I'm not going to wear a bow tie like Deacon Dick. I am NOT." This was thin ice, but bets were on the effect of the speech and the amount of work put into preparation. Mom fluttered about straightening his collar, tucking things, a pesky housefly on a mission. Des waved her away, or at least attempted, and thumbed through his index cards, as if he didn't have them memorized. One or two words per card, he had done the research. Just research sugar? No way. This was Desmond. He researched sugar and everything all around it. Including how to give speeches. Write it all out on the cards and you tended to just read the stupid things, head down, way too fast, no eye contact with the audience, DUD SPEECH. And he was going to WIN THIS FREAKING THING.

See, top prize was a bike. Which he had never even been on. A bike. Serious wheels, one for the girls, and one for the guys. Mrs. Herringbone had a picture of them prominently displayed beside the homework board. Sneaky. They would be right up there on stage, apparently. Podium in front, glaring spotlights, bikes behind. Sort of the whole Human Ecology thing in one image. Grave, scholarly consideration of food topics, children and community involvement, pollution free transportation, exercise, the whole freaking shebang.

And win the thing? Whole shebang leading to serious bang in the family. Serious leverage. This could even be WIN THE GAME.

Des had won the bow tie thing. Wedged between his folks, the talks wafted over his head while he waited his turn. The food pyramid. Farm to table living. Pasteurization. Interesting blurb on margarine, apparently lipids never found before in nature. What the heck were people putting into their bodies, anyway? We were all going to be turned into purple spotted alien things with antennae. Right. As if. Butter was better anyway.

Refined flour. Ok, that was the talk right before his. Heard it before in class, rehearsal day. All serious new age educational theory. Group work, do your own research, listen to the others present in rehearsal, hear it again polished, rehash the whole thing the next day, la tee dah ta dah. As if. As if Reginald, dear Reggie, was going to take that bike.

Talked to him the day before. Made it plain, that bike was his. Chrome, candy apple, eye candy. His. He saw the look in his eyes. Reg got it. After all, he was...THE ROLL. That last school move was his last. It was a name that garnered respect, gained all at once on that schoolyard and honed ever since then with a steely glare here, a lean on a desk there. Before, there was 2-Gulp. Now there was THE ROLL. Gulp didn't last long after that day. Without DEE-kew and Keebler to back him up, he was nothing. Next year went off to Nottingham Hills, the next school district.

Good riddance.

Henchmen? Who needs 'em?

What was happening? The lights went down. What the heck? Saw Mrs. Herringbone at the back with a slide projector. Oh, come on. This was not in the rubric. Right there, Desmond could see it in his mind. Not one thing on there about smoke and mirrors, electronics, or ...

Props? What was that? A table? He had bags of flour on the stage!

Desmond turned to look at Mrs. Herringbone. Fish-face. F— head. She gave him a sweet smile and gestured at the stage as if to say, "Don't look at me, your job is to listen to your classmate..."

Listen. Right. Wish that egg was still in that little pouch, could almost feel it in his fingers...

"Refined flour is a man made, corrupted, cheapened, bastardized, almost profane version of a natural..."

Bastardized? Where did he get that word? Did Fish-face allow that one? Cranked his head around, looked at her, seemed taken aback, just a bit. Profane? Serious thesaurus work here. This was shaping up to be more than a polishing of that version in class.

Lost the next few bits. Concentrate. Got to BEAT this guy. Sure, could squash him the next day. But that would still leave that bike in Reg's garage.

Images of turn of the last century gristmills, black and white, all very charming...

"... ago were built around natural, environmental circumstances and topography. Towns sprung up around falling water, where grist mills could be built, where a turning wheel could set into motion grind stones. These monstrous stones would turn against each other, grinding grain into..."

Okay. Someone had yanked this whole thing around. Des looked over his shoulder at Fish-face, and glared. As if this guy could come up with those words. What did he have, a freaking master's degree in English?

Reg was gesturing to his table, first pointing to a burlap sack, holding it up, nice obviously FAKE antique, way to go, PRISSY, then a bag of who cares grocery brand flour, like who doesn't know what a bag of flour looks like, JERK-OFF?

"...people were leaving the countryside, attracted to the urban centres for work and higher wages. It was called the Industrial Revolution..."

OK, serious trouble. He was going completely off of HOME EC and into history, pulling in stuff from other courses. Des slumped in his chair. This was A+ stuff. Fill all the rubric criteria, A. Pull in other stuff, shot at A+.

Going for it, was he? Des grit his fingernails into his palms.

"...Flour was processed in huge, centralized plants that filled bags destined for the far corners of the country, where they would sit on the shelf until..."

Now he was talking not only flour. Not only how it was made, or pulling in history. The guy was pulling in economics. Urbanization. Freaking geography and human dynamics.

"... wheat germ, high in fat, would deteriorate and destroy the flour. In essence, it would go rotten. What we have today in enriched, refined white flour is NOT real flour, but just the endosperm of the wheat grain, basically just the sugars. A lot of the natural goodness of the grain has been taken away, for the sake of shelf life. Vitamins, sure, you can add that...."

Squashing was too good for this guy. He was going to have to win this thing. Fair and square, only that would show the twerp. A little idea hatched...

Thunderous applause. Desmond clapped, and looked at Reg. Their eyes locked. Des smiled.

Reg paled.

Mrs. Herringbone turned off the projector and flustered up on stage, still clapping. "Ladies and gentlemen, Reginald Brownstone, let's hear it for some originality!"

Thunderous applause. All the junior grades were clapping, suddenly awake after sleeping through several other speakers. Brownstone. Yeah.

Mom nudged him. "You're next Des. You'll do great!"

Des eased his body mass out of the chair and moved to the side of the stage, awaiting Fish-face to beckon him forward. Which happened all too quickly.

"And here, ladies, gentlemen and esteemed judges, is Desmond O'Brien, our last speaker tonight, to talk to you about... Well, we'll let him tell you!"

Salty sweat sprung out on his forehead, heart thrashing his sternum and intercostals. Blood coursed to his cheeks, must make him look like a freaking cherry.

Des bit his tongue on the side. A taste of copper bit the back of his throat. He forced that tongue over to DEE-kew, that empty socket on the left, and remembered. Remembered what he'd been through, what made him what he was today.

Grit. They drove it into his forehead. Now, it was him. Watch this.

"Ladies and gentlemen, parents, esteemed classmates and fellow students..."

Des looked at his cards. A hook. He had to get a hook. There was no hook, no grab 'em by the ears, by their very freaking necks kind of zinger, on those three by five dog-eared recipe cards. Desperate times called for desperate measures. His heart hammering, his brow moist. Cards...it wasn't there. Looked up. They weren't going to help him much now, as he was going straight off the reservation.

I was enthralled with several of the speakers before you today. Margarine. Who would have thought of the potential problems? Imagine your cells, all bounded by phospholipid membranes, incorporating these very man made, never seen before on the planet lipids into that membrane? When we know now how dynamically active the membrane is in cell function, metabolism, communication...well, the possible implications are myriad."

Which is how Stilts should have ended his talk. Didn't even talk about the membrane, dufus. How'd you like that one, Fish-face? Myriad. How'd you like THAT? Phospholipid membranes, as if they even touched that one in biology. How's that for pull?

"And flour. I had no idea that every slice of bread, or mouthful of pasta was basically sugar. That a great deal of the nutrient value had been stripped away from the product. Sugar. Which we drink down in our Big Gulps."

And there's a nod to our dearly departed...

Des looked down at his card. The molecular structure of sugar. As if anybody gave a damn. And A+ demanded cross-links, pulling in other courses, other ways of looking at things. And that's what it was going to take to pull this thing out of the fire, out of Reg's fingers. Deep breath.

"Let me take you back to medieval times. Marco Polo travelled from Europe to Asia in the 1200's. The Silk Road brought treasures to Europe: silk yes, but also military devices, exotic animals like lions, porcelain, paper, jewels, many other things... and spices. The most valuable, lightest and easiest to transport items were preferred.

"Myself, I think transporting a lion would present some difficulties."

Des grinned and held out his arms. People chuckled, on cue.

"Before the year 1500, ladies and gentlemen, sugar was so expensive it was considered a spice. Most spices nowadays can be bought for only a few dollars. An interesting exception is saffron, which still is incredibly expensive. One would have to work many days, perhaps weeks, to buy a pound of saffron, not gold, not diamonds, but a mere spice. It's difficult to discover how much sugar cost back 500 years ago, but let me tell you, it took more than 10 minutes of work to buy a pound.

"Sugarcane has given mankind juice for many thousands of years. About 2000 years ago, actual sugar crystals were refined in India. It's quite possible that Marco Polo may have hidden sugar in the lining of his coat along with those jewels on his way back home."

Okay, veer off number one, done. And Fish-face thought he was asleep through that history class. He looked past his parents but couldn't see, stage lights fading the audience and his teacher to dim silhouettes. Big breath.

"What is sugar? Sugar is sweet. Sugar is put into things, and is in things. We modern humans get sugar out of sugarcane still, and the sugar beet. Wars were fought over land that could be used to produce this substance. It's thought that slavery was largely perpetuated because of the man-hours needed to process sugar cane.

"It's funny. Before 1500, sugar was a spice. People used honey, which is still sugar, to sweeten things. Honey was not easy to get. Until the 1800s when technology improved, you'd have to destroy a hive to get the honey out.

"Something seems to have changed. Is it that we humans want what is hard to get? Somehow, sugar became thought of as a staple food, something necessary to have in one's diet, right up there with water and potatoes."

And that was for my mom. Mom and her potatoes. Des was the peeler, the smasher, the masher. On every plate. Stories of that potato blight in Ireland every St Patty's day. Health meant potatoes. A plate without potatoes? Not in the O'Brien house!

"Currently, the yearly average intake of added sugar is about 150 pounds per person in the U.S. You may not think that's right. You may only put a bit on top of your grapefruit, or on your cereal. It's in stuff. It's put in stuff. That's where you get most of it!"

Des could hear some murmurings in the audience. Maybe push this a bit. Tell them once, then tell them again they say...

"I'm not a good example. I'm a bit heavy..."

Murmurings, chuckles....

"But most people eat their weight, per year, in sugar. Come to think of it..."

Gulp.

"Maybe I do, too." Laughter, straight out laughter. He had them!

"So where is it? Ketchup! And that's my favourite vegetable!" Absolute guffaws!!!

"But I'm getting ahead of myself. Sugar is an overall term for a number of different carbohydrates. Simple sugars are called monosaccharides, one sugar. Chains of sugars are called disaccharides if composed of 2 molecules of sugar, or oligosaccharides with longer chains of sugars."

None of the other kids had asked questions. Maybe...they seemed to be paying attention, heck, they were freaking laughing! Maybe...

"Give me a simple sugar, anybody..."

Stunned silence. They weren't expecting that one, were they!

"I have trouble seeing with these lights." Des put a hand over his eyes. "Come on, intelligent people, give me a simple sugar! Name one!"

"Sucrose!" Came out of the audience.

"GOOD! THANKS! I thought no one was going to say anything. BUT WRONG!"

Laughter. Des could just see someone stand up and bow.

"No, sucrose is table sugar. It's the natural disaccharide in fruit. It's a mixture of glucose and fructose, 50:50. These two monosaccharides are bound together. Sucrose is a disaccharide."

"Stevia!"

Desmond's dry tongue suddenly felt like one of last year's insoles: worn, cracked, and stood on way too often. Come on, what was it...something had grabbed him about that.

Suddenly the teeniest tiny sunbeam poked its ruddy finger through the nimbus.

"Stevia is sweet. Really sweet. Sweeter than sugar, but sugar it is not!"

CHAPTER TWO

It was the same guy. The one who had bowed. Probably embarrassed. "What is it then, chemicals?"

Gotta get this guy onside. "Sir, I want to thank you for helping make my talk come alive. Stevia is from a plant, and although it's been used for a long time in some areas, scientists don't know much about its action in the body. Very sweet, sweeter than table sugar, but not sugar.

"Sugar itself has a basic chemical structure with carbons and oxygens in equal number, and hydrogen twice that amount. For example, glucose has 6 carbons, oxygens and 12 hydrogens. Your body, every cell of it, uses glucose. Your liver, however, and only your liver, has the ability to use fructose. It changes fructose into glucose for the body's use. A lot of this liver processed fructose ends up in triglyceride, a fat which often plugs up your liver, and free radicals, which can hurt you. Let me stress, the body sugar, the one your body uses, is glucose. Glucose, that molecule your brain, your muscles use, is less sweet than fructose. Put them together, glucose plus fructose to make sucrose, and that's in the middle for sweetness."

"Which is great English. My apologies, Mrs. Herringbone."

"So, sweetest, fructose. That's what goes up in ripe fruit. Green unripe grapes, for example, have a lot more glucose, proportionally. Ripe grapes, more fructose than glucose. Fruit has all three: free glucose, free fructose, and sucrose, which is fructose and glucose bound together. Honey has almost entirely monosaccharides, glucose and fructose. Or I should say fructose and glucose, as there's more fructose."

Mr. Heckler, not content or assuaged in any way by the complement, or maybe truly interested and disinhibited, just would not let things go. "So who cares, glucose or fructose? Who cares?"

Fish-face moved towards the commotion.

"Mrs. Herringbone, please, it's ok. If I can't answer questions on my topic, then I don't know it very well. My friend here is letting me have a dynamic, interactive presentation!"

Applause! One clap, two, droplets of clapping built to a ripple, and then a curling wave.

Des flushed, and bowed from the waist.

"It matters, because of what happens to these monosaccharides in the body. Glucose is the basic energy molecule the body uses. Fructose goes to the liver, to be changed to glucose. Which, through processes completely above my brain level, preferentially appears to be stored as fat, those triglycerides I was talking about!

"So fructose makes you fat?" Hisses and a few chuckles. This guy was going to be with him to the very end. "What about fat itself? Doesn't eating fat go to fat?"

Des removed his jacket. This was it. Stage lights probed his eyes, beat down on his head like a mid-day's sun. The sweat was real. Arcs of sweat, vertices just above his waistband, glistened. Sweat. Sweat was him. Had been for a long time. Sweat, more than anyone else, on a summer's day. Sweat, till it drips, on a spring day. And yes, sweat in the middle of winter. Add some adrenaline and a stage.

"I'm big. I learned a lot during my research. Things I've been eating have made me what I am. Ladies and gentlemen, I may not have an audiovisual high tech presentation but, I have but one prop. Myself.

"Fat is simply a storage form of sugar. Fat is made up basically of triglycerides, long chains of sugars. If you eat fat, you're eating a storage form of sugar and some complex molecules called cholesterol. The energy your body uses, basically, is sugar. To overly generalize, and this isn't completely accurate, but only when there is no sugar, no sugar stores, no fat stores, does the body use other things for energy, like protein.

"For years, sugar intake has gone up on our planet. So has mine. Some feel that fructose goes straight to fat. Has it been the fructose rich syrups that go into the pop I drink, or just the total calories I eat that has made me this way? Don't know. Probably doctors don't know. Clearly, if you eat too much straight glucose, if you eat more than you need, it is stored as fat. Any excess sugar, glucose or fructose it matters not, any sugar not burnt up for energy, is stored as fat.

"What's clear is, that things have changed in our modern society. In order for our industrial society to make flour sit on the shelves for months, it's been refined and altered. And made less whole, less healthy. Even today's store bought whole wheat bread is highly processed. Many whole grain breads are not fully whole wheat, either. New foods, never seen before, like margarine and high fructose corn syrup, are in our refrigerators, and on our tables. What's it all going to do?

"My talk is on sugar. People like sugar. I like sugar! And we eat too much of it. A spice that has become a staple.

"What we clearly need to do, is start thinking.

"I have to start thinking."

If the clapping started as raindrops before, Desmond now witnessed a wet monsoon. As he reached down and picked up his jacket, he wondered just what he had jammed himself into.

* * *

No, he couldn't ride it. Didn't seem to matter, though. The O'Brien's drove on ahead, as Des pushed his prize home. It probably could have fit in the ocean liner, but Des wouldn't have it. Candy apple red. His. His bike. Streetlights found some sparkle. A light rain fell. Droplets stood on the frame, perfect little domes that reflected his face. He couldn't quite recognize himself.

Step by step, one at a time. Walking, it appeared, was actually exercise. He stopped and took a deep breath.

And truly saw his neighbourhood, streets he really hadn't seen before.

* * *

Coach was right behind him in line. Little guys in front, elbows, most with pants half pulled down. Leaning, posturing, and trying on life. Stainless steel troughs and Plexiglas. The cafeteria served up the usual fries, dogs, burgs, fish sticks, pizza, pop, some chili, dinner rolls. Special today was Beau-Yar-Dee ravioli. Must be some southern speciality.

Yum.

"Des! Heard you last night. You've got some serious stones."

Des looked up. Well, not that up. More over the shoulder. Enormous went in more than one direction. Raised a brow.

"I couldn't have done that. Stones, serious stones. Look, I know you've never been in gym. Looked into it this morning. Some kind of doctor's note. Look, I want you to look into this. Got a big hole in my defence. Massive. Getting killed out there."

Pretty smooth. Buzz cut. Creased forehead, laugh and worry lines. Did guys that old have muscles like that naturally? What was he on?

"Coach?"

"Des, I need you on the team. I mean, if you can move. You've got the guts. Sorry. I mean, you've got the chutzpah. You can stand up there and take it. On the line. We have a hole. A hole in the line. Defence. You'd be unstoppable. We'd be unstoppable. I'm talking maybe State, with the other guys we got."

Des flushed. Des was seldom rendered speechless. And Des DID NOT FLUSH. Holy crap.

Fries, pizza, a few slices, and … milk. Chocolate milk. For the muscles, right?

CHAPTER THREE

"Football team? You OK with this Des, Mrs. O'Brien? You were the one asking for that note again this year."

Mom's eyes could really bug out. Bug-out, neat term. Really big, but not probably compound. Not really bug eyes. Bugs have these eyes, called compound, that have hundreds of visual receptors, sticking right out there.

They had made the appointment immediately, but it was still a week ago. Daily finger wags had admonished rest until Doc gave the OK. But finally, they were there. Reception line, leave your name, take a seat, which was too bloody small. And then wait again for Doc.

"Des. Stop looking at your mom. Somebody talk to me. I'm sitting here kinda shocked."

Doc was shocked. Doc? Him? What about this guy? This guy right here, fresh off couch city. Thinking he can actually play football...

"Coach thinks I can help."

"Well, the question is, Des, whether or not you can survive this."

"Doc!" Mom dropped back into her chair, in a complete bean bag slump. Body sag, but those compound eyes kept a-bulging. "Doc!"

Interesting. It must be the carotid. That little bulgy, throbbing thing in mom's neck. Probably about, oh, a hundred, a hundred and ten.... "Mom, take it easy. If it's at all dangerous, I won't. If you don't want me to, it's ok."

SCORE. But what did that mean now? Sugarless gum?

"Look, we don't need to beat a dead horse. Sorry. Bad metaphor. Don't need to go over and over old ground. And I've got to watch my mouth. Survive this? Did I actually say that? What an idiot. Me. Hey, I'm a classically trained doctor. It seems we're trained to be idiots, throw bombshells like that. Sometimes I forget and slip up. I'm sorry.

"Des, you carry the weight of a full grown man on your shoulders. And your sneakers. And your heart. Let's just start with an exam and some blood work, and go from there. Mrs. O'Brien, do you want to wait out in the waiting room for us?"

"Seems like doctors are always asking me to take a seat, somewhere else. That's ok, Doc. You bet. Des is a young man now. Des, be straight. No smart stuff."

Smart stuff? Des? Come on.

Mom got up, actually cracked the door open before Des stopped her. The relief was painted on her face as she resumed her chair. Young man or not, she was still mom.

Des looked at Doc as the door closed, and shifted in his seat. "A full grown man, Doc? Get real."

"Well Des, I'm known for real hyperbole, but what I said was not an exaggeration. Let's measure you up, and look at some statistics."

OK. Obesity class 3. His BMI, which is Body Mass Index, or the height divided by the square of weight, was over 40. Morbid. They say morbid. Ghoulish. Sick, weird, gruesome.

"Morbid, eh, Doc? They call that morbid, right? Let's just use a better adjective, like...let's use unwholesome."

"Words matter, don't they? Labels. Pegs and peg holes." Doc had this annoying habit of looking over his specs. Probably readers.

"You got it, doc. I've been called fat all my life. Heck, I've even got nicknames."

"So, Des, since we're trying to watch our language and be non-distortional, are you fat, or do you have excess body fat? Extra stored energy?"

"What's the diff?"

"The DIFF, Des, is how you think about it. It's human nature. It's the brain! How it works, how mine works, how yours works! The left brain oversimplifies things, labels things and distorts things. Look at how I just screwed up. Imagine me, a healthcare provider, saying something like, *will you survive this*? Idiot. Forgive me. But look, everybody else has labelled you as fat. I don't want you to mentally, emotionally, carry that label. Because if you do, you'll do everything day to day to fulfill that self-definition. If you have a fluorescent badge on your lapel that says, *I'm fat*, then you'll act to make that true. What do fat people do?"

"Huh?" Questions? Is this school? "Labels?"

"Peg hole. You know, jam the peg in the hole. Use a hammer if it doesn't fit. We've all got to be categorized, right? Just think of all the labels you've got. Son, student and now recruited football player! I don't want you to categorize yourself, label yourself, as FAT. Des, think. What do fat people do? How are their lives different than that of a thin person?"

"Well, that's dead obvious, Doc. They eat too much and don't exercise." Shrug and a hand flip. Obvious.

"Got it. Right. Bang on. So, if you've defined yourself as being something, you live that way. If you're calling yourself nicknames, then you'll eat too much and not choose to move, not exercise. Understand? It's a subconscious thing. All labels are false, two dimensional oversimplifications. Lies. You need to Defy-the-Lie! Or, at least use better labels! It's better to use more positive self-descriptors, like perhaps...imposing! Even enormous is more powerful, more positive than the word fat."

"So you think I'm calling myself fat. That I should work to rethink this, to recognize I've got too much fat stuck on me because of choosing to eat too much, and not move. That I'm not intrinsically FAT. That actually I could be a powerful, fit guy underneath all this. And more, that perhaps I'm overeating and under exercising because *I call myself fat.*"

"Yes! You're bringing up a great point, Des. The medical word, obesity, has connotations in the English language. It's like the word depression. That's a medical diagnosis, not a crash in the stock market or a dip in the road. It's a homograph. A word that is spelled the same, sounds the same, but has a different meaning. It's unfortunate. It's difficult, because the medical word obesity still deals with that which the English word describes, an excess storage of adipose or fat. Morbid is an even worse, unfortunate modifier, but it's what we were stuck with until we came to rely more upon BMI. Words can hurt, and I'm sorry if I offended you. Labels. All very much inaccurate, lies. Diagnoses are, too. BMI is an improvement, but it isn't everything, often distortional in itself. BMI isn't the be all and end all, Des. Look at something here. Look at these calves."

Doc grabbed his calves, right above the slip-ons. No shoelaces for Des. Yeah, they were big. Calves like footballs. Footballs. Great.

"See how little superficial fat there is there? Nothing. At ALL. Now, there's probably some fat in here, but there's no hiding this huge muscle."

"So what are you saying, Doc?" Doc was clearly balding. Watched him crawl back up his legs and assume a sitting position.

"Des, you've got a severe weight problem. I won't try to diminish that. But BMI has to be taken with a pinch of salt, especially in mesomorphic people, like you. Mesomorphs are very muscular people. I think if you tried to hit what we term as normal weight, you'd be losing a lot of muscle. In essence, you'd be sick. Schwarzenegger doesn't fit on this BMI scale, and neither do you."

"Schwarzenegger?" Hardly.

"Des, I'm not trying to blow smoke at you. You're not Arnold. You are severely overweight, and it carries real risk for you, especially in an aggressive sport like football. Let's look at things a bit more. Are you stressed out, any conflicts, anything…and here, have an M&M, I have a few left over in the box. Like red ones?"

Shook the box, smiled and dumped one out, just one, into a big meaty palm. His patient's.

Mom gasped. Choked. Shuffled about in the chair, big breath. Started to flush, stand…

"Mom, there's a point here. I've been your doc a long time, right?"

Mom sat down, not in the least mollified, the red flush continuing up from her collarbones. This had better be good. Des popped the M&M in the gob, gone.

"See how that happened?" Doc stood there, typical doc pose, short sleeve arms crossed, leaning against the desk.

"Huh?"

"I just gave you an M&M. What happened?"

"Well, I ate it!" More questions, looks like philosophy 101, right here on clinic central.

"I gave you one. Did I ask you to eat it?" Doc looked affronted.

"Doc!"

"Not trying to give you a hard time, big guy. Look, I'm going to give you another one. This time, I want you to just hold it in your hand."

"Another red one! Don't you eat those, Doc? Leave them for last?" And what the heck was he doing with M&M's on his desk. Halloween leftovers most likely and that was months ago. Stale. The freaking thing was stale.

"You bet. Don't you? Now, feel that M&M in your hand. Describe it for me."

"Red."

"Come on, Des. Play along. This is theatre arts class. What's it like?"

"Small, smaller than a dime. Thicker though, smooth. Fat in the middle." Took a nibble. "Candy coating on the outside. It's actually white, with the colour, the red colour on the outside. Bit of a smell. Not obviously stale. But it is, right, Doc? Not bad… never noticed. Actually, I don't think I ever bit one before!"

"Before you bite the other half, describe what you feel in your mouth. Yeah, it was from Halloween. My last secret weapon when a kid won't get a vaccine. Won't kill you. The M&M. I don't think."

"Ha. Okay, a crunch. Sweetness. Sticks in my teeth a bit."

"Move it around your mouth."

"Sorry Doc, it's gone."

"Take the other half, then. Describe how it feels in your mouth. Move it around with your tongue." Doc was leaning on his desk again, seemed intrigued.

"Like a piece of something, a fragment, a bit sharp, melting. Chocolate. Sweet." Swallowed.

"Do you ever eat without thinking about it, Des?" Scratched his chin.

"Huh?" What can one say? Favourite word today.

"Most patients that are overweight are actually nutritionally deprived. Weird, huh? Lots of calories, no nutrients. Think of that M&M. Compare it to…a blueberry! Think of the nutrients in each, the calories in each. Stunner, huh? And then there's simply the speed at which we all seem to eat…Ever sit down in front of the TV, you know, with a pizza ordered for the family and just, wham, all of a sudden it's gone?" Raised eyebrows made his eyes bug out this time.

Mom looked at Des and cleared her throat, looked down. The flush was dissipating, only to return. She piped up, "Nutritionally deprived??"

"Sorry, mom. Obese patients eat a lot of calories in food that just isn't very good.

Food that's simply nutrient-poor. Like M&M's. Not blueberries. Bread, instead of veg.

So you end up putting on a lot of fat to try to get those nutrients. If you focus on consuming foods of high nutrient density, things often take care of themselves. Believe it or not, a lot of obese patients are actually malnourished. Vitamins, minerals, omega-3's, you name it. Try to focus first on food quality, and then the calories."

Des looked up. "Yup. Think that's sort of an O'Brien thing. Quantity is a big one."

Mom put her chin up. "Yup. It is. We eat a lot of food, fast. Fast food."

"You can't change a habit until you become aware of it. Let's throw something in here that may help. Do you always eat, let's run with that pizza example, pizza with your fingers?"

"Always. Only idiots don't."

"Des. Don't call people things. You don't like being called fat, right?"

"Right, Doc. People that eat pizza with a knife and fork, just don't get them." Des shook his head, seeming a bit off balance with this line of questioning.

"That's what I want you to do."

"Huh?" You can try to stay impassive. Say nothing. But that darned air. Always gets out. That's huh. Exhalation with vocal tonality.

"That's another Huh! Yes. That's what I want you to do. Change up how you eat. Eat pizza with salad tongs or something. Break it up, become hyper aware. Try it with everything you eat. Some people suggest trying to eat with baby utensils. That gives you less food per bite, but I think more than that, leads to this hyper aware state. Really tune in. Your food intake should drop. Really process those bites in your mouth."

Conflicted? Of course. Didn't he remember those sutures he took out, those vaccines he got? Said something about the body being the battlefield for the brain. Or some such mumbo jumbo. Who was he kidding? But normal blood pressure, normal heart sounds, fairly normal blood work. In the end, Doc gave Des consent to play ball.

And then mom's eyes really bugged out.

* * *

Cutting out pop, salad tongs, other ridiculous utensils, and some more regular exercise brought something new to Des. He never did actually ride that bike, but achieved weight stabilization. For the first time ever, his weight did not go up. Coach got him an XXL adult uniform that fit.

Running out with the guys was a blast. Looking at the other, scrawny team, second blast. Realizing that his size, his presence, turned the tables was the atomic blast. The guys actually volunteered to tie on his cleats. He was their "Big Guy."

Not-so-secret weapon. Braden looked at him differently. Looked up.

Suddenly, his nickname meant something completely different. Bedsheets with clumsy, gigantic letters spelling, "ROLL", began appearing in the stands. There was the chant.

Things changed.

Pizza post games. And the guys didn't drink Perrier. Initial weight stabilization, perhaps even a bit of loss, led again to weight gain. Des learned how to impose, to intimidate, and not move too much. XXXL. Just roll and make it look good. Heck, he was there to hold the door closed. He could do that with his eyes shut. A mesomorphic, morbidly obese teen that finally looked a bit more in proportion with massive shoulders.

The guys just laughed when he peed in the shower. Didn't know his personal problems in the toilet, usually the disabled stall, as there was more room. Then it was just the team thing to do. Bonding, guy style.

Mom got diabetes, got depressed, got anxious. More than before. More than he could believe. Worried about her kid? Worried about the pills? Worried about life. Dad, prediabetic. More diets, pills, pills and more pills. He learned how to inject his mom with glucagon if she got too low.

They got to state. Won state. Won acclaim. A girlfriend sort of, for a while. More of a hanger-on.

Helped his mom get over the mood thing. Turned out this peg-holing thing happened to everyone, and ended up getting her sick. Got her back. Got a university scholarship. For football, of all things.

And a heart attack, sophomore year.

CHAPTER FOUR

The sun slanted through the window pane, rising low on the horizon. Sediment from early morning smoke stack emissions turned the sky a bit redder. Buttes of steel and glass corralled lines of cars, brake lights still bright on the apparent ravine floor.

Images of styrofoam, cardboard, memories of swamp water and ketchup came unbidden to mind. Rays of sunlight always seemed to do that. Memories of Schwartz upchucking. Des smiled. Great memories.

A dust particle, suspended in mid-air, turned and sparkled. Shadows were long in the apartment, creating a parody of the scene below. Stacks of pizza boxes threw shadows across the carpet. Empty beer cans littered the space between, glinting in the sun.

Different digs, same pill bottles.

All lined up on top of the tube, which was a ginormous. Called it, "Wrigley Field." Aspirin, the nickel a pill lifesaver. Snort. It would be better if it came in tooty fruity flavour, in a roll. A roll! Snort number two. Ramipril, for hypertension. Rosuvastatin, for cholesterol. Metformin, prediabetes.

But that was a few months ago. Des looked at the lab requisition in his hand. The sugar was slowly creeping up. That's what Doc said. He had felt real bad about that MI. Seems he half blamed himself for, what did he call it, pointing the stick at him. But hey, as they say, poop happens.

And it always runs downhill.

And that's where he was.

Sitting in it.

He had gotten through university. Seems like they had felt real bad, too. Free tuition, his grades hadn't hurt. Now he was a lightly paid graphic designer, hoping to be someday moderately paid. Hence the apartment, hence the who-cares attitude. Why clean up some place you're just going to leave?

But that's life though, right? We're only here for a little while. So why bother cleaning up?

Des chuckled, philosopher stuff. Becoming a freaking philosopher. Graphic designer come Goethe.

At least his furniture fit him. No wedging, un-wedging here.

Flippin' batteries gone on the damned remote, again. Des pulled himself up, ambled over to the set, and flipped it off. Freaking land mines. Ronnie still made a great burg and now what it came in was all recyclable. If he bothered.

He'd expend some energy on that later in the day, his nose demanding some action. Desmond snaked his way to the door, turned the handle, and looked down.

Every freaking day, on the floor. Call the circulation department, speak to the manager, the same thing every FREAKING DAY. There's something right on the wall, right at eye level for the paper! Why not USE IT?

Des looked up and down the hall, leaned against the doorframe and kicked the newspaper into his room. Big one, lots of ads. Stupid thing should be illegal. Not one tree existed, except for those stupid little ones on the sidewalk in their metal cages, out that window. Probably they were all used to print this stupid thing. Threw out all the ads anyway. What a waste of living, breathing tissue.

HIS. He had to kick the stupid thing over to his chair, ease himself down and then pick it up. One of these days these stupid papers would be absolutely defunked. No more trees falling, none of this printing, distribution, delivering, bending over to pick up the damned thing, just news on the screen like it should be.

Des shook his head. It was his life, but still something hard to get used to. He played college ball, for heaven's sake! Tense edema stretched the skin at his dusky ankles. He pushed a digit into his foot, leaving a deep thumbprint.

Ugh.

He had gotten up early for that blood work. A few minutes to kill.

THE TIMES. How many papers were named that? Isn't that some kind of copyright infringement?

Big glaring headline, OBESITY PANDEMIC KILLS.

Well, we'll see, but certainly HYPERBOLE SELLS NEWSPAPERS.

Des flipped it open in his lap, looked at the clock…

Obesity: a disease in pandemic proportion, now striking even developing, emerging economy countries. Possibly the most common health problem facing physicians, obesity seems to have a clear and obvious, cost-effective solution, that people simply don't take.

Eat less, exercise more.

These words leave the lips of every practising physician. Those few that achieve weight loss seldom maintain it. Changes in behaviour, including both calorie intake and changes in activity, seem to mitigate any loss achieved (Ludwig & Friedman, 2014). Why doesn't this simple solution work?

The Global Burden of Disease 2013 Obesity Collaboration reported no individual national success tackling this problem in the last 33 years, and no successful "population-level intervention strategies to reduce exposure"(Ng, Fleming, & Robinson, et al., 2014). Among the most affluent countries on the planet, obesity is a serious problem. In Qatar, arguably the richest country in GDP per capita, fully two thirds to three quarters of the adult population are overweight or obese, with 17% of the population struggling with diabetes in 2007 (Bener, Zirie, & Janahi, et al, 2009). Now using this country as an example may be unfair, as there is a fair bit of consanguinity in the population: there may be a substantial genetic factor, just now being elucidated (Tomei, S., Mamtani, R., & Al Ali R., et al., 2015).

The United States, so called melting pot of the world, may be a better example. 2012 data from the USA show more than a third of adults suffered from obesity. Taken altogether, two thirds of American adults were overweight or obese. This problem does not start in adulthood, however. 17% of those aged 2 to 19 were obese, with over 30% overweight or obese (Obesity and Trends, 2015). Over 9% of Americans had diabetes, one of the conditions highly correlated with obesity, in 2012 (American Diabetes Association, 2014).

Although very apparent in the United States and many other wealthy countries, obesity is certainly epidemic planet wide (World Health Organization, 2003). Health care organizations worldwide trumpet the importance of confronting the issue. Family doctors feel they are wasting their time, as some research implies (Barnes & Ivezaj, 2015; Lorts & Ohri-Vachaspati, 2016). Super-sized big gulpers Google sixpackshortcuts.com, while female entertainers are accused of using spray-on fake, "abs". Billions are spent on research, treatment, supplements and gym memberships, all to no avail.

Des looked up at the clock...

Time to go. Rolled up The Times, AS IF, someone should sue these guys, as if it's the real Times. At least they had some references, which he was going to read.

The elevator at least was around the corner. Just beside the stairwell. Dicey looking thing, that stairwell. Last summer he had cracked that door open and was sure he had smelled urine. Enough of that. As if, anyway. Not as if he was on the second floor, so come on.

Jammed his finger into the button again. Type A. Well, maybe. Jam, jam.

Des smiled and slid in. Typical faces, all a bit horrified looking. Heh heh. Hey, he got to use the elevator, too. Butt-heads. All so superior. Sharply indrawn breaths. At least they could thank him for the straight ride down. The doors opened a couple of more times, but they closed right back up: ride was straight down.

At least he got off first. At least. They streamed ahead, curving around both sides like the Venturi effect personified, charging through the lobby and out the front door. Which is where he was going.

Double front doors, nice. One of the reasons he picked the place. That, and the bus stop right in front, man, was that sweet. Sure, a regular door was fine. He was going to get on the bus, they only have one door, sure he could do it. But why struggle?

Perfect timing. Had it down to a science. Could set your watch to these buses, as if anyone wore a watch any more. Unless you could swing one of those iWatches, and who the heck...

"Sir, I'm afraid there's no seats. You ok with standing?"

Knew the guy. Decent enough sort. At least to say hi. Little guy, big sideburns, looked like a chipmunk. Big wad of gum in his cheeks. Couldn't be tobacco, he'd have to spit.

"Sure, sure. Used to play ball for state! Sure, I can stand. Just a few blocks."

And Des would always do that, too. Bluster. Laugh.

Lie.

Des worked his way to the back of the bus, waddling one way, turning a bit, grunt. Straps along the ceiling helped. On a left turn, the lady to his right almost screamed.

Heh heh. At least he could laugh. Poor thing, looked embarrassed squashing herself next to her husband there, leaning over so far.

Remembered squashing. Learning it in the doctor's office that first day, repeating it in the schoolyard the next. Then coming damn near close to getting paid, big time, to do it. Before that stupid heart attack. He should probably say something.

"Sorry lady, tight bus, eh?"

She flushed a bit, murmuring something. Husband stammered, waved his hand a bit, was nothing.

Well, it was something. Something imposing. Massive. Enormous. All much better labels. Doc was such a hoot. He felt the newspaper under his arm. Pandemic?

Looked around. Well, depends on how one defines things, right? All in a definition. But there was a kid on the side. Man that could have been him. Nobody around him, mini massive. Mini imposing. Mini…

"Hey, kid…"

The kid looked up. Chewing something, wrapper in his hand. Crinkled it up. "Sorry, finished it."

"No, no, kid. Hey, I don't even know you! Think I'd ask for a piece of your candy bar?"

"Yeah. I do."

Des looked down. Well, not too far down. Feet must have been down there somewhere. Starting to burn, hot. "No, no, kid, just wanted to say hi. Seems no one sitting around you."

"Well, you know what they say. Like the old joke, So how fat's your mom? She's so fat, when she sits around the house, she…"

"Sits around the house, yeah. So you're good with jokes?"

"Gotta be, in this world. Gotta be funny. Gotta be quick. You know, when you're like…" Donnie moved his hands, moved about in the seat a bit. Uncomfortable, and not just the upholstery.

"Us. You mean us. It's ok, kid."

The city clicked by. "So, you take this bus often? What's your name?"

"Donald. Some call me Donnie. I don't care really."

"Des. Desmond." The two shook hands, the newspaper transiently wedged in Desmond's mouth. "Look, this is my stop. Could you hit that bell for me?"

"Sure, man. See you again."

Lurch to a stop. All buses do that. Lurch. Des bus surfed a couple of steps, then moved to the stairs down. One… two… three steps.

Now it was just getting into the lab.

Gotta be smart, gotta be funny.

Gotta sit.

* * *

At least he had something to read. Did everyone come at once, first thing in the morning? What's the big deal with morning blood work? At least there was a BK next door. Hoped they had some morning sandwiches. Or anything. That they were open. Maybe a drive through, if he could walk through it. Tried that before. For some reason there was some kinda car rule.

As if.

Des looked at the number 39 in his hand. THIRTY-NINE. Looked around. All shapes and sizes. Tall ones, short ones, and someone else sort of like him.

But no one matched his. Enormity. Heh. At least that paper... Des flipped it out like a windshield. There was one way to get some privacy.

...On one hand, one wonders where the common sense has been misplaced. On quite the other, one looks at the acceleration of the problem and wonders if some other factors are at play. It's not only more and more people becoming overweight, but it's faster and faster.

Many patients are surprised by the disease classification. Some clearly take offence at the placement of the word on their chart medical problem list. Obesity was classified as such in 2013 by the American Medical Association. A disease, as defined in Dorland's medical dictionary is, "any deviation from or interruption of the normal structure of function of any part, organ, or system (or combination thereof) of the body that is manifested by a characteristic set of symptoms and signs and whose etiology, pathology and prognosis may be known or unknown." Certainly obesity seems to fit here. Obesity itself is defined as, "an increase in body weight beyond the limitation of skeletal and physical requirement, as the result of an excessive accumulation of fat in the body." The modern working clinical meaning of obesity is a BMI of over 30, overweight having a definition of a BMI of over 25.

BMI is simply a person's weight, divided by the square of their height, expressed in kg/ m². This partially helps account for height in evaluation of obesity. Of further assistance is body waist size. Obesity is inferred if waist size is over 40 inches for men, or 35 for women. This measurement carries some real clinical impact, as someone carrying their body mass in front (more visceral fat) are at increased risk for heart and sugar problems compared to those pear shaped individuals with a heavier bottom (more subcutaneous fat, see below). And clearly, a heavily built muscular weightlifter would appear falsely to have a weight problem based on BMI analysis without consideration of waist size. So, mass counts. Shape counts.

Perhaps the term pandemic should be addressed. Is the use of this word hyperbole, a mere effort to whip up emotion? Pandemic infers a widespread epidemic, throughout a large region, continent, or across the globe. In 2014 the WHO (2015) reported over 1.9 billion afflicted with overweight and obesity. Out of a world population of 7.2 billion, that's over 25% of all persons. Of those 1.9 billion, fully 600 million were obese.

Of all adults worldwide, 39% were overweight or obese, 13% obese (World Health Organization, 2015).

"... Thirty-nine... I'm calling THIRTY-NINE..."

Whoops. Imagine that. Kismet. Gotta be smart. Gotta be funny. Gotta get a lotto ticket.

"Sir, sir, its ok. Don't get up! I'll come to you! How are you this morning?"

Wow, who is this ray of sunshine? Sunbeams would usually pull back Golden Arches memories for him. Not this time. That's not Styrofoam, cardboard and Schwartz spewing, that's Sunshine.

"And they say service is dead! My goodness, thanks, hun! How long you been working here? Like 2 minutes? Not burnt out yet?" Let's just say this one had cute cornered. Tiny!

Sunshine looked over her shoulder, whispered confidentially. "No, I've been here a while. Saw you last time. Went to State...a few years ago..."

Des flushed. Yes, Des never flushed. Worse than that, Des hated when he did it. Damn.

"Well, that was a few years ago."

"You were amazing. All the girls had a crush on you. On the CRUSH. No, it wasn't that, it was something else cool, something…" A tourniquet appeared out of nothingness, conjured from the air itself, the magic of day-to-day life. Of which he hadn't seen much in a while. Magic.

Or life.

"The ROLL. Capital letters. That's me."

Sunshine smiled, nodded, tightened up the tourniquet.

"Hey, Mr. Roll, whatcha doing holding your breath?"

"Huh?"

"Trying to get ready? That's a sure fire way to get more keyed up! That's panic breathing! Look, all that air has to come out anyway, right? Some of it's mine! You can't have it all!"

Des breathed out and laughed as she deftly took the sample, turning over one of the tubes up and down, up and down. The tourniquet was gone, tucked into some mysterious fourth dimensional pocket.

"Well, don't be a stranger!" brightly and scooted off.

Well, miracles do happen. Des sat there a minute and watched her skirt. Scoot, that is. Didn't even ask him what happened. Told him, in a roundabout way, that the girls had a crush. On him.

Well. Well. Well. Well be damned, anyway. Well.

He got out of that chair with a vestige of his old vigour. Didn't lean, didn't tip, didn't climb his palms up on his knees and thighs. Just stood. For the first time in…way too long.

She was gone. But suddenly he felt something, and it was more than his screaming muscles, knees and sweat.

He looked at BK on his way by. Started for the bus stop. Hesitated.

Back to BK. Hey, he had given blood. Looked at his wallet. 30 bucks, enough.

Ok.

* * *

Des got a seat on the way back, his arm thrown over the back of the seat. The facial sweat got a chance to dry as the concrete, graffiti, neon, cars, vagrants and commuters blurred past him.

41

Other sweat areas...no such luck. Billboards. Happy hour. Ronnie's. Donuts. More donuts. Pizza shack, pizza shed, pizza to go, three for one. Somehow a neon soda bottle, bubbles sparkling, as that cap came off, spun up, soda pouring into a glass, mesmerizing...home, it seems.

The bell chimed. That straggly dog ambled by, glancing up.

His stop. He must have struck the bell out of habit. The dog turned his head. Time.

He stood again, no pull, no leveraging, no cheat. By the time he was out, his bud was gone, as usual. Up and down the street, gone. One day. One day.

He'd been up a while. Up early, bus rides ... Sunshine. Dog tired was an understatement. Despite the loose ties on his shoes, his feet were taking it. Taking it big time. But right through those doors, to...

The stairwell. He had no pretence of doing them at all. Humph. We'll just see. He was going to do the stairs properly, one step at a time, no yanking up, no dragging up, no slumping. Des put his hand on the handrail, took a big breath, up.

Funny how you describe Sunshine. Next step. Light, bright, radiant. And painful. Muscles screamed. Des felt for the little bottle in his pocket, there. He was ok. Stopped for a moment, breathed. Breathed. And up.

Just one flight. Okay. He leaned against the wall and smiled. No pain, at least in his chest. Probably stupid, but life. Pounding in his chest, throbbing in his neck, dripping down his sides. Life.

* * *

On Channel 6 Doc Martens, black tights and stupid poses. Channel 7 some guy out of the 80's with a loopy afro, clothes out of what-the-heck daymare, lots of overweight women trying to follow him. On 8, solo, precise, again in tights, presentation, outside, green grass. Must be the time of day. Every channel, different flavour, same thing.

Looked at his feet. He'd never get Martens on those Flintstones.

Well, there were exercise programs and Dr. Pulpit, or whoever, trying to sell special edition Bibles. Five hundred bucks would get you special prayers and a front line ticket for the eternity express. No checked blazer, no hair deficiency, no, couldn't be him...

Des sat in his chair, his exercise routine done at about minute two. Sweat stung his eyes. He took another big slug of chocolate milk, while fingering his automated blood pressure cuff. His heart rate was back down to normal, again no pain. Breathing rate ok, time.

There it was again. 170, 180. For a guy in his early thirties? No good.

He picked up the phone and called.

CHAPTER FIVE

Doc had a big video screen in the waiting room. Big flat screen, yesterday's technology, not as big as Wrigley, but pretty close. HD it wasn't. Doctor's hours, nurse's hours, secretary's hours. After hours, big hang up with hours. Wear a mask. Wash your hands. And thankfully a channel switch. Weather, golf and news, or an opinion piece...

...Not hyperbole. Pandemic.
Children unfortunately have no immunity to this affliction. Again, in 2013, 42 million children under 5 years of age, worldwide, were overweight or obese (WHO, 2015). Interestingly, developing countries with emerging economies had childhood rates of obesity 30% higher than developed countries.

Images of overweight, obese kids...kismet. Talk about kismet? First the newspaper, then this.

Enough said. Big problem.
But what is the problem? Not aesthetic, certainly. Heavy is not necessarily unattractive in the eyes of society. One must remember that the new normal is overweight. For the first time, in 2016 a strikingly attractive "size 16" model graced the cover of Sports Illustrated. Many suggest that Marilyn Monroe was a size 16. Is size

16 overweight? Probably close, but certainly this was no skin and bones model. Heavy is certainly not new, either. In the millennium following the year 500, obesity was actually a sign of wealth (Berry, Stenesen & Zeve, et al, 2013). Look at the renaissance subjects of Raphael, or da Vinci that close out this period.

All superimposed on Marilyn, then the Sports Illustrated cover.

Certainly, it isn't fair. Our species has struggled to move beyond mere survival. In many areas planet wide, this has been achieved with great success. Shelter, warmth and a full refrigerator are now taken for granted. We have time, finally. No break of dawn chores, no mucking out stalls, no struggle to just get by. For most of us, food has evolved beyond sustenance to become a glorious celebration, a bonding, a togetherness, family. Food is love. Rest itself is that thing sought after all day and when adequate, can be peace, tranquility, creation. Rest is...rest. Putting down the load from the day's video screen cognitive tasks. Muscles are no longer tasked.
But too much food, or rest, is just too much.

And here he was, vegging in front the TV...

Unfair is more than inequitable. Of course it's not fair to people struggling to find a crust of bread, or clean water. That's certainly unfair, a huge problem for humanity in itself and an ongoing humiliation and embarrassment to developed countries. But it's clear that obesity, on a worldwide perspective, wastes. Wastes more than food. It wastes resources, wastes health care dollars, wastes human potential. The McKinsey Global Institute report of 2014 on obesity suggests the yearly global financial cost of obesity to be 3 trillion dollars, in essence equal to that cost incurred by effects of tobacco or armed violence, war and terrorism and more than alcoholism (which comes in at 1.4 trillion) (Dobbs, Sawers, & Thompson, et al, 2014).
The way we're living our lives costs us.
Obesity costs. Americans spent more than 13 billion on mere dietary supplements in 2013 (Millman, 2015). The US weight loss

market is estimated to be worth over 60 billion (Overweight and weight loss statistics, worldometers, 2016). Much more than this, obesity costs its victims through job discrimination, higher insurance premiums, poor physical functioning and just those day to day, life limitations (Seidell, 1998). It's remarkable the amount of societal stigma related to this diagnosis in the face of its pervasive nature. Self-image suffers.

But more than this.

Obesity kills.

Well, that was right on cue, wasn't it?

"Des? Des O'Brien?"

Des wondered if he'd see Maisey. True grit, that one. Then wandered down the hall after the secretary they called, "the runner".

She did. And was in the room prepping the computer, finishing her last tidy as he came in. An absolute whirlwind of secretarial force.

"Have a seat! Doc will be right with ya!"

Des smiled, shaking his head at the boundless energy. And saw the chairs. So sat on the examination table.

"Doc, you gotta get better chairs."

Doc sort of flustered in, seemed in a rush as per usual, Kramer without the hair. Not much hair at all, that is. "Des! Long time! Get that blood work?"

"Yup, few days ago. Got my BP up yesterday after a bit of exercise. The girls wedged me in today."

Doc opened his electronic medical record and started typing. Big Apples. iMacs. Must be nice. Chiclet keyboard. Wireless mouse. Nice to be a Doc, better computer than he had, and he was doing freaking graphics, wondered if he could trade. Managed to keep his eyes on Des, though. Nice. Mavis Beacon, probably…

"How high?"

"140/90 average. A 170. A 180. I know not that bad, maybe I panicked."

"Oh, high enough for your age and your medical problems. Let's check."

Doc brought back his automated cuff, some kind of wobbly thing on a tripod, called it C3PO, Ho Ho, set it up, big cuff size and let him stew for five. Wasn't as bad, 136/82.

He came back in, pretty glib. Rolled the wires back up, folded the cuff. "Not bad. That machine is way more accurate than yours. So what's this about exercise? You?" Stuffed the cuff in the front basket, cracked the door open and rolled it outside.

"Funny, Doc. Played ball, remember?"

"Des, it's me. Me. You told me all about it. Said you just stood there and occasionally squashed people, not that I'd know anything about that."

Des laughed. "Yeah, you've been my doc a long time. Yeah, I'd squash people. Didn't really have to move that much. But I was a lot better before. Since that MI, it's just slowly gotten worse."

"What?"

"Everything. My weight, my energy, my weight, my sleeping, my weight, my life. Doc, I can't freaking bend over to pick up the bloody newspaper anymore."

He flipped it out there on the table. That Obesity Pandemic piece. That had been driving him nuts. The next part was about, "Adipose…" Fancy way of saying FAT. Des.

"Are these pills doing it to me? Are they making me fat? What about this diabetes preventer, this metformin stuff?"

"Des, those pills are helping you. You're getting worse despite the drugs. Metformin is not associated with weight gain. You're right, insulin is anabolic and will put weight on. The sulfony-lurea class, for example, puts weight on. But you're not on those. Simply put, and I've said this before, you're too big because of thermodynamics, plain and simple."

"Doc, I'm a college grad, but not physics. Thermodynamics?" Des leaned forward from his exam table seat and remembered the first squash. That was physics, straight ahead Newtonian. It didn't seem to fizz on Doc.

"It sounds complicated, but it really isn't. Know what a calorie is? Energy. The amount of energy required to raise one millilitre of water, one degree Celsius. It's a measurement of energy. If you put more energy in than you burn, then you end up in positive balance and put on more energy stores, which is adipose, or fat. If you burn more than you take in, then it's in a negative balance and you lose stores, lose weight, lose fat." Well. Didn't that sound dead easy? Right.

Despite Kramering in, he was giving him time. Had to give credit where credit was due. Even if he didn't need all that freaking computing power.

"Eat less, move more. If I hear that one more time, Doc, I just may go..." Nuclear is what he was thinking. But that was then. This is now. Might just go. Leave. See ya.

"Des, you sound upset. Must drive you nuts, almost a professional athlete, with a fist full of pills every day and now not being able to pick up the newspaper."

His shoulders slumped. Hard to stay mad at this guy. And he was really angry at the whole thing. Not just his weight. His apartment. His towers of pizza boxes. His inability to get up more than a flight of stairs. Wearing sandals, all the bloody time. Sunshine. Or, rather, his utter lack of anything like it.

"Seems like something has changed, Des? We've talked a lot about this, but I sense something else is going on here."

"I'm a young guy, Doc, living the life of an old man. I want it back. I want my life, back. Doc, I can't even wipe my own ass." Desmond's face crumpled, shoulders heaved and sighed, huuuuhhhh, huuuuhhhh. "Doc, I can't even breathe right. I wear a flipping space mask at night. C3PO? What about Darth Vader time. Listen to me! People ask me if I'm ok."

"All right. I'm here for you. Let's clearly define where we are, so we know our starting point. What's your end point? What's your goal?"

"Doc, you're trying hard, but you didn't hear me. Life. I want it back. I'm living in a bachelor's apartment, strewn with pizza boxes. I take a lineup of freaking pills, every day. My blood pressure's going up! I can't go up one stupid flight of stairs, much less stand up from a chair! Showers are exhausting! Public bathrooms terrify me! I would like to have a young man's life. I had it for a couple of years in college, then it all went down the crapper."

"You want a girl. And eventually a house, with a dog and a kid. To play football with."

Okay, maybe the guy does have ears. Des gave a big breath and felt his head slump forward on his chest. Maybe not doable.

"Got it. That's our goal. That's our end point. Now, let's look at where you are and we can then plot a course. Just like flying a plane. You need to know where you want to go, but you also need to know where you are. Let's look at this blood work, do some measurements."

Doc flipped his computer around and walked Des through the lab results. At least he used the graphing ability. If he hadn't, with all that computer under his fingers, Des may just have suffered cataplexy. Turns out the blood work was still pretty ok, still not frankly diabetic. Just that thing called prediabetes.

Before his heart attack, he was pre everything. Pre MI, pre-diabetes, pre-stroke. That's what was called metabolic syndrome, sort of an overall precursor condition.

Not to do things in half measure, he was way past that, post MI. He was no longer merely metabolic syndrome. Proven *vasculopath* they called it. Plugs. Plugs that had done damage. Plugs in his blood vessels that prevent blood and its oxygen from getting to where it's supposed to go.

That's what had happened in his MI. He was actually running, him, Des O'Brien, during that fateful game. The demand for blood, for the oxygen carried by his blood was simply too high for the heart blood vessels to supply. Part of the heart muscle died.

And with it his athletic career. And a lot more. Hope just seemed to die. Before that, he was THE ROLL. Indestructible. A steamroller.

Doc continued, reviewed his lipids, blood pressure, waist circumference and of course his weight. The little tiny funny scale in his exam room seemed to have trouble... the beam worked...they hoped. He said the max was...unbelievable. The little pointer thing wasn't absolutely stuck, it did drift a bit. If he wiggled. Must have been ok. The numbers? High. All of them. Meaningless numbers. What was his number? His number was that he couldn't even put his belt on after donning his pants. That was the first thing. First thing was the belt into the pants, then put on the pants, and that was his waist circumference.

"Doc, I like numbers. I like good numbers, too. But really, I don't care. I want my life back. What's that number?"

Doc smiled, listening to his breath and heart sounds. "Nail on the head, Des." Let his stethoscope dangle and stepped back.

"So, did you get up that flight of stairs?"

"Well, yeah. But holy cow!"

"Do you realize how much you did, though?"

"Huh?"

"At your BMI, small changes have great leverage. Think about it. How much good would going up one flight of stairs do a marathon runner?"

"You mean..."

"That was a phenomenal workout. Any changes you make, any cuts to your intake and any bump in your day to day movements, have great leverage. Fat acquisition often seems to accelerate as you gain more and more adipose. But it can come off in a similar accelerated way."

Des looked a bit...nonplussed at this. Could say flummoxed. Bewildered. What the heck? Doc moved on.

"What kind of job are you doing again?" Doc scratched his head.

"Graphic design."

"Big downtown office or something?"

"No, that's for the plebes. I don't make much, but I've been around a while. Some benefits. Let me work at home."

"Huge, huh? Don't have to get up at any certain time, all flex time?"

"You got it."

"Work with your bunny slippers on?"

"Pretty much! Between games of League of Legends. It's pretty easy. Could do it in my sleep. Frankly, often do. Boring often. Fall asleep at my screen sometimes."

"4000 calories."

"Huh?"

"We've talked a bit about calories, but probably not enough. A farmer burns 4000 more calories a day than you. Easy."

"How do you know? What are you talking about?"

"All movement counts. Bet you don't move much. A farmer moves a lot and sometimes with great physical exertion. He's also probably up more hours, up at dawn, you know? That's what all those personal devices are about. The iPhone with the step monitors on them, I think other phones, now, heck, there's even little straps, devices that you can wear on your wrist that will measure your steps. It's called Non Exercise Activity Thermogenesis. It's burning calories in your day to day life, not just on your little episode of exercise. You have an opportunity to burn way more in all that other time in your day to day life, outside that which you put aside for exercise. You don't need to wear Nikes to exercise, you know. Even doable in bunny slippers!"

"Ok, Doc, enough with the bunny slippers. Do you think I could get any that could fit these Flintstones?"

Doc took off Desmond's slip-ons, looked at his dusky feet, gently pushing a finger into one of them, leaving an impression. "That hurt?"

"Well, it's not comfortable, Doc." Typical freaking Doctor. What did he think?

"Your blood is basically water, you know?"

"Huh?"

"Your blood is basically water. With things floating around in it. Proteins, nutrients like sugar, blood cells, but basically water. Over 90%. Basically, your urine is just blood water, processed. Your kidney processes the water and makes urine. Anyway, I'm off topic. Your heart, a big two cycle engine, pushes blood actively down muscular arteries that also help push blood down to your feet. The blood then enters small blood vessels called capillaries.

51

Some water leaves here, through the capillaries. Venous blood is carried away from the capillary bed in thin walled vessels that take muscular contraction to squish the walls, to move the blood back up to the heart. No muscular contraction, the blood sits there. Varicose veins, like this and this. If your body is big, if you're system is trying to manage a huge column of blood, just passively sitting in your veins, veins will get bigger and more water will just leave those blood vessels at the capillaries. The system tries to move the water back up along lymphatics, a parallel system of collapsible channels, but sometimes there's just too much."

"I've got too much. Water, and a big body above my feet. My skinny blood vessels are trying to hold up a swimming pool worth of water."

"Yep. Gotta get this weight down, Des. You know it." Gave me one of his serious looks. What's he do, practice that in the mirror while shaving? One beady eye half closed, give a guy a break.

"Doc. Thanks for repeating the dead freaking obvious." Typical.

"Sorry. Easiest way of course is to not eat it."

"What?"

"Food. Don't eat as much! You can gain weight by eating pretty much anything, but patients suffering from obesity tend to be nutritionally deprived."

"What?"

"There's that word again! I remember that's what I called my daughter, what girl. Yup. Remember, it's just calories. Thermodynamics. Calories in, calories out. And, of course, nutritional density. Obese patients tend to eat calorie dense, nutritionally poor food. If you eat too much of almost anything your weight will go up. One of the biggest problems, though, is the choice of junk food over nutritious food. Lots of calories, not much else. Vitamin, mineral, omega 3 deficient junk. Just whacks the calories on. Think of it, there's just as many calories in a slice of bread as a cup of veg! And what do people reach for first? BREAD! Sure, there's talk of other factors, like environmental contaminants that get caught in your fat and change how it acts. Your fat, your adipose tissue, is actually an organ. But we're getting way too complicated and almost philosophical here. What you need to hear is, *eat less*. Eat less junk and mind the fiber for health! You don't juice, do you?"

"Well, yeah. Of course. Hate vegetables, but I can drink carrot juice."

"Really? How many glasses of carrot juice a day, Des?"

"Hate veggies, but I'm not stupid. Gotta be smart in this world. Probably every meal. Gotta be smart, eat veggies!"

"Des, you are smart. Don't mistake now what I'm going to say, but you should Google this. How many carrots does it take to make a glass?"

"Oh, depends on the carrots, of course, but probably 3 or 4."

"Des, can you eat three or four carrots all at once?"

"Are you kidding? I'd not be able to eat anything else!" Des laughed, then hesitated…"I'm eating about 15 carrots a day. Easy."

"Des, you can gain weight on good food. Broccoli. Tofu. Lean bison. Blueberries. It doesn't have to be bacon grease, or candy floss. But it's tough. Incredibly hard. I'm talking bushels of broccoli. Who could eat that? Des, you're taking all the fibre out of your carrots! Your gut flora needs that! Fibre doesn't just help you save time in the bathroom and decrease the risk of hemorrhoids. It makes your tiny little buggies in your gut happy! Happy intestinal flora, better health! And, that fibre really slows down the sugar hit of the carrot, which is one of your vegetables with the highest sugar level. If you just ate 3 carrots a day, one with each meal, you'd be cutting down probably about 300, maybe 400 calories. Right there. That's a lot."

"So if I did this. If I managed to cut off my carrot juice and just had carrots, 3 a day, and made no other changes, what would happen? To my weight?"

"Good example, Des. You'd have to Google all this and check the calories. I really don't know how many calories there are in carrot juice, for example. But it's a safe bet you'd be cutting down a few hundred calories a day. For every 100 calories a day you decrease a day, either through not consuming it, or burning it off with movement, you lose 10 pounds in a year. 5 pounds in 6 months…"

"So if our guesses are right, cutting down 10 carrots a day could decrease me three or four hundred calories a day, which would be 30 to 40 pounds in one year. That one maneuver."

"Yup. Well, sort of. We haven't talked about your metabolism, which has a bit of a *nasty surprise* for you. IF your weight is currently stable… and forgive me, but you and I both know it tends to keep going up. Held it stable a while there in college, but since then, you've been gaining. But do us both a favour and check the numbers, right? But basically know this. It's a whole lot easier to just not eat it, than exercise it off. I'm a big guy, too. I can eat two of those muffins you can get from our friendly every neighbourhood has one donut shop in about two minutes flat. Or about 1000 calories. Bang. Right there.

"Took me an hour to run 10 Km on a treadmill last week. Big accomplishment for me, hurt my knee. I'm an old geezer. But guess how many calories on the display? For running an hour, exhausting myself, sweating to death. Exhausted for the rest of the day."

"Okay, Doc, I get it. You were pooped. Huge exertion. What, couple thousand calories?" Twenty questions. Thirty. The guy needed one of those Magic 8 balls.

"Less than 900. Run for an hour, or not eat those two muffins. It's easier to not eat it."

"Well, how much am I supposed to eat? And…what's that *nasty surprise* you were talking about?" Des crossed his arms and leaned back.

"The *nasty surprise* is that your metabolism, right now, is WAY higher than it will be when you lose weight. That's why all those calculations never seem to hold up. You start burning off weight, then your metabolism actually DROPS. The overweight person has a HOTTER, FASTER metabolism than the thin person. Weird, Huh? So you lose weight, and then your burning rate drops and your weight starts to drift back up again. Basically, with weight loss, you need to continue to increase your activity,

54

forcing your calorie burn up as much as possible, or that weight comes right back on.

"...Now in regards some simple diet advice...you want to know what to eat. Why don't you look at it like how we often teach diabetics to eat? Look at your palm."

"This?" Des demonstrated his hand, palm up. Remembered when he had calluses...pretty pink, now. Pudgy. Even his freaking hands were fat. And that metabolism thing just seemed wrong. Didn't fat people have slower metabolisms? But this was Doc talking...

Doc took it and made sawing motions with his hand. "Take your hand, cut off the fingers, and the thumb. Your palm. It's got a surface area, but also a thickness, see?" He showed Des his hand.

Doc continued, "That's a quarter of your plate. I want you to have a quarter of your plate protein, one quarter starch and 2 quarters, that's 2 palms, veggies, every time you eat."

"So my plate is four palms big?"

"You got it. Every time you eat. You can have a piece of fresh fruit after your meal, in addition. And a glass of milk if you want. But that's it. If you go somewhere for Thanksgiving and they put out some kind of real ultra-healthy snack before dinner, like hummus and whole wheat crackers, then the crackers go in the starch palm and the hummus...well, I'd put it in vegetables."

"Your snacks count in your plate."

"You got it. Now think. Let's say you go out for a chicken dinner and they ask if you want a whole wheat, or a white bun. Since you're getting so health conscious, you pick a whole wheat roll. Well, Des, that's your starch, probably close to the whole thing, the whole enchilada, right there. That means no potatoes for dinner."

"But that's a vegetable!"

"Yes, sure, it's a vegetable. But for the purpose of this plan, potatoes are a starch. As well as all grains, or anything made from them, from flour. Like noodles."

"Then I eat no vegetables at all! Only carrot juice!"

"Carrot juice isn't bad in itself, Des. It's how much you eat of it. Smoothies are a bit better. At least they have the fibre. The problem with them is there's no chewing and less body processing. Think whole foods. Remember that red M&M I gave you? No food, really, in itself, is bad. How big's an M&M? Not that big of a deal, in itself. It's how much you eat of it, versus how much you're burning. Healthy choices, Des. First, think nutrition. Highly nutritious food just simply is better. Usually, less calories too. A blueberry, or that M&M. Carrots are veggies, but even if you were trying to fill half your plate, I don't think you could jam four carrots onto it."

He looked at his palm. Four of those, with each meal. Wow. That was a small snack. That was an after dinner mint. Doc must not have any idea of how much he ate. Thirty bucks was the minimum at a fast food joint. 30 bucks.

He didn't seem to have an off button, a full state. Food consumed his thoughts, was the pivotal event around which everything else was planned, the biggest rock in the bag. The first priority.

Easy, this wasn't gonna be.

"Des."

"Doc."

"There are some other options. I'd be derelict in my duties if I didn't tell you about some other options. There is surgery. Surgery is a real, clear option here. We should consider it."

"We? WE having surgery, Doc?" Heart started to pound, just a bit.

"Des, there's bypass surgery, sleeves, all sorts of things. A simple band the surgeon could put around the top of your stomach, a fairly small procedure with a scope. Would cut your intake down right away and give you a real leg up. Your weight is a real health issue. This isn't cosmetic surgery! It could help save your life. Won't stop you from drinking high calorie fibre deficient carrot juice, though. Still just a tool you have to use properly."

Doc handed him an info package and suggested a website. Gulp. This must be serious. He'd look at it. But surgery? Might be the smartest first step, but his pockets weren't quite deep enough, not on his graphic designer salary. First the diet, exercise option...

They talked as Doc finished up his note. The goal for the next week was to start making small changes, daily. Des wasn't really quite sure of this leverage idea, which sounded like smoke and mirrors, if not a straight lie. If thermodynamics was real, calories in and calories out, then this acceleration thing didn't seem to wash. He could understand that for a fixed amount of exertion, like that set of stairs, then he would burn more calories than that example marathon runner. One set of stairs almost destroyed him. It made utter sense that he expended way more calories doing that than that marathoner. The eating thing he really couldn't get, just yet. The idea of a bit of a diet really pulling his weight down fast was like pie in the sky. Pizza pie. But it was encouraging, because Doc wouldn't pull his chain.

Not Des. He hoped. Mind you, he never had had the opportunity of leaning on his desk. Maybe he should try it sometime. He remembered the squash. Des grinned at the thought. He may be sick. He may have a heart condition. But he had big, like rice had white.

And big, Doc just said, had a metabolism to match. And Des was...BIG.

Grinned. Maybe there was a little benefit of being...Big.

He wasn't going to weigh himself at home, just yet. Not that he may be able to. Might need to go to Walmart for a scale. If they had them. But what he was going to do, was eat less and move more. Focusing more on nutrition would help big time. That cup of vegetables would go a lot further than the bread and fill him more. Interesting. Imagine, Des O'Brien, being nutritionally deprived. Was that why he was so freaking hungry? Was he just trying to fill his quota of nutrients? And this intestinal flora business. Really, that important for health? If that was the case, his flora were pretty unhappy. Sound like they needed all that fibre he was just pitching. Interesting theory...but clearly, there was one thing he would have to do.

Just start. Eat less, eat better. And move more.

CHAPTER SIX

Des had to stand again. Standing. Something else people...not of his heft...took for granted. Walked out of the doctor's office, down the elevator, out the front door to the convenient bus stop. You'd think they'd look at the number of people using public transit and put enough freaking buses on the routes to pick up the people. Well, suppose there was. They all got on the bus.

But there he was, standing again, gripping that dangling strap. He could see Donnie at the back, a glimpse between moving obstructions. He gave him a wink over the heads of those lesser plebes in front of him. As if he could move back there. As if Donnie could move up. But the kid grinned. Gave him a thumb's up.

But how Donnie got a chair every time was beyond him. And wasn't he older? Weren't most people older than the kid? What's happened to society, anyway? Tucking him away into a seat was probably better though than having two Tessie's jamming up the aisle.

He looked down, listening to his mental chatter. Wow. Entitlement. Think he should get a chair, just because...he was older than the kid? Because...he was bigger than the big kid? Because... he was a cardiac patient? Plebes. What did he actually think of these people around him? Really? They were plebes?

What was that, in ancient Roman times? Oh yeah, the bottom of the heap. So ..."other plebes..." So did that mean he, too, was at the bottom of the pile?

Well, of course he was, he was on the freaking bus, hanging his derriere in the face of some vagrant who just managed to scrape up enough coin to ...

Des shook his head. What was happening to him? Tessie's? Him and Donnie? Calling people vagrants? Where did he get off? He looked around him and counted the number of people chewing. Candy bars, Donnie was one. Some just chewing, gum. Hey, wasn't there some sort of rule? No eating on the bus? What about that pop? And for heaven's sake, more than half of them seemed heavy. Just like before.

Wow, talk about mental chatter. Thought about thinking. About all the labels that automatically come to mind. What did Doc call them? Lies. And the stupid tape recorder in his head. Tape recorder? Where did that word come from? As if he'd even seen one of those.

Des swung by the neon soda pop sign, noticing how the lid flipped over and over. Sparkling. Filling the cup. Then saw the kid with the Coke. And the one with the Fanta. And the one that had a six pack under his arm. Bag with groceries, but all he could see was crap.

Des hit the bell and surfed to a stop. Yup, there he was again, that little mutt that was never on the street by the time he got out. Up and down the street, gone. Must have run. Walked towards the building, past the stairs this time, enough is enough.

And wondered what was in his fridge.

* * *

Later. He'd look at the fridge later. Collapsed into his chair, his chest heaving. Legs up on the ottoman. What relief. Palpable reprieve from pain. Peace.

He flipped open the paper. Des had walked by that one in the hall. Actually, had kicked it in the door. But this one, getting a bit dog eared now and thought about his buddy on the street, amazing how his brain worked, serious mental discombobulation happening. Heh, Heh...this one had the article. Adipose. Next section on fat, itself.

First, know thine enemy.

Battle plans.

Page 2...

Adipose.

Fat: commonly despised, an enemy to be sure. Or is it? Adipose is stored energy, padding and insulation and more. Fat is not bad. In many parts of the body, it fulfills functional roles beyond mere padding. How would an eyeball stay suspended properly in its socket? Doctors are well aware of the great frequency of foot problems later in life, just through loss of fat pads in the soles. Could one exert as much pressure in a grip without some fat padding? Joints themselves need some fat to operate properly. At a cellular level, there is some research that indicates an adipocyte role in control of stem cells, in skin and bone marrow sites.

It's not a thing you can just cut off; it's not inert; it's not just your "spare tire". We try to cut it off in our great haste for change. Doctors suck it out with a procedure called lipolysis. Lipectomy: the tummy tuck. Except it doesn't work. Our understanding is incomplete, but it appears that other fat sites get bigger and the very site that gets cut out regenerates (Berry, Stenesen & Zeve, et al, 2013).

Adipose tissue is now recognized as being metabolically (chemical transformations), immunologically (antibodies, etc.) and endocri-nologically (hormones) active (Booth, Magnuson, & Fouts, et al, 2016). Too much of it you get sick. Too little you also suffer. Anorexic patients can suffer from arrhythmias, heart failure, anemia, fractures, mood problems, hypogonadism (the effects of low sex hormones) and many other problems. Long distance female runners, as fit as they are, often suffer from amenorrhea and infertility as well.

Back during the Olympics, Des had been struck by the female marathon runners. Sure, the guys were skinny, some like toothpicks. Different body type, for sure. Sure. But then thought of what those athletes were sacrificing.

Fat tissue is largely made of something called adipocytes, cells whose function is largely the storage of energy in the form of triglycerides. We are born with fat. Fat cells are formed in the fetus and keep forming throughout life. Obesity is caused from both an increase in number of adipocytes and increase in the size (up to 3 times in size (Berry, Stenesen & Zeve, et al, 2013)) of the actual adipocyte cell. Triglycerides are formed in the liver and in adipose itself, from sugars and glycerol. In essence, a triglyceride is a "tri-sugar chain". Three long chains of sugars are bound to glycerol. Sugars essentially come from plant sources.

The fat we consume from animals consists of basically saturated fats (triglycerides with chains of glucose molecules joined by single bonds) and cholesterols, which are a more complex molecule called a sterol. (In contrast, vegetable fats are basically unsaturated fats... having double bonds, with some exceptions such as the tropical oils, coconut and palm). Whereas molecularly, triglycerides look like just 3 long chains of sugars bound together, cholesterols have the appearance of chicken wire, or a net. Cholesterols are needed for life but when consumed in excess, are either excreted in the gallbladder or stored in adipose. Up to half the body stores of cholesterol can reside here. Cholesterols are found in cell membranes and are metabolized into steroid hormones, vitamin D and bile acids. Recent research suggests that cholesterol is preferentially taken up in visceral (abdominal) fat, not at the subcutaneous sites (Chung, Cuffe, & Marshall, et al, 2014). Both types of fat, triglycerides and cholesterol, are found in atherosclerotic plaque, the blood vessel plugs that lead to heart attack, stroke and other vascular problems (American Heart Association, 2014). Many feel that the saturated fat is more dangerous in this regard.

Des remembered that model of the heart Doc had on his desk, with the fat globs plugging up the pipes.

Total body fat can represent as low as 2-3% to up to 70% of body weight (Berry, Stenesen & Zeve, et al, 2013). The two basic types of fat include white adipose tissue (WAT) and brown adipose (BAT). WAT stores fat for energy production, while BAT is used for heat production. The percentage of BAT in the body falls with age and was until recently felt to not be found in adults. Large accumulations of fat are found around internal organs, underneath the skin, in the breasts, between muscles and in bone. These accumulations can more easily be conceptualized as a separate organ, however fat is not always found like this. Ectopic fat is that fat found where it really shouldn't be, like inside the liver, the heart, the pancreas, or within skeletal muscle.

There are real differences in the types of WAT found in the body. Energy is stored first subcutaneously, the excess then being stored viscerally and elsewhere. Subcutaneous fat does not act like visceral fat. There are several defined places where fat accumulates, for example between the shoulder blades, in the groin, around the sex organs and inside the abdomen itself. Under the microscope, these tissues appear different, have a "different molecular signature" (Berry, Stenesen & Zeve, et al, 2013).

Fat found around the heart is felt to be different metabolically, as is the fat found ectopically.

Sometimes subcutaneous fat is called good, visceral fat, bad. Pear shaped fat distribution is often called female, apple shapes male. Are these categorizations appropriate? Certainly, it appears that individuals that are more pear shaped (subcutaneous fat) have better health outcomes than those more apple shaped (visceral fat). These shapes tend to run in families, inferring a genetic trend (Shi, H. & Clegg, D.J. 2009).

In comparison with visceral fat, subcutaneous fat has more new fat cell creation and adipocytes with more rapid turnover. These younger cells are thought to be more metabolically normal (Berry, Stenesen & Zeve, et al, 2013). Interestingly, transplantation of subcutaneous fat into the visceral area led to health improvements in mice (Tran, T.T., Yamamoto, Y., Gesta, S. & Kahn, C.R., 2008).

Those with more visceral fat exhibit more resistance to insulin than those with more subcutaneous abdominal fat (Preis, Massaro, & Robins, et al, 2010), seeming to infer a different metabolic, or endocrine function of this subtype of adipose tissue. Subcutaneous tissue appears to release more leptin and angiotensiogen (Berry, Stenesen & Zeve, et al, 2013).

In times of relative insulin deficiency, energy requirements are filled by release of glucagon, an opposing hormone. Glucose is released from its storage form, glycogen. Fatty acids are released from adipose. Glucagon has many actions, including starting the production of new sugars and encouraging the body to mop up debris.

The hormones work opposite to each other: INSULIN UP, glucagon down. GLUCAGON UP, insulin down. When sugar is up, insulin goes up and sugar enters the cells, the excess producing fatty acids which are stored as fat. Insulin down, glucagon up, fatty acids are released…when no sugar stores are available. Insulin and glucagon, those hormones involved in regulating blood sugar, are therefore heavily involved in obesity.

When no sugar is available…interesting. Come to think of it…probably at no time during the day, the way he ate, which was all the time…except when he was asleep! Or just getting up. Wonder… what about a walk before that first meal? Would that push that glucagon up and start a bit of fat burn?

After a meal, insulin is released. It is released faster and in greater amounts after a sugary meal. Sugars come in different forms, from the most insulin inducing simple sugars (refined sugars, as in candy floss), to starches (anything made of flour, potatoes, rice, grains), to those sugars found in fruits and finally in vegetables, where one finds the sugars inducing the slowest release of insulin.

Potatoes? There it was…a starch. Half of his normal plates of food. Well, his normal several plates of food.

One tends to forget other hormones involved in obesity, with insulin's powerful lead role. Adipose is actually an endocrine gland itself, a tissue that releases hormones. Amongst several others fat tissue releases leptin, a hormone called a cytokine that tends to vary inversely with insulin. As insulin goes down, leptin goes up. And vice versa. Leptin enters the brain, decreasing eating and energy expenditure.

Why doesn't leptin work in obesity and diabetes? Resistance occurs to both insulin and leptin. There's more to this story than we currently realize, with adipose now being recognized as a producer of many circulating hormone like molecules called adipokines and cytokines. They are important in healthy regulation of not just food intake, but metabolism itself, immunity and inflammation (Booth, Magnuson, Fouts, et al, 2016). They also have more physiologic roles, such as hypertension (Yiannikouris, Gupte, Putnam, & Cassis, 2010). Factors that relax blood vessels (perivascular relaxation factors) come from adipose. Resistin, an adipokine found in fat and felt at one time to only slow insulin's action, may have a role in hypertension as well. Angiotensin, once felt to be only released from the liver and the target of many of today's antihypertensive medications, appears also to be one of these adipose related hormones.

Analysis of adipose itself may lead to some answers. This fat reservoir is a magnet for fat soluble chemicals from the environment. Many researchers feel that the explosive growth in obesity must be due to more than just the effects of a sedentary lifestyle and tasty treats (Regnier & Sargis, 2014). Although this perspective is not helpful for patients struggling to initiate personal life changes to overcome obesity, there may be real, tangible, outside factors at play. Environmental contaminants may be disrupting both the formation and function of adipocytes.

Pollution. That's what they're talking about.

Des threw the paper on top of Rushmore, his biggest pile. Pizza boxes, still there. Pizza, his go-to dinner. Lunch and leftovers breakfast. Call 'em up and it was there. Speed dial. Answer the door and it was there. Hot. All of them, the whole stack, hot. As if, leftovers. As if, how often. Crusts. Finish what's on your plate, starving kids in Uganda. As if, thought about Fed-Ex-ing his left over pizza crusts across the ocean. His feet hurt. Probably would be stale. The crusts, not his feet. Probably would eat them anyway. Actually hurt, just from that stupid doctor's visit. His feet. Or could have been the staircase.

Now, that was stupid.

Sat back and thought about that one. Was it stupid? Thought about what had happened. Was it all on Sunshine's shoulders? Was he that taken with her?

Maybe it was just the feeling, the heart rate increasing, the stir he hadn't felt in so long. Was it an error? He knew that feelings could be distortional. Memories of his mom's depression and talks over the decaf coffee pot, pot after pot, night after night. She really wasn't into books, but Doc had wanted her to work on that Cognitive Behavioural Therapy workbook. Des had helped her do it and learned a bit on the way. No, feelings weren't necessarily all, "correct". He had a feeling, though, that this one may have been right. And that a lot of his hardness, his resistance to change, his decisions to self-isolate, well, they sort of felt like the warped ones now.

He started looking at his thoughts. Why hadn't he even tried the stairs on the way back? Once burnt, twice shy? Why not just one step up, maybe two, then bail and use the elevator? Well, guess... it just wasn't done. Nobody did that. You walk into the foyer, push the button and wait. It's how it's done. The stairway was semi-dark, chipped paint on the door, cobwebs... now who would use that? What if someone saw him? What if, when he got out the door at the second floor...what if someone saw THE ROLL, the college athlete, the next big best thing in the NFL, staggering through?

It wasn't just the thought, the decision to get active and eat less, to make the change, to lead a different life. It was everything else, much more everything else. It's what everybody else was expecting from him and from everybody else. It was if his thought, his decision, was like a tiny little piece in a much bigger whole. In order to change paths, he would have to consider that whole and make plans.

But how?

Des moved to his computer, his window on the world, his eight hour a day work, four-hour-a-day recreation tool. He'd heard about this from one of his online buddies.

Standing, just standing was supposed to burn calories. Now, if what Doc was saying was true, simply standing for a period of time when he was at this point in his body recovery program, could just move some calories. Standing...at his weight, using this online calculator...an extra almost 100 calories an hour. If he could just stand all day, just think.

He could probably just prop up his computer on a couple of boxes. He had enough pizza boxes to work with.

Des sat back in his chair, his usual day to day exercise. Wonder how many calories that took, leaning back! Ha! As if standing was substantial work! But probably at his weight, it was.

Stood up and timed himself. He could do a bus ride, about eight minutes, walk into a building, but then that was pretty much it. Chairs were his first target. Didn't move, just stood there. No grab bar to hold on to like the bus, no lurching around, no steps, just stood there.

And collapsed in about 3 minutes. Des shook his head. This stand all day thing may not be for him. He would have to move when he stood.

Pulled his computer towards him and worked on a prompt. Made it cool, heck, he was a graphic designer! In about an hour, he had a little flashing pop-up that reminded him to stand up. That's how he could do it. None of this embarrassing himself out in the lobby. Just stand up in his own apartment and sit back down.

Programmed it for every ... eight minutes. That would mean he'd have to stand up 7 times an hour, sixty times a day. Couldn't find how many calories that was on Doc Google but it was a lot better than he used to do.

He made another decision. Action. Doc had always said the whole thing runs backwards, too. Sure, there was belief system

-> thought -> feeling -> behaviour. But it also ran the other way. And, faster he said. Change behaviour, change everything.

He was going to document it all. Well, some of it. And a picture was worth a thousand words, they say. Humph.

"Ok, Instagram, you got a new putz." Signed up. Obrien. desmond. There. He'd take responsibility and start documenting what he ate, what exercise he managed to do.

There. Started.

* * *

There was a fridge. In that kitchen. Around the corner from the TV room. Not to mention the mini one next to the couch. The beer fridge. The dip fridge.

Typical bachelor pad. Typical home, nowadays. Wrigley Field flat screen, click-clack couch sitting the prescribed distance, coffee/ chip/ pizza/ beer/ crap table. A balcony, under those windows stuffed with junk. Torn up lawn chairs, golf bag...did he ever use that a second time? Couldn't remember. Boxes. Beer cans. Bric-a-brac.

A vacuum somewhere in the back of a clothes jammed closet. Garbage, too small. Couldn't pitch 'em. Sure, he'd wear them again. Right.

Dust bunny tumbleweeds. But that TV was clear. And with the lights out, what did it matter? Crystal plasma clarity.

Laptop on the couch. iMac in the bedroom, not as big as Doc's but decent, big desk bigger clutter. Coffee rings, sugar grease stains, comfy couch chair.

Probably stunk.

But you get used to it. It was his stink. Gotta wash dishes one day...

But the fridge. The fridge freezer.

Lots of ice cubes, ice cream bars, Haagen Dazs, pastries, more pizzas, minis. Corn dogs, pop tarts, pancakes and waffles. TV dinners. Bag of frozen corn.

FAT

Hmm. Corn. Veg, right? Ice cream… dairy. Corn dogs… meat and veg, right? Pastries…but still had fruit. Same goes for pop tarts. TV dinner, 'nuf said, they have professional dieticians, right? Pizza, tomato sauce…cheese is dairy, bacon, sausage, onions, mushrooms…that's why pizza is the go to! Well, it's a meal! Doc talked about nutritional density. Whatever that was. Fibre.

He took out the pancakes, waffles, obviously clearly junk.

Freezer done, the fridge itself was easier. More beer. Maple syrup. Catsup. Ketchup. Whatever. Bacon.

Well, you didn't throw out beer. Come on.

Des swung it shut. This was a bit tougher than he thought. Do you throw out something that took what, gallons of sap? Underpaid guys standing around in the snow, probably half frost bitten, poor horses dragging the stuff on sleds through the trees. But you had to put it on something.

And threw the pancakes, waffles, back in there. Didn't have to eat them now. That's what freezers are for. They'd keep.

* * *

Tough to work at home, in a way. Really didn't matter a damn when you got up, or if you worked half the night. Never had bad feedback from the boss.

Alarm went off. Cuffed it off the table. Stupid thing. As if. Set the thing last night, thinking he'd get up thirty minutes early for a walk. Sure. Glared at the machine purring away on his side table. And the mask he always threw off.

Leaned back into his pillow, then shoulders up a bit, then leaned back, shoulders up again, rocked the momentum and swung his legs around and down.

Still had it. Athlete at large.

So, he was up at his regular time, which was in time to watch Family Feud reruns. Gotta have something on in the house, no one else making any noise. Stung a bit, that one. Stood looking there at Richard, scratching his stubble with the remote. He had quite the routine.

CHAPTER SIX

Get up late, lounge around the 'Feud with a couple of danishes and double doubles, slowly get around to creative genius work. You can't rush creativity, right? Try to jam that and it all just falls apart. Creativity has to blossom, germinate and grow.

So he didn't push it. Petticoat Junction after that, running around in frilly dresses after a pie eating contest, then the Hillbillies. Jethro with his mixing bowl full of corn flakes. What a pig. And how did he stay that thin? Food pornography, so help him. Damned food pornography. And then there was James Bond, during his little graphic arts work break in the afternoon yesterday, Mr. Prime Secret Agent hitting the bottle and never slurring his speech, able to run across that girder full speed, gun in his hand and not slip. What BS. Food pornography, alcohol porn. All those girls in the bikinis drinking Bud and eating fried chicken, some sort of beach oyster bake, now get real.

Sort of fun though. Nice if it was real.

It wasn't. It wasn't real. It was societal BS. It was part of the net, part of the bear trap he was in. It wasn't just what he decided. He was caught in a trap called society. He'd just been lapping all this up, for years, like a thirsty dog at a drainage ditch.

Thought about all those chemicals. Looked at the smokestacks, way down the road. Used to just look past them. Not anymore. Suddenly it felt like the veneer was ripped off. Looked at his chairs. All grouped around the freaking TV. Like that was the focus of his life.

It probably was. WAS. That's the key word. WAS.

That article, where was that? Was starting to get into toxins. Toxins and adipose. Fat. Toxins in fat? Where was that stupid paper?

Turned from Richard and went to his fridge. And how many 6 packs did one single guy need, anyway? Doc said water, or milk. As if milk would keep in his fridge. He'd have to drink the stuff. Milk. What was that, anyway? Wasn't lactose sugar? And...if you did low fat milk, what happens there? Wouldn't sugar go up? But protein...there *was* protein in milk. This was getting complicated!

Grabbed the beer, the maple syrup, pancakes and waffles, throwing them in a bag. Doing this in TOP SECRET mode wasn't going to work. Family next door had some little kids. Torn clothes, running up and down the hall yesterday.

Care package. And not just crap. They needed some food, any food. And he could afford real food. Better food than this, anyway. TV dinners and corn dogs. In the bag. Corn. Corn was a grain, not a vegetable. It was even in those TV dinners! Cheaper, right.

In the bag.

Looked again at the Haagen Dazs. Big sigh. Yeah, dairy. A bit. More societal hogwash. Probably a ton of sugar...looked at the label. Man. First time for everything. Des O'Brien, looking at a food label. What! One cup, 42 grams of sugar. Remembered as a kid, his big seminar. Yes, him. Des O'Brien. Probably did eat his weight in sugar. 42 grams. An ounce and a half. 40 grams of fat! 600 calories! And as if he only ever ate a cup! Nutrients? Well, some calcium. A bit of vitamin A...

Threw it in the bag. Basically, crap. Nutrient dense it wasn't.

Well, that's pulling down his pants. That's waving the flag, look at me, the Fat Guy.

Well. He was. He wore society's label. And he was going to DO something about it. DEFY THE LIE. That three letter word, FAT, did *not define him*. He *was not the label*. He was a flesh and blood, whole person. With excess energy storage.

Defy the lie. He was going to do it. Do what "FAT", and he really *resented* that label, what FAT people don't do. But doing it without any kind of societal interaction just wasn't going to wash. Society helped make him like this. He was going to use it to get back his life.

Big breath. There's thinking it, then there's action.

He had started. It was there, in his plastic bag. The remnants of his old eating habits. Stunner. That's what it was. Apart from pizza crusts in boxes, that was all the food in his house. Besides the bacon. But come on, it was bacon. Cupboards were bare. In one step, he was symbolically making a shift.

But going down the hall was another matter. Knocking on that door, looking at Kit's eyes, eyebrows raised, the confession.

And threw that plastic bag back in the fridge.

But at least found the stupid paper. Grit his teeth at the smokestacks out the window and sat to read.

...adipose itself may lead to some answers. This fat reservoir is a magnet for fat soluble chemicals from the environment. Many researchers feel that the explosive growth in obesity must be due to more than just the effects of a sedentary lifestyle and tasty treats (Regnier & Sargis, 2014). There may be real, tangible, outside factors at play, biological forces that stack the odds in favour of increasing adiposity. Environmental contaminants may be disrupting both the formation and function of adipocytes.

Des looked at the grime on his plastic table, out there on his balcony. Absolutely black, couldn't wipe it off without some sort of cleanser...which of course he didn't have. Garbage in his apartment, refuse on his balcony, sediment in the air. He was living and breathing this pollution thing and realized he was part of it...

Called generically endocrine disrupting chemicals or EDC's, these are chemical compounds that affect an aspect of hormone action (Chamarro-Garcia & Bloomberg, 2014). They have been shown to have an effect in fertility, on the thyroid gland, and now appear to be involved in changing energy metabolism. To be clear, much of this is pollution and chemical exposure. Animals in industrialized countries have demonstrated weight gain and increased adiposity, both wild and domesticated. EDC's have been proven in the lab to increase obesity in lab animals. These chemicals, dubbed obesogens, include PCBs (now legislated away, but are they gone?), tributylin (a fungicide, now banned but also a persistent environmental chemical), lead (still have that crystal decanter?), BPA (bisphenol A, that chemical that made us throw out most of our plastic cups that year), organophosphate insecticides (standard chemicals used in farming), atrazine (herbicide, apparently popular) and trifumizole (a fungi-cide) (Chamarro-Garcia & Bloomberg, 2014).

In February, of 1998, the first Olympic gold medal ever awarded for snowboarding was stripped from Canada. Ross Rebagliati tested positive for marijuana, despite not having used the drug for almost a year (Lapointe, 1998).

Des remembered back...how mad he was. Stripped from him and hadn't used in months! Now was that in any way sportsman-like? Well, if those black barnacles were on his plastic balcony tables...and that stuck on...he looked at his pannus and wondered. How much of it was in him? And what was it doing?

There was discussion that he may have been exposed to second hand cannabis at a party a month earlier. THC is stored in adipose. Truckers attempting to maintain their special license are aware of this problem and desperately avoid exposure, even second hand. Adipose acts as the perfect storage site for fat soluble compounds. The more fat there is, the more chemicals are stored.

Not all obesogens are EDCs, but all obesogens are chemicals which increase adiposity by either acting directly on the fat or indirectly, affecting things like satiety and metabolism. These include alcohol (Hetherington, 2007), estrogens, organotins such as TBT and others. TBT is found in some seafood, plastics, farming chemicals, textiles, etc., as well as in house dust, which is human skin. Experimental exposure of lab animals to TBT resulted in increased adiposity in the next three successive generations, the last of which had no direct contact at all with the chemical (...the primary having exposure in utero, the second in germ cells...) (Chamarro-Garcia & Bloomberg, 2014).

It appears that fat, metabolically active, fully engaged hormonally in the body, is affected both directly and indirectly by chemicals. Many chemicals we are exposed to on a day-to-day basis increase fat accumulation. More than this, fat is a prime target for poisoning. Fat soluble chemicals target fat. They enter, accumulate, and they stay for a long time. We know that the adipose in obese patients operates differently. One wonders not if accumulated toxins have a role, but how much.

Des folded the corner over, ROLLED the paper back up, flipped it on his crap table. Coffee table. Pop, chip, crap table. Put one Flintstone on the edge and heaved it across the room.

Stood up. Well, the only way to get the barnacles off the tables out on the balcony was more chemicals and elbow grease. To get the crap out of him, only one of those components would work. Elbows, he couldn't quite see. But grease, that he was well acquainted with.

Sat down. Breathed hard, big breath. Leaned forward and heaved again, himself this time, and stood back up. Heart pounded. You know, you kind of get used to it, then recognize that merely standing up is difficult.

He'd have to just dive. Des recognized his feelings and acknowledged them, just like that book said over that decaf coffee pot. He remembered his mom, trying to push away those toxic feelings, trying to deny them, close them out. Never worked. Just started clobbering at her head like a battering ram. Trying to shut them out just made it worse.

Okay. So he was embarrassed. He wanted this to be his problem, not everybody else in on it. But didn't everybody else know? Sure, he wore black. Even had some vertical stripes. But as far as camouflage went, pretty piss poor. He was a big guy, bigger than big and everybody saw it, felt his presence, knew it.

Somehow it seemed to just start to roll off his shoulders. Yeah, he was big. He was an ex college athlete, the next big thing for the majors, now struggling to stand up.

But he was also Desmond O'Brien, and he was going to do something. NOW.

There's the belief, the thought, the feeling but it's all for naught without the behaviour. NOW.

He grabbed the bag out of his fridge and made his way down the hall.

FAT

* * *

The door looked a lot like his. Peep hole at belly button level. Paint from the last decade. Big Des knuckles rapped out a beat.

"Des! Wow! I've never seen you at my door! Looked out my peephole and just saw... BIG! So what's up? Ooof! "

A couple of little rascals had charged up and ran into Kit's legs, grabbing on like koala bears. Not much money, but those kids were happy. Kit's eyes sparkled.

"Yeah, I'm big. Sorry I've never come down. You have. You've always come down with mail, or a misdirected newspaper, or ... a piece of pie. I've never reciprocated."

"That's ok, Des. Guys don't do that as much. It's ok!"

"Look, Kit. I've got to do something. I have to get some of this weight off. I wonder...could you help?"

"Me? What could I ..."

Kit saw the bag behind his back. "You want me to take that, don't you?"

Des slid the bag around in front, holding it open. "Some stuff for the little guys. Mini pizzas, corn dogs, ice cream. Maple syrup, pancakes. And a couple of 6 packs... I know you guys don't drink much, don't think..."

Kit burst into tears. "Des, I didn't know what I was going to do for supper! Thank you! Kurt's been out of work for a few weeks... we're living on dribs and drabs. Thank you!"

Des awkwardly returned the hug, feeling one of the koala bears transfer over to another tree. Flushed.

"And you did this just because you're trying to help me, aren't you? Or... did you really need some other help?"

"Kit, I'm glad I can help you. Really, it makes me really happy. But I need to stop. I need to stop eating all this. I mean, it's ok for you, look at you. I can't eat this. It's ok for the kids. But look at me, I'm no kid climbing a jungle gym all day!"

"Well, we're glad to take it. Look, I'm going out for groceries at the end of the week. Kurt's brother is coming, just for that,

74

helping us out. Want a ride, get some real food? Maybe I can help you pick!"

"You wouldn't mind? Your car…"

"Is a van. You would fit, don't worry. It's a plan, Friday night at the grocery store! It's a date! And thanks! Gotta get the little guys into the tub."

They waved through the closing door. Des put a hand on the wood, and a forehead against the doorframe.

Who would have thought?

* * *

Des worked his way into his shower. An ordeal.

People never talked about this. All his visits to the doctor, no one ever asked about hygiene. How it was…well, done.

The answer was, of course, very carefully. He had taken down the glass door ages ago, simply not usable with his mass. Replaced it with a hanging plastic affair, little beige palm trees in a repeating pattern. Of course the water got out, the shower head being below shoulder level. Lots of towels on the floor prevented puddles. Dangly soap dispenser completely out of the question.

Won't talk about the grout. Managed to spray some stuff in there once in a while, run the water and hope. Splashed some bleach down there the other day.

Sandals. But then you could slip on those blessed things, too. Step on an edge, blow a flip flop like that Key West singing dude and fall on your head. Or hit your head on the side of the shower and get freaking jammed in there, with the paramedics trying to extricate your body. Jaws of Life. Probably would need a sledge hammer, and go at the very wall. Maybe even try to spray in some oil to slide him out.

He sort of slid in with one shoulder, turned, one leg in, drag the other one up, then there was turning on the water. There frankly wasn't much room. Jam the small of the back into the wall, pull the knob, splash it around a bit, then it's off as your body turns. Had to get right out of the shower, turn, rotate the other direction, spray the other shoulder, quite the production. Wash cloths helped afterwards, sitting on the toilet first, then lying on the bed to finish. Deodorant covered up the rest.

The bed. People didn't talk about this. To dry off, he put towels all over the bed. And rolled around. Sat up on his bed, shaking his massive head. Thought of the contortions he had to do to just reach his privates. Disabled stalls weren't really enough.

Thank God he worked at home. Want his life back? How about just a little sliver of a life. How about just being able to easily toilet?

Des looked at his washcloth and considered the skin cells that must be there. Those researchers had found toxins in dust. That's skin. It was in his body, in all our bodies.

He lurched up (he did a lot of that, this lurching, this rocking back and forward, leaning, precipitous movement… a lurch) and stood on his scale. Said he wasn't going to do it, but hey, he was naked and it was there.

Pretty close to what Doc got.

He thought about the toxins and realized he still really didn't understand all the diet advice. Looked at his hand. Cut off the fingers, the thumb and use that to measure…

Okay, sort of got that. But this protein, veg, carb thing really still messed him up. Calories in, calories out, thermodynamics. Got that. Got the leverage idea with physical exercise, that one made sense now. Sure, just standing on the scale, for him, was a work out. He was burning calories just showering, where it wouldn't even fizz on a fit person.

Time for another appointment, anyway. He needed the brass tacks.

Des looked up the national Food Guide. Good graphics, simple pictures, way too many clicks. Interactive site, hover your mouse and find out. Listed every vegetable, protein, starch source known to mankind, and what a portion was. And how many portions. Irritating pop up that kept telling him to stand up, what a pain in the…ended up with a huge pounder. Right between the eyes. You mean he'd have to keep looking up this thing? Carry a stupid iPad around in the grocery store? Must be an easier way.

Doc seemed to have a simple handle on this thing. Looked at his hand again. Was that half a cup? No way Hosay. Jose. Whatever. Sigh.

Back on black clothes. Black, again.

Went out to the Wrigley Field room, the TV amphitheatre veg out chamber, and looked at the mountains of pizza boxes. The tin cans idling on the floor between them, their tail lights glinting in the sun.

Very nice mock-up of the scene out his balcony window, complete with pollution. Bugs. Probably Bugs. And it did stink. Well, it may be polluted outside, but it didn't have to be in here.

Picked up an armful and walked to the door.

CHAPTER SEVEN

When he was a kid, it was Johnny. Heeere's Johnny! And Big Ed. Weatherman turned late night staple and his henchman. After that, Letterman. Or Saturday night, Cone-heads and cheeseburger, cheeseburger, cheeseburger! No Coke, Pepsi!

Some habits were just hard to break. Sometimes, a slow bend is better than a shatter. Dropping Carson was no biggie, as it wasn't even around anymore, nothing like it. For years. Infomercials. Dice 'em slice 'em super vacuum cleaners. Some kinda skin cream. Always a gap, waiting for Letterman.

Sometimes reasonable stuff. National Geographic. The History Channel wasn't bad. Or moving to Costa Rica, rural France from Dallas, culture shock. Sometimes it was just channel surfing while waiting.

Or an interview.

Easy chairs, suits with loose ties, the late evening chat. Even a fireplace. Cups of, must have been, decaf. Or, of course, a canned session.

Intense, curious interviewer, laid back expert.

Nutritionist?

"So why doesn't it work? Why doesn't just eating less and moving more, work?" Sat back in the chair, gesticulating in frustration.

Calm, assured smile. Shock of ink black hair standing on end. "There is no eat less, exercise more diet. Lots of hits on the Internet exist, however. Separating wheat from the chaff, the gist of the musings seem to indicate that although it works out on paper, it just doesn't work. Calories in, calories out. The predominant feeling is that it's just too easy and that if it held true, everyone would do it. One of the biggest reasons for the cycling of weight, the loss, then the regain, is the fact that metabolism slows with weight loss. It's more complex than it seems. According to a viewpoint in the prestigious JAMA (Ludwig & Friedman, 2014) which sums it up well, the two contrasting camps are, "... eat less move more vs chronic overeating as a manifestation... of increasing adiposity." In this latter position, weight loss is not sustainable without coming to grips with, "...biological drivers of weight gain, including the quality of the diet" (Ludwig & Friedman, 2014).

"Timing of that meal seems important. Shift workers have more problems with weight, implying impact of the circadian rhythm on adipose (Laermans & Depoortere, 2016). Those that skip breakfast had more problems with obesity than in those that ate dinner within 3 hours of going to bed, itself a risk factor for obesity (Watanabe, Saito, & Henmi, 2014). This new kind of inquiry has been dubbed, chronobiology."

"Chronobiology, Dr. Hu? This is television, not some academic paper! Can you put that in words I can try to wrap my brain around?"

"It's not just calories in, calories out. It's also when those calories are consumed and when those calories are burned."

"So it matters when we eat and when we exercise?"

"One of the biggest issues is that we sit around, all the time, like we're doing now. We're made to be moving, almost constantly. Hunting, gathering, searching for that hard to find food and running away! Now, food is at our elbow...," Des pushed away the cookie plate at his elbow.

"Maybe a topic for next time, chronobiology. Any little tips, of when to exercise, for example?"

"Any exercise helps. Stand up at work! Go for a walk to talk to your co-worker. Park farther away, or leave your car at home! Walk to get those few groceries, to mail your letter. Most people that exercise burn actually very few calories during that isolated exercise event. You have more opportunity to burn calories during the rest of your day. For example just standing at work, instead of sitting, for an overweight, out of shape individual, can burn an extra fifty calories per hour. Doesn't sound like much, but over an eight hour day, it builds up! Four hundred calories is equivalent to jogging for almost an hour."

"Dr. Hu, you should go into politics. You answered my question by saying exercise all the time!"

"That's my answer. Move, all the time. Take short breaks of rest, but otherwise move, or at least stand. There are some trials inferring that morning exercise, before breakfast, may be the most powerful at burning fat. But forget that. Exercise all the time!"

"Didn't mean to divert you. You were starting to...," the interviewer gesticulated, "...expound...on diet and obesity..."

The man in the tweed jacket, apparently flustered by the questions on exercise, obviously a sore topic, sat back in his chair, took a breath in and sipped his coffee, becoming contemplative.

"It appears there are many pathways through the forest in regards diet, with ongoing research on all fronts. The hottest diet right now, the paleo diet, does come with some impressive research. The prestigious ADA has jelly fished its stance, allowing different approaches, but emphasizing calorie restriction and increased exercise.

"It makes sense to pull essentials from more than one camp to come up with an approach to teach someone suffering from obesity. Clearly, intake of less calories is paramount. More leverage can be achieved if lower glycemic load carbohydrates are chosen, with less straight sugar period. Lots of fibre slows the sugar hit and feeds gut flora. Protein clearly plays a major role in insulin sensitivity. Choice of fat matters.

"What if the glycemic load diet, famous for having no portion restrictions, was so modified? People need clear guidance for portion choice. Perhaps going with the palm of the hand as a basic measuring device could help (Wax, 2014). Four palms per plate, with one palm representing meat or alternatives, one starch, and two a variety of vegetables."

"Palms, Dr. Hu? From Mr. Scientist? That sounds pretty fuzzy!" The interviewer took his turn sipping java. Hot chocolate, perhaps, as he looked as if he had a remnant of a moustache.

"Palms are portable and always with you! They vary with the size of the individual, very appropriately. A big person will get a bigger serving. Exchanging olive oil for butter is a clear move, borrowing from the Mediterranean diet, which is one of the only two diets for which we have really good outcome data. If you want to go with one diet, as a basic structure for your eating decisions, this one is probably it. DASH, the other diet with really good data, emphasizes salt restriction and good nutrition, foods that help lower the risk of high blood pressure. DASH stands for Dietary Approaches to Stop Hypertension. If you're interested and want to just learn a couple of diets, do these two. The Paleo diet's exclusion of processed foods is a wise one. There are some foods that humans were simply not made to consume at all, or in their current quantities. Margarine contains fatty acids never before seen in nature. Refined flour, a bastardization of the industrial age, has wheat germ and husk removed, allowing for better shelf life but suffering from decreased protein. And sugar! Prior to the year 1500, sugar was so rare it was considered to be a spice. Now one can buy sugar more cheaply than fruits and vegetables."

"Outcome data? Come on, Doc, remember who you're talking to! And, you infer that margarine is plastic? Bread is just sugar? Which, by the way, we should only sprinkle? What is this, Doc? Would the government let us eat plastic?"

"Not plastic, but certainly not natural. It is fat, but the lipids that make it up are simply not found in nature. Your body uses lipids in its structures. Myself, I don't want a man-made chemical forming any part of my cell membranes! And yes, bread is just basically sugar. And yes, each North American eats about 150 pounds, often almost their weight in actual sugar, yearly. Way, way too much.

"Outcome data is what it infers. Outcome. Many diets can get your weight off. But what really counts? Being thin? Or dropping cardiac risk? Cancer? Dementia? Depression? Heck, many feel the Mediterranean diet has better data for diabetes than the diabetic diets!

"150 pounds?" Must have been the hot chocolate: Buddy was examining his coffee cup.

"Yup, that's three pounds per week. That's about a half pound per day. Mind boggling."

"So we should just cut these out." His eyes were clearly bulgy.

"I'm tempted to say that but the thought of complete exclusion of some types of food, however, is fraught with risk. For example, the basic tenants of the paleo diet are logical. Why eat food that is not meant to be eaten by humans? Raw foods should take more metabolic energy to break down and metabolize. However, despite the burgeoning supportive research on this diet, it appears that the diet is fairly difficult to adhere to (Jonsson, Granfeldt & Lindeberg, 2013). The WHO reports that regular consumption of processed meat or meat that is cooked at high temperatures, such as on the barbecue, is associated with adverse health consequences, including cancer, indeed the level of proof indicates causation (WHO, Oct 2015). We must also acknowledge the lifespan of ancient man was shorter than it is now, by several decades. Lives lived were very different, as was the environment. Neither do we know, exactly, what was consumed. No dairy? Can one imagine an ancient man not consuming milk found in a hunted animal? Current researchers now muse that grains did play a significant role in the paleo diet (Hardy, Brand-Miller & Brown, et al, 2015). Rules. Rigid rules. I need to emphasize that there must be an individualized approach to diet. There's no one size fits all solution.

"We also must acknowledge that these processed foods are here. Chocolate brownies exist. Mac and cheese is pretty easy, comes in a box for 99 cents, and does fill those corners. Perhaps it's all just a problem of proportion. The rare chocolate brownie is unlikely to cause problems. Just like the rare exercise event is unlikely to help..."

Des snapped off the big screen and stretched. Managed to stand through half of that one. So there.

Seemed like the guy heard his grade school speech.

Scratched Letterman.

Bed.

CHAPTER EIGHT

He was a rascal, anyone could tell.
No collar on that one. Street-wise. He just had a look about him.

Savvy.

Could have been a yellow, or maybe a chocolate. Hard to tell. Would swim at the park on warmer days, but that was a while ago. The rain would come, but best to stay out of it. Just too cold sometimes. Shivering burned them up. The calories.

Knew the cars, the bicycles, the motorbikes. Knew the street vendors he could lounge beside, the ones that would chase him with a stick, or attempt to land a boot. And attempt was usually the word. Kept clear of the vagrants, most of them. One old codger always seemed to have a cookie. Knew which doorways to sleep in, some to steer clear of.

Too many of them, what people called strays, and just not enough. Not enough, really, to get by. Food. Had to fight, not only dogs, but cats. Five, six times as many animals as homeless people. Stayed alone, fed up with the pack, the dominance non-sense, the mounting. Bigger than some, but not all.

He knew restaurants that threw out the best stuff and how to get into the dumpster. Playing cute with little girls, rolling on his back. Sitting up straight and proud for the guys, down at the park. Chip bags, hot dogs, pieces of pretzels. Believe it or not, sometimes one had to fight off birds; dogs usually won.

They said Labs could eat anything. He tried. But when there wasn't enough, ribs pushed through. He'd lie quiet, in a sunny spot. Curled up. Had to conserve energy, precious calories. Kept the nose up and watched for opportunities. The man approaching the garbage pail. The kid with the tottering ice cream. Usually he'd find something. People. These tall, big people. Always eating. Always throwing away some of it.

It was one of those times. Some days, and it was days, there just wasn't anything. Water out of puddles dried up, his buddy the street vendor out of wieners.

And then there was the big guy. Kept seeing him, went through the doors across from his favourite cubby. He was always alone. Always looked at him. Threw him a crust once.

Remembered. Remembered his bigness, his scent. He remembered all the scents, all the people that threw a crust his way. People that looked at him, that saw him, that didn't look through him.

Survival.

At night it got cold. Curled up, shiver.

Fleeting images of horses, a girl that took care of the runt. A nipple, milk from a bottle, when all his sibs pushed him out. Freckles, she had freckles.

But that was a long time ago.

No one. A piece of paper fluttered by, startle. Maybe the man, maybe a crust.

Looked across at the big glass doors. No. So still.

Wind.

Curl up.

CHAPTER NINE

Felt like a field trip. Even had a bag. A real Muscovite. Carry the thing around, scrounge for deals.

Heard that grocery stores were starting to charge now, for the plastic ones. Not a bad idea probably, seeing all the crap on the sidewalk out the window. Cigarette packs, butts, even from here. Sheets of paper and plastic. Water bottles. Energy drinks. Blown up tires, strips of rubber lying in the gutter like beached mackerel. Coffee cups. Just more planet garbage. Des had found his big backpack from State. Official team swag, emblazoned with insignia. Could fit an Austin mini into the thing.

Walked down the hall. The Kit direction, seldom taken. Same ratty carpet as the other direction. Stains on the wall from Lord knows what. Buddy must have had curry...

And arrived at the door, knuckles primed, but must have been on automatic setting, as it swung open before him. Little guy with an ice cream bar swung from the handle, grinning.

"DES!"

Kit accelerated around the corner, and pried him off his leg. "I told you about just opening the door! Hi, Des. I'm all ready. Fred is going to stay with the kids. Let me just grab my purse..."

Des stretched, and tousled the kid's hair. Freckles, right across the nose. Must brighten your day. Your life. Kids, that is. Not the freckles. Him, Des, would look stupid with freckles...

mind, cognitive processes clearly melting...thought about what he was doing.

Desmond O'Brien, actually buying foodstuff? Not online? Not delivery, him? Himself?

"Come on, Des! Harold is waiting out front with the van, just called me. Imagine. Naming two kids, Fred and Harold. Can you believe it?"

Kit trotted down the hall, jamming some grocery bags into a huge over the shoulder multi coloured purse/bag/haversack.

"Whoa there, little sister, my running days were left at State..."

"Sorry Des, I'll run ahead and get the elevator."

Good move. Less standing. One way up the hall, then all the way down the other. Should have called her, met her, Alexander Graham Bell would have approved...Kit, I need you...elevator opened.

"So Des, got an official State bag there! I think I could probably fit inside!" Kit grabbed both sides and stretched, demonstrating the vast proportions.

"Yup, heard they charge for plastic."

"Just a couple of cents, but it's the principle I think. You know, green planet..."

"You mean, there is one?"

"Yes Des, there is one, green and blue. We're in a little, tiny concrete corner. It's out there."

Elevator doors were personalized by some idiot, who was trying to popularize a phone number. That gave access to certain products. Tacked up notice about a card table for sale. Candy wrappers on the floor, right beside the sticky area, which he desperately tried to keep his size 14's out of.

"Well, that corner is pretty flipping big. And getting bigger. Heard about it on the TV? Papers? Oxfam kids, and we're using way too many resources. North Americans, like many times everybody else. Feel like a parasite. In this thing, a trapped parasite. Watch, the doors won't open. We've had the veritable tea biscuit. Goners."

"Well, isn't that a positive descriptor! You, my friend, are starting to go grocery shopping and sharing a ride, with me. You're taking a step away from pizza boxes and beer cans. And taking steps! Good on 'ya!" Made to punch him in the arm, and stopped short.

The elevator chugged to a stop, and they walked out. Dusty dingy van awaiting, Harold waving.

"Yup, that'll fit." Des sighed a breath of relief. What they called vans nowadays...but this one was straight up. Not vanesque, but definitely "van". Indicated with his hand and eyebrows, front seat?

"Yes yes, you sit up front. Think you could get your massive self in the back, do you?" Kit laughed, a clearly merry thing.

Where do you find these people? She was fairly dancing around, greeting Harold and popping into the back. More energy in her than ten people. Des swung into the front passenger seat and shook Harry's hand as he took the wheel and turned the key, Harley Davidson key fob.

"So you're Desmond O'Brien, huh? The ROLL? You're him?" Harold fairly ogled.

"State fan?"

"Oh, from way back. Saw a few games. Man, you were unbelievable. People just bounced off you. Nobody, I mean nobody, could take you down. And once, so help me, I saw you plow, right through and absolutely nail the quarterback. Right through all those guys..."

Yup, that was the day. Had chewed back the nausea, the pain, the sweats, the feeling he had to have a dump, right there on the field. No fuss, that was Desmond O'Brien. At the end of the game, thank God. Had mentioned it to the trainer.

Who had called that ambulance? The day. The last day.

"Thanks. Long time ago. Hundred pounds ago. Thanks, man, for the drive. Appreciate it..."

Harold was fumbling around for something behind his back.

"Think you can sign a ball? My kid, it would mean a lot..." And suddenly there was a football in his hands, a black sharpie being offered to him. Raised eyebrows accentuated his sheepish look. Guessed he came armed and ready.

"Oh, sure man, no prob, happy to…" Memories of doing this. Wow. Ancient history. Remembered the attention, the people looking at him, just…different. Scribbled his name. "What's your kid's name?"

"Harold, like me."

Inscribed "*Harold*," above his signature and handed it back. "Two Harold's?"

"Yup, should hear those angels sing for us at Christmas!" Threw his head back and absolutely guffawed. Family joke, must be, Hark the Harold's, sure. Harold chucked the ball to the back of the van and pulled out into the street.

"So Des, do you have a shopping list?" Kit chimed in from the cheap seats.

"Shopping list? Like you write stuff down before you go?" Strained against the shoulder belt, grabbed the back of the driver's chair to turn, look at her.

"You have no earthly idea what you're doing, do you, Desmond O'Brien?" Let the seat go and half rotated back into his seat. Here we go. Des heard vague echoes from his mother in that voice. Must be a female thing. Genetic. X chromosomes must be wired straight to the voice box…

"Teach me, neighbour. This is your gig. Sensei."

"Desmond-san. If you just walk into a grocery store, and especially if you're hungry…" eyebrows raised. A mom thing. For sure.

"Kit. Do I look like a guy that struggles with hunger?"

"I don't know, Des. Good question. Do you get hungry?"

Good question indeed. Sometimes he wondered. Habit, or hunger? Or something else…boredom? Sure, he got hungry. Ravenous? No. But that tank was hard to fill. He just sort of kept going once started. Thought about those rats in his neuro class, the ones with part of the brain nuked out with a wire. Just kept eating. Must have brain damage…good Lord, how did he get this big? Like who was he talking to, who was he asking?

"Yes Kit, I get hungry. But thanks for looking out for me. You're suggesting, if I enter a grocery store without a purchase plan, that I'll spend too much?"

"Yes, for sure. But more than that, you'll buy the roast chicken because it smells good, although that's not a bad purchase this week, on sale I think, but everything else that looks good. Need a plan!" Kit screwed up her nose, jabbing a bony finger into his chest.

"Ouch!" Was automatic, but got to thinking. That was the first touch, from anybody, painful or otherwise. Then there was Sunshine, but she had that phlebotomy needle. Not really the same thing.

"I think there's some muscle, under all...that..."

"Fat, Kit. Fat. That's what it is. I eat too damned much and don't move enough. Simple math."

Kit turned her head. "Listen, big buddy, everybody's got problems. Just different ones. You wear some of yours, right out front, where everyone can see. Just can't see mine."

Kit and Des sat there and made faces at each other. Managed to engorge veins and even change colour. Hard to beat Des, as he simply had more face. The blowfish usually brought 'em down. Nevertheless, Kit won.

"Your list. Can't distract me. Whatcha gonna get?"

"Breakfast, lunch and dinner. Snacks." The nag. Here it comes...

"Not good enough, big buddy. Talk to me. What are you gonna get?"

"Kit, stop the grilling. Figure I may go Mediterranean. They say it has the best outcome data. Sorry. TV... Don't know. Tell me."

"You want suggestions..." Yes, well, duh...

"Yup. Lay it on me. I've been screwing up, big time. Obviously."

"Okay." Kit sat back and put out her chin. "I won't ask how. Well, maybe a bit. Just need to know items. Do you cook at all?"

"Not much. Dial it up. Pizza, usually. Pizza Buona, Pizza Hacienda. Pizza Station. Pizza Pizza Pizza. But they deliver a lot of other stuff out there, some do burgers and chicken, too."

"And fries, and corn on the cob, and buttermilk biscuits, right? And Peppers. I remember your Peppers. So you don't cook."

"Nope. If you want a one word answer. Nope. Maybe I'll get some olive oil and a can of tomatoes. You know, Mediterranian.." Blunt. Sometimes ya just gotta be. Sometimes that's all they get. Blunt.

"Can't lose weight on take out. Yeah, the guy from that sub place. Sure. Couldn't do that myself. Mind you, you sort of live on pizza, I guess maybe you could. At least there's a measured amount of calories, whatever, in each sub. Sort of puts a cap on it."

"Not doing that. Considered it, but no delivery, to be frank. And anyway, want to do this myself. Three subs a day can't be healthy. I want my health back, not just my weight off."

"So you know the general principles? Do you understand that Mediterranean diet? Look it up? You know the eat five to ten fruits and veg rule? Know what a legume is? Just eat less crap?"

"I think no crap would be best." Everybody trying to be gentle. This big guy need gentle? Would gentle even fizz on this?

"Easily said. Right. I get it. I'm going to give you real help."

The van pulled into the literally jammed parking lot and the two got out. Imagined having to walk from the far corner. People had no idea. What, three wheelchair spots? One car there with no permit. Hackles rose beneath his collar.

Harold had other errands and would meet them in an hour.

"Want to share a cart?"

"No Kit, I'll take one, if you don't mind. I think I need quite a load. And to be frank, I can lean on it." Des felt the tips of his ears start to burn. Even now, the sweat was trickling down his sides, his shirt damp, in just all the right places. Bloody embarrassing. Burning at one end, drenched on the other. Tried to move his arms subconsciously, to hide the stains.

Kit rattled another cart over and patted his hand. "Got it. Stick with me."

Right in front was the fruits and veggie section. Half a football field, easy. Front line was celeriac, little funny squashes with multi-coloured hats, pomegranates and kiwis. Things he'd never seen, much less heard of. Cheap bananas, the loss leader as they say.

"Pretty imposing, huh? If you want to go full bore Mediterranean, you gotta get comfie in the fruit and veggie section." Kit grinned at him. "Follow me." Grabbed some yellow ones, barely stopping.

Right over to the side, where there were clear, jaunty plastic tubs of spinach, lettuce, leaves that looked like ditch weeds, bottles of salad dressing. Kit held up a plastic bag.

"Look at this. Some things are dead easy. Salad in a bag. Done. Open up the top and pour it in your bowl. Take a couple of these. Look at the expiry date...take three. You eat a lot, right? This'll fill you up. Get hungry, eat this stuff. Take four. Once you get in the groove, I want you to make your own salad, from scratch. Who knows how many chemicals are in these things, preservatives, you know? And this light salad dressing. What do you like?"

Des grabbed the blue cheese dressing and pitched it in. Big bottle. Grinned.

"Now, Des... got to watch it there. I know there's a lot of this Cro-Magnon stuff going on...and I suppose choosing fat may actually be better, though..."

A familiar face suddenly appeared at his elbow, turned up, looking at him.

"Donnie, how're ya doing? What are you doing bending over like that, trying to surprise me or something?"

Donnie stood up straight and turned. "Trying to show you my smaller version..." He was with his mom, little thing, turning pink to one side.

"Holy crap man, you've lost some! How much? Come on, it's me!"

"Fifty freaking pounds, man. Cro-Magnon stuff? Look at me! Went Paleo, hard core. Breakfast bacon, lunch chops, dinner steak. Green beans. Tons and tons of beans. Headaches man, like you wouldn't believe. Shakes, couldn't get over the freaking shakes. Thought I'd peg off the board, but did it. EVEN FASTED! You know the new fasting thing? Fifty freaking pounds. Know how much that is? Just piled up fifty pounds of butter over in dairy. Take a look, I left it there. It's a ton!"

Still heavy. Probably still, "morbid". But he was down. Sure as hell. Down.

"So how do ya feel? Donnie, this is my neighbour, Kit. Helping me shop. See?" Held up the salad bags.

"Good on ya, man. Hi Kit."

The two shook, Donnie enveloping Kit's in his massive baseball mitt of a hand.

"Hey, know what? Kit is teaching me to cook. How about I do dinner, sometime? Invite the two of ya?"

Kit screwed up her face in the winning position. "Now, how am I going to do that? I don't mean teach you to cook, which if I'm not wrong is an elevation of the proffered assistance, but don't mind (and punched his shoulder)... But I've got kids, ya doofus, and a husband, and how the heck are you going to get all of us in there in that bachelor pad?"

Shoulders fell. "Right. Big aspirations, no common sense." God, what just came out of his mouth? What was he thinking? Sometimes it felt nowadays as if the whole universe was shredding, something in the past solid, now a cotton ball to squish between his fingers. Like doing a spacewalk. New territory didn't quite cut it.

Donnie grabbed his mom by the shoulders. "Des, this is my mom. Kit, mom."

More baseball mitts and tiny hands. All around.

"Mom won't mind if I go. You know, guy's night."

Mom, still a bit flushed with all the unexpected attention, gestured no, no...

"Nice to meet you, mom! Donnie, you're on. Call ya?"

The two big men exchanged numbers, then Donnie turned to proceed to checkout. "Don't forget, it's a commitment!"

Des waved, and started to flush himself. "Now, what have I gotten myself into?"

Kit grinned, "Do it all the time, myself. A social commitment like that gives you a deadline, a constraint, a plan, all in itself. Just think. What did that little invitation just mean, for you and your life? That one little invitation?"

Jammed big sausage fingers into his hair, then rubbed off his hand. "Don't know...gotta clean up the place...get food... cook it..."

"Yes, and that's only the grossly obvious ones! What else? What else did you just commit to?"

"I don't know! Hey, we could use that night as one of his FASTS! How about THAT? Oh well, I guess I gotta learn this Paleo thing if he's hard core. Sort of like inviting a diabetic over, don't make chicken and waffles. Though that's a shame."

"Yes, and learn to cook. And be active this whole time he's over, since he's the guest! And be an example! He clearly looks up to you."

"Yeah, this whole football thing, probably."

"Whatever, it's there. See it in his eyes. Anyway, back to the veggies..."

Kit proceeded to load bags of apples and some clementines into his cart. "Now these, these are some snacks...," and went straight to the veggie section. Held up a bunch of asparagus.

"What's this?"

"Well, asparagus. I know what things are, Kit. Well, most things."

"Know how to cook it?" Held it like a knife, pointed at his chest.

"Yeah, ya don't. Ya leave it in the store. Disgusting."

"Cooking lesson number one. Boil this at your risk. Good chefs might be able to do that, hear they somehow tie 'em together and put them in a couple of inches of water, base down. Some kind of steaming, never done it. Boiling usually kills asparagus. You can try frying in some olive oil, on a frying pan, 'ya know? Or you can try broiling. Not boiling, broiling."

"Weird! Never heard of that! Just dump 'em on a cookie sheet, or something, and broil?"

"Well, not that easy, Des, but close. Need some olive oil on top and a touch of salt and pepper. Or, you can just bake it at a high temp, like 400 or so. For 7 or 8 minutes. You won't believe how much better it is."

Made a mental note to check the olive oil shelf and took a couple of bunches. During Kit's soliloquy about veggies, during which she continued to extol the virtues of raw eating, she taught him how to broil other veggies, like zucchini, broccoli, eggplant...

"Eggplant! It's purple!"

"Des! Never had moussaka?"

"Sure, love it!"

"Eggplant! Look Des, you're like my kids, when I'm making chocolate cake. They look at the bowl, with the flour and the egg and say, Yecch! Come on! Do you like avocados?"

"What, the green hand grenades? Wanna get fragged?"

"Gonna roll one under my bed, soldier?" Kit punched him again.

He started to like this. Weird woman. "So, okay, I'll play along, what's avocado in that I like?"

"Ever eat Mexican?"

"Kit, I'm not a cannibal!"

"Ho ho ho. Think of the green garnish you like with your tacos. Guacamole!"

"Oh, I could never make that. Come on. You're trying to give me real help."

"I am, big guy. Wait till this is soft, then scoop it out and squirt some lime juice on it. Just cut it up a bit. If you want to get fancy, put in some cut up onion. A few tomatoes. There, cooking lesson number two! And a side dish for your Paleo buddy!"

"Impressed, Kit, impressed. And with the eggplant, how do I wrestle up moussaka?"

"Now that, that's a bit much. But you can cut this in one inch thick slices, pour some olive oil on them, sprinkle with salt and pepper, and broil as well. If you like moussaka, you'll like that! Now that's three things! Three things to cook!"

The big and the small walked down the aisle, the big leaning, the small often dancing about, fluttering up and down aisles to get this or that. Like those legumes. Whatever the heck that was. Mediterranean, right. Yogurt. Desmond learned about something called "nutrient density", or the amount of good stuff crammed into a food. Pretty simple. Veggies high, same calories really as a slice of bread. Which had no nutrients to speak of!

Looked down at his hands, leaning down forcefully on the cart. Felt the sweat under his hands, the bit of a slide on the plastic handle. Looked up at her, his tiny neighbour, literally jitterbugging through the store. Thought about movements. His movements. How much more he was doing today, compared to most days in the last year. Compared it to her. Her movements, not exercise, just movements. Didn't even realize how much she was moving. Did she? She didn't see it. Didn't register. Didn't see it at all, didn't know it, just bet, just natural, all those movements.

Kit would talk about food, about cans, about the deli and the do's and don'ts. Lots of don'ts. But basically, the advice was to eat what you cook and eat whole raw foods when possible. In her mind, if your body had to work to chew it up and even move it to body temperature, it burned more calories. Made sense. Kit emphasized this by chomping on an asparagus stalk all the way down the butcher aisle.

"You gotta remember, we cook for a reason. Looked at the History channel the other day. Looks like our species wouldn't have survived without cooking! Makes the nutrients more available. So don't go raw nuts. Raw crazy. Do some raw, some cooked. You like meats, right?"

"Yup, I guess a closet Paleo Cro-Magnon type. No one would guess."

"Too much meat is too much. Try to cut it down, choose other things."

"Like lamb? Pork?"

"All meat from four legged animals is meat. Meat is meat is meat. Sure, Buffalo and venison have less fat, but from what I heard about from that WHO scare on meat, it's all the same. Too much, ya get bowel cancer. Or something like that. Or your risk goes up, whatever. Just eat less."

"So how much would you say is less?" Des screwed up one eye and gave her a beady one.

"Probably a lot less than what you're eating. But way more than me. Has to be proportional to you. I don't know, probably for you, eight ounces? Don't know. A good doctor question."

"Okay, less. But fish...never had the family thing going on that. Never had it at home. All seems weird. My house, meat and potatoes. Well, potatoes and meat. Which we actually didn't get."

Des looked over his shoulder, as if to turn back.

"Des, I walked by them. You've talked to me about this before. Potatoes for you are all apple pie and ice cream, but not only that, they're mom's apple pie, right?"

Wow, and did that sentence ever pull in some items.

"Yeah, suppose. Sort of a staple."

"Try to eat some other things, Des. It's not that potatoes are all that bad, it's just that we fry them in butter, oil. We cut the skins off, which is half the nutrient value. Add mayo, sour cream, whatever. Just a starch. Let's try to go with some brown rice this week, you know, the slow cook pain in the ass variety. For some of it. Variety. Variety is important to optimize nutrition. Why not black rice next week, red rice...maybe wild. Maybe it'll shake things up a bit. Bet you can't eat as much rice as potatoes."

"Wow, this is gonna be a leap. But that's what this is. Cannonball time. You'd like my cannonballs!"

"I can just imagine." PUNCH.

Now, that was starting to hurt. But thought he wouldn't mind the bruise. Memento. Reminder. Talisman.

"Fish. Cooking lesson number... What, five? Want a quick meal, this is it. You wouldn't believe how quick fish is to cook on a frying pan or baking in the oven. Useful for more than just warming pizza! Easy. Put some of that no stick spray on the pan, or on your cookie sheet and plop it on. Maybe some lemon juice, salt and pepper on top. I usually use an electric pan, setting it for about 300. Doesn't burn if you watch it."

"How do you know when it's done? Don't you get sick from raw fish?"

"Ever heard of sushi? But sure, you can. If it's really fresh you can undercook it a bit. If you use a fry pan, you need to flip it over. Of course! Myself, I just flake it a bit with a fork, you know, stab the top and look inside, you can see if it's cooked. Done! Cooking lesson five! Fish, Des, fish. Wanna go Med? Go FISH!"

By the time they were done, Des had to get some plastic bags. Knapsack was stuffed. Olive oil, and wasn't even sure if he had salt and pepper outside of leftover little paper pockets, thrown in his junk drawer with surplus paper napkins, straws and stir sticks. Food, and basic kitchen stuff. A real load.

Harold pulled up in the big Dodge caravan and slid open the door. "Hey, did ya buy the whole flippin' store?"

Glad of the van, Des put out his hand and solemnly shook. "Man, you don't realize what you guys have done for me today. Honest. First grocery shopping trip to an actual, non-virtual, tactile, here in the now grocery store. Have had some stuff delivered before, but not this."

Harold beamed with satisfaction, popped open the front door for Des and helped pack in the supplies. Des let them, unable to do much more than collapse in the front seat.

"You okay, Des?" Kit wasn't pulling a face, this time.

"Yeah, yeah, Kit. I'm ok. Thanks for all the help. And the cooking lessons! Harold, thanks for helping load the stuff."

"Least I could do. You rescued me last week, remember?"

"Oh yeah, Haagen Dazs for the kids. Right. Sorry about that. Junk."

"No such thing as bad food, Des. Thanks, really, the kids loved it."

"Kit, you didn't let me buy potatoes!"

"Potatoes aren't bad, Des. Didn't you see me buy some? I guess I'm just playing junior psychotherapist, trying to jolt you out of a habit. You're used to eating a ton of potatoes, right?"

"Half of every plate Kit, and I have big plates. Sort of a family thing I guess, a heritage thing. O'Brien, right? Great potato blight? Saint Patrick, all of that? Sort of sacred."

"Oh Des, sorry! Did I stomp on your traditions?"

"Well, maybe a bit. Maybe I needed it. I know, it's the amount of food and the type it is, proportioned to and compared to other food I'm eating and the amount I've burned off, right?"

"Uh, yeah. My kids, why not eat Haagen Dazs? They're like Tasmanian Devils! They burn it up like mad! Fuel and flame. But pile too much food on top of that campfire and what happens to the flame?"

"Huh? What kind of metaphor is that?"

"Clumsy one. Sorry. But fuel and food kinda have to match. If you've got a campfire going and there's not enough wood, the flame goes out, right?"

"Well, yeah. Of course. Gotta find wood."

"And if you dump a whole wheelbarrow worth of wood on top of your little camp fire, what happens?"

"So that's how you think of it, huh?"

"Whatever works, Des. Probably not scientific at all. But food and burn, fuel and flame, they gotta match!"

CHAPTER TEN

B us trips were a different animal now. From the window on his left, then the one on his right, Des swung his head and looked under the proverbial rock. It actually wasn't easy to lift. That rock sat nicely, and preferred the stock-still position. No one on the bus actually elected to stand if there was a seat open. No one. Including Des O'Brien. Few people on the street were walking, except door to door along the shops. A lot standing about, talking, waiting. A few dog walkers… looked for his little canine fantasy buddy, not to be seen. The occasional jogger, a couple of clumps of said enthusiasts.

Now if Des O'Brien had decided to stand… wonder the reaction. Would people have moved away, afraid of the impending squash? Kersplut? Tidal wave? Better just to sit and remain inconspicuous. As possible. But if he was lighter, if he was thin, he would have stood.

And ads. All over the place. Garbage pails overflowing, shattered glass right beside them, cigarette butts strewn everywhere. He'd heard that in Paris, they collect 350 tons of butts on a yearly basis, equivalent to greater than the weight of a blue whale! And signs. Wooden signs, illuminated signs, flashing lights, street signs, neon come-ons, window signs, metal street signs.

Most of them, the non-directional, non-street sign official type signs, seemed to deal with junk food! Was he in some kind of alternate dimension, or was this the red VW beetle effect? You know, buy a red Beetle, see lots of Beetles? Get hit by a red Beetle, that's all you see? Well maybe, there was that sign for the all-inclusive in Cuba, the Big and Tall Man's shop, but restaurants, all you can eat, donut shops, coffee shops, fast food meccas, one after another. In between buildings, a couple of guys on the down and out, just in the shadows, paper bags hiding the bottles in their hands. Loose paper fluttering around, cardboard slice holders, tin cans and bottles.

St. Vincent de Paul, where are you? Wide open church parking lot the next street over, probably empty, big closed doors. Funny.

Newspaper on the floor, *Subsidies on Cash Crops Leads to Obesity*, sub-heading: *Since the mid 1980's, the cost of healthy food has risen dramatically compared to that of carbonated drinks, sugars, fats and oils...*

Des thought about the former food guide's recommendation for what, 6-11 grain servings a day. Sure. It was lower now. Slumped back on his chair. Did the government have some kind of an agenda? Was the former food guide tilted towards grains, in order to support the big national cash crops? With over 7 billion in agricultural subsidies for only corn crops in 2005 (wheat, tobacco and soybean were essentially tied at almost 2 billion each...a subsidy for tobacco??) one started to get suspicious. Grain and grain products were the base, the foundation of the food pyramid?

The scene outside drew his eyes again. He knew he was big. More than big. Enormous. And everyone was smaller than he. Knew it. Knew it in black and white and capital letters. But it looked more and more that everyone was big. What were those numbers again? 39% overweight or obese? Right now it looked like a wee bit more than that.

Lady across the aisle, must have been 75 if she was a day, blue hair to boot. Shopping bags strapped to her walker, folded up beside her. Knees were...enormous. Good word. Not as big as his but huge. No business being on those legs. Cankles. Distended varicose veins. Huge, sat on that chair like a pyramid, tiny little head perched on top of a body that kept getting bigger as you went down. She rang the bell, looking a bit panicky.

And Des knew why. Bus stops weren't very long. And she had to not only stand up, but flip open her walker, make it to the door, and then get off the damned bus.

And good luck.

The bus slowed, shifted and rolled to a stop. Des couldn't sit and watch. Stood up, offering a big hand to a big lady.

"Ma'am, let me assist."

Her relief was palpable. Almost broke into tears. Blessed him. She was big, but little for Des. Simple physics, a grip and a tip. Up she came, like the Titanic. Did they raise the Titanic, or was that some horror flick he saw last week? Anyway, simple work for the big guy. Flipped that walker open and tossed it to a guy on the curb, eased her down the stairs... Just had to tip and use those orangutan arms, lean forward and semi hoist her by the nape of her coat. Just like a puppy.

She was able to turn, look up and wave a thanks. His buddy the roaming mutt peeked around the corner and looked up into the bus, tilting his head as usual. The door closed. Des watched blue hair waddle painfully away.

75, female and way shorter, but a glimpse into a possible future. He shivered and watched the bus slip down the road, towards that clinic. Pushed the bell one stop early.

What the heck.

CHAPTER ELEVEN

"Hi Des, you're a bit early. Take a seat. There's the TV on or some magazines."

Des grunted, looked at the familiar sitting area. That's what you do, sit. There wasn't a standing area, but a sitting area. That's what you do.

So he did, watching all the other sitters. Another grannie in the corner, knitting. Two kids watching the Teletubbies, or something else complete with fluorescent outfits. A couple of kids, Goth, mouthing each other in the other corner. A bunch of zoned out nondescript people.

Pamphlet. Always Pamphlets...

Obesity: Associations with Disease

Those with an elevated BMI have increased health risks. Although there may be that rare exceptional person, the patient group called overweight or obese has elevated health risk. Adverse health outcomes occur even in the face of normal metabolic features (Kramer, Zinman, & Retnakaran, 2013). This means that despite normal blood work, overweight and obesity is associated with health risk.

How much risk? Overweight and obesity is associated with risk. It's difficult to pin down absolute risk without considering associated illnesses, age, smoking, alcohol use, etc. However, overweight (BMI 25-29.9) increases relative risk, with obesity (BMI 30 +) increasing it even more. Increased waist circumference (35" for women, 40" for men) increases risk in overweight from increased to high and in obesity class one (BMI 30-34.9) from high to very high. Class two obesity (BMI 35-39.9) has very high risk. BMI greater than 40, obesity class 3, or extreme obesity, has extremely high relative risk (National Institute of Health, 1998).

Health problems seen in obesity include cardiac disease where fatty sludge builds up on arterial walls, limiting blood flow, increasing blood pressure and increasing risk for heart attack. Myocardial infarction damages heart muscle, leading to decreased heart power.

A similar event occurs in the brain. Blood vessels narrow with plaque predisposing to a plug, leading to stroke, which is damaged brain tissue.

Diabetes is highly associated with obesity. There are two basic types: Type 1, in the past called juvenile onset diabetes, has little association with obesity at its onset and is the kind children get. In this kind of diabetes, the pancreas is attacked by antibodies. There are genetic and likely environmental factors involved. People get on insulin very promptly, the hormone that is lacking in diabetes, which rises in response to increased glucose.

Type 2 diabetes is the adult onset kind, usually seen in the setting of obesity. Here there is no autoimmune destruction of the pancreas. Again, there are genetic and environmental factors, the latter felt to be more important here. In type 2, cells don't use insulin properly (called insulin resistance) and blood sugar rises. More and more insulin gets released to try to handle the burgeoning sugar load, until the pancreas can't release enough to keep up. Initial therapies in type 2 diabetes focus on lifestyle changes, including appropriate diet, which limits the load the pancreas has to deal with, and exercise which burns sugar. Often, with adequate weight loss and muscle conditioning, medications can be limited, or avoided for some time. Diabetes affects every tissue in the body and can lead to kidney, eye, and heart disease, and also stroke.

Obesity is associated with cancer: including that of breast, endometrium (uterus), colon and gallbladder.

Other conditions associated with obesity include gallstones, osteoarthritis, hyperlipidemia and sleep apnea.

"Okay, Des, your turn, walk this way."

Couldn't help but think of the Monty Python skit. Should be dragging her leg behind her, or walking with a funny bunny skip. Unconsciously started speeding up steps to at least keep in time with her.

Same room as last time, crammed up chair with arms, and one without. Hadn't noticed that before. Did notice the lack of upholstery, the sterilizable oh so comfortable black plastic. The magazine rack devoid of magazines. Pictures of his kids on the wall.

Same room, same entry line:

"Hi Des, what's up?"

The response of course should be, "What's up, Doc?" but those were old cartoons, probably heard several thousand times, so said instead, "Hopefully not my weight."

Doc walked with him down to the beam scale and verified that he, Desmond O'Brien, was actually down three pounds. Which was absolutely shocking, as he hadn't done anything to speak of. No hour long walks in the woods...speaking of which, he didn't know of any. No crash diet, but he had been cutting back on volumes.

Walking back to the room, which was thankfully on the same side of the clinic, Des noticed Doc watching his gait.

"Doc, do you ever just stop? You were watching me walk there!"

"Des, just part of the job. If I saw you walking on the street, sorry, that goes in the noggin, too. Those couple of pounds could be a large bowel movement, some water weight, or actually some adipose loss. But I'm glad it's not up. So do you have something you would like to talk about?"

"A couple of things, Doc. I just want to talk to you, to try to save time. I'm trying to read a bit but it's a bit overwhelming. There are just so many diets, styles of eating. And not eating! Fasting is in, apparently! It may just be easier to have the boiled down version. Could you have a crack at the diet thing again?"

"You mean what and how much to eat. You're interested in specific diet types."

Eye roll and a nod, from Desmond.

"Okay, basic principles. Want a data based diet? DASH and Mediterranean. That's about it. Most of these other diets are just like different religions, ways of eating based on theory. Might get your weight off, but will you be healthier? Who knows. Beliefs and religions. Different ways through the forest. Choosing any one of them may help get weight off, but choosing a religion doesn't necessarily get you to God quicker. If you eat more than you burn, weight goes up. If you eat the same amount as you burn, weight stable. If you eat less than you burn, weight down. That's easy, right?"

"Got that one. But it's hard to figure out how many calories I need to eat in order to lose the fat. That I just don't get."

"That's too difficult, Des. Just cut food off. Focus on eating to be healthy, with a nutrient dense diet. The weight will drop. If your weight is stable as it appears to be now, or even down, then all you need to do is tip the scale and things start to move. Either eat less, or move more, or preferably both."

"But how much less?"

"Here's where some of the calorie stuff will help you. Do you remember what we talked about before, the palm being a good measuring instrument? Do you remember the 100 calories per day, 10 pounds in one year rule? That rule that really wasn't perfectly correct?"

"Yeah, Doc, I'm a college grad, right? I remember. But I still don't get it. We talked about how carrots were bad."

"Des, we were talking about juicing, not carrots! There's absolutely nothing wrong with carrots! Frankly, there's actually no bad food, and juice isn't necessarily bad! Some foods certainly are more nutrient dense, some more calorie dense, with differing amounts of fibre. The nutrient dense foods are simply better. But bad food? Is one M&M going to throw the whole plan off? One chocolate bar? Of course not. It's how much is eaten, in the setting of your amount of daily activity."

"Oh, damn. Right. Forgot the juicer. Out it goes."

"So if your weight is stable and you want to go down 50 lbs in one year, you need to take off 500 calories in a day. Eat less, or burn it. Now, that's what the calorie rule says. It's not quite right, because as your body shrinks, your metabolism DROPS. You need to keep amping up the exercise to keep that fat off.

"That's the basic reason people have yo-yo weights. To keep the weight off, you need to keep cranking up the activity, then maintain that very active lifestyle and eating habit."

"Ok, Ok, I guess I have to Google it. Google all the different foods. Learn the calories, and just get moving. Hoped I could get away without doing that."

"Des, you don't have to. Just look at the volume of your hand, your palm without the fingers, and use that as a measurement of your protein serving every meal. The same size carb and double that veggies. It's a close enough approximation. Don't have to Google it all. Just stick to high quality, nutrient dense, high fibre choices. You certainly can research however, to start learning the calories for various foods. Start comparing them. A cup of vegetables, or a slice of bread. What's better? Think nutrient density, all the time. I think knowing calories may help more when it comes to cheating, you know, snacking. You should know how much you're blurring the lines with your diet."

"Ok, ok. I get it. I'll do it. But I'm having trouble categorizing foods. I just shovelled out my freezer and gave the whole lot to my neighbour, but some of it may have been good food. I'm having trouble identifying what goes in each section of the plate."

"Alright, Des. Easy. A lot of this is horse sense. A blueberry, or an M&M? You know a lot of this stuff. But maybe I can help. There are three types of food molecules on planet Earth. What are they?"

"Uh, veggies, fruit, meat, umm, and grains."

"No, smaller than that. Think building blocks. What are the smallest components of food? Macronutrients. What's your muscle made of?"

"Fat."

"Ha ha, Des. Protein. I'm thinking protein. In obesity, fat can and often does invade muscle, but I'm thinking protein. Of course it's other stuff, too. But protein. But yes, fat is another molecule. So there's two molecules. What's the third molecule?"

Des looked blank.

"What do diabetics have trouble with? You're prediabetic, right? On Metformin, right? What food group do diabetics struggle with?"

"Sugar!"

"That's right. There's protein, fat and sugar. That's it. I'm not talking about water, of which a lot of your body is made, or minerals, or fiber, or vitamins. Barring those things, your body is basically made of protein, fat and carbohydrates. So where's... platypus?"

"Huh?"

"If you were going to eat an Australian marsupial, where would you put it if you had to categorize it, protein, fat or sugar?"

"Protein?"

"Yup, and fat. Where would you put aardvark?"

"Doc, you've got to get real here. Protein and fat."

"Yup! And fish? Let's say salmon."

"Protein. A lot less fat."

"Right. And candy canes? What are those?"

"Sugar."

"Yes, simple sugars. And pie?"

"Sugar."

"And all day suckers?"

"Sugar." All day sucker. Like Des O'Brien. Couldn't believe he was sitting here listening to, and even participating in, this elementary school grilling.

"And broccoli?"

Des hesitated. "Protein?"

"No, a carb! A high fiber carb!" Doc looked delighted. Must be his number one joke.

"Oh, come on, Doc. Broccoli?"

"I said that one to trick you, Des. But yes, anything grown on planet earth is basically a sugar. There are some wrinkles, like avocados and nuts, but plants are basically sugar. Now, broccoli is a great sugar, but it's still sugar. I want you to eat broccoli, don't misunderstand me, but you need to know what it is. And what it is, is a highly nutrient dense, fibre rich...sugar!"

"Why is this important to know?"

"What food group do diabetics have trouble with?"

"Sugar."

"And what hormone do diabetics have to use, to survive? What do they inject before a meal?"

"Insulin?"

"Yes. Insulin. Insulin works by storing sugar. Either it pushes it into cells where it's burned up, or if it's in excess, sugar is stored as fat. Insulin is an anabolic hormone. It makes you bigger, increases your fat stores. That's why in diabetes, that once someone starts using insulin, the fat seems to start accumulating. More sugar, more insulin, more insulin, more fat. Actually, weight loss is a symptom of early diabetes. Lack of insulin."

"Well, it's fat that I want rid of. So then I just eat protein and fat? That's called Atkins or something, right? Is that Paleo? And how do vegetarians exist, how do they even survive, if all they eat is sugar?"

"The Atkin's diet isn't just pork chops and eggs. Even in Atkin's, you eat vegetables. And you're right, there's protein in plants. Of course there is. I'm trying to give you rough principles. Think low fiber carbs, like sugar, versus high fiber carbs, or produce."

"So broccoli is actually a sugar protein."

"A high fiber carb! With vitamins and minerals galore. Nutrient dense. These sugars are ones you should aim for! Have you heard of glycaemic index?"

"Nope."

"There's the low GI diet, heard of it?" Paleo, low GI, what next?

Doc encountered a blank stare and continued, "You can stick a catheter in someone's arm, give them a spoonful of sugar and then time how long it takes sugar to hit that catheter. Then, you can measure all sorts of foods and get how long it takes sugar to hit the catheter, and compare it to simple sugar. Some foods are really fast, almost like straight sugar, and some are a lot slower."

"Like broccoli."

"Yes! Like broccoli. Fast sugars are the simple sugars and starches, slow sugars are veg, and the ones sort of in between are fruits."

"So what's the diff.? What's the big deal? A calorie is a calorie, right? You told me before that you could gain weight eating too much broccoli!"

"Well, that's a stretch. If you ate buckets, sure. Not possible, probably. But any food at all eaten in great quantity can put weight on. It's how much you eat in the context of what you do. That's correct. But you need to consider what your body does with the food. Remember that fat storage hormone?"

"Insulin."

"You've got it. And the food diabetics have the most trouble with? The one that needs insulin the most, the fastest?"

"Sugar."

"Right. Eat food, then insulin goes up. It goes up the fastest and the quickest, with sugar. If you eat straight sugar and give yourself a tidal wave of sugar in your blood, then you spank your pancreas and insulin goes shooting up, really fast in response. It goes up so fast that it actually bypasses glucose, rising still as sugar starts to be pushed down. Insulin comes after the sugar, in response to it. It sort of overshoots. In many cases, after eating a very sugary meal, the glucose gets pushed below normal by this huge insulin spurt. Pick the low glycemic load veggies and fruits. These nutrient dense, excellent choices induce the least amount of insulin release."

"And...if your sugar is low...isn't that good?"

"Your brain needs sugar, Des. Let's say your brain gets this great sugar hit. You've eaten candy canes, or something. Insulin overshoots. Pretty quickly the blood sugar is low, lower than normal. Your brain wants at least a normal sugar level. What does your brain tell you to do then?"

"Eat."

"Yes, and eat sugar. Your brain likes a quick hit. Have you ever eaten a fairly large meal and for some strange reason you're still hungry? What turns off, just shuts down that hunger?"

"Sugar. Dessert."

"You got it. Usually after a big meal your brain doesn't get you to keep asking for more and more dessert; the body has enough calories."

"I do. No kidding, Doc. Full meal, full pie. Full tray of brownies. Not kidding."

"You'll need to retrain your brain, Des." Maybe shocked. Doc? Frowning...

"And how do I do that? Don't I need the brain changes first, so then I eat more sensibly? That's why I'm here, to get information to train my brain."

"You're right, Des. If you can change your belief systems, then your thoughts will change, your emotions will change and then your behaviour. Remember, though, that it goes backwards too. And a lot faster. Impose behaviour changes. Do it now and keep it up. As you do, your feelings will change, then your thoughts and finally that brain."

"Ok, Ok, Doc. Ok. Just stop eating. Right. Heard it before." Des started to lever himself forward off the exam table.

Doc put a hand out on his shoulder. "Des, you're upset. I'm sorry. I'm trying to help. I'm not telling you to just pull your socks up and get on with it. I'm asking you to engage in some therapy for your brain. The therapy is behavioural and I know it won't be easy. But as you eat less, it'll get easier. There are some tricks, though."

"Ok, tricks! I'm all for that!" Des sat back down and folded his arms.

"Number one, and it might sound weird, is the Washington Apple Diet."

"What?"

"Really popular, a few years ago. You know, these diets, fads. You can often learn something from them, though. There was a man, really overweight, who didn't like vegetables or fruits. His trainer was trying to come up with some way for him to eat healthier, to lose weight. Asked him if he liked any fruits or veggies. He said he didn't mind apples. The trainer then suggested he eat three apples a day, so at least he'd get three fruit servings in."

"And he started to lose weight? Eating three apples a day started weight loss?"

"Yes, because she asked him to eat those apples before his meals, with a full glass of water."

"Oh, so his stomach was half full before he started eating. So he would eat less. Sort of fooling his stomach."

"Yes, and it gave his brain a bit of a sugar hit to start, to help turn off the hunger feelings."

"Okay, I could do that."

Doc folded his arms, mimicking Des, and leaned against his desk. "You can improve it."

"The Washington Apple diet?"

"How many calories is there in celery?"

"With cheese wiz? Buckets!" Enough of the trick questions, for Pete's sake.

"No, plain celery. Plain celery has almost nothing, being a lot of fiber and water. One stalk of celery gives you six calories. An apple, about a hundred."

"So if you ate a stick of celery before a meal, you're putting a gob of fiber in your gut, filling your stomach, with next to no calories."

"And water, to make it swell a bit. Yes. Not much sugar hit to your brain, though. But overall, it's 300 calories less. And that fibre…your little friends in your gut just love it. Happy gut flora, happy person."

"Okay, that's a good trick. Yogurt help, too? I could do that celery thing with every meal, to try to restrain my appetite. And, eat a meal that is proportioned according to the palms idea. If I eat carbs that are low on the glycemic index, my insulin should be lower. Lower insulin, less storage of carbs as fat. I get it. But you said you had a couple of tricks. You just gave me one!"

"Well, two. We haven't talked much about your gut flora, your intestinal bacteria. Improve that, improve your health. Yogurt, sure. High fibre, whole grains. Less stress. Happier flora! You wanted to know about fasting, right? That can kick start things. Some people stay on that regime as a lifestyle. Basically, there are a couple of ways to do it. Remember, this is not substantiated like the Med diet. Recall that trial I told you about, the one where people gain less weight eating breakfast? Things aren't quite squared away, here. But, whatever. You want it, you got it. One fasting technique is to eat from about 11am till about 7 pm. No breakfast. Then absolutely stop. No snacks, no "free veggies" or fruit later in the day, or on rising. Give yourself a good 15, 16 hour fast, and ideally go for a hard walk before you eat. Exercise at the end of your fasting period really pulls up glucagon and jolts you into fat oxidation. Or, you can fast a couple of days a week, say on Monday and Thursday, or something, eating only 5-600 calories. Same thing. Glucagon goes up, fat gets broken down. Does a lot of interesting things in the body. Some researchers feel that this fasting process actually breaks down a lot of the garbage in the body, you know, cleaning it up!"

"So that's fasting. I get it. Don't know about that one, Doc. These were supposed to be easy tricks!"

"You told me once you ate a lot of pizza."

"Pizza champ, Doc!"

"How many slices could you have at once? Champ?"

"Oh, a huge number."

"I bet you buy all mediums, each with different toppings."

Des sat back, astonished. "How would you know that?"

"Well known principle, Des. If you have less flavour variation, your appetite drops. You've been able to eat a great deal, Des. You're changing up the flavour!"

Eyebrows raised, but a nod. Swami. Guy should work at a circus, no crystal ball needed.

CHAPTER TWELVE

They told him he desaturated something like five thousand times an hour. Well, a lot. Oxygen levels fell while in bed, because he stopped breathing. Nocturnal desaturations, they called it. Had spent a whole night in a sterile mock-up of a bedroom, his brain wired up to a machine, his finger plugged in to some kind of infrared clip for monitoring. Thought he hadn't slept at all. He learned otherwise.

He'd heard the rationale, the reasons, had the counselling sessions. Ad nauseam. Still didn't like the whole idea. Strapped up like some kind of astronaut, spaceman, freak, some Darth Vader wannabe. The first guy that told him just to lose weight and come back for a reassessment. That didn't happen...the weight loss part. Shrugged, like of course he didn't lose weight, the bastard, and gave him the script. Insurance kicked in for some of the machine.

Air. All around, and all you had to do was suck it in. Problem was, with a heavy chest wall, air really preferred to go out. And preferred to stay out when faced with a just as heavy jowl. His jaw actually moved backwards, contributing to the constricted passageway the air had to take to get to his lungs. Heavy tissues in his neck finished the job. Sort of like a one way valve. Without active, muscular work to move the bellows and keep that cave door open, air just wanted to go out. Stay out.

CHAPTER TWELVE

Not only could he not ride a bike, a horse, ride in a glider, a corvette, go on a slide, or sit on a freaking lawn chair. He couldn't even sleep without being plugged in, couldn't even breathe at night on his own. Didn't have a choice, they said, not with his cardiac history. Sort of use it or die kind of threat. Sure, hyperbole, but they had to say something, something to break through that Cro-Magnon skull. Didn't blame them for it. Could have even contributed to that first heart attack, they said.

The mask fitted over his nose, soft plastic. The use of regular nasal spray and the bubbler apparatus (the air was bubbled through water before it hit his nose) kept the nasal tissues from cracking and bleeding. The sleep doc had told him the pressure, just short of the setting needed to blow the mask right off his face. He had tried it. Hey, there was a knob, why not play with it? As it was, it had taken a few masks to find the one that didn't allow the air to escape.

But no. That wasn't enough. Not enough to have an electronic babysitter/ monitor/ girl repellent, with a perfectly sized mask, plugged in right beside the bed. As if. No. He had had to find a way to keep his jaw shut.

The face masks didn't work. No, he had devised bunny ears. A pillow case, because dish towels weren't big enough, wrapped about his head, under his jaw and back up the other side to tie up on top of his head. To keep his jaw shut. So the air wouldn't find its way out. Through his mouth.

A two tonne Easter Bunny.

Looked at himself in the mirror. The Roll. The Bunny Roll.

As far back as he could remember, from being kicked in the gut by Dee-Kew, to now this. As hard as he would try, as hard as he could suck it in. The air always found its way out.

CHAPTER THIRTEEN

"BALL PARK FRANKS! PRETZELS! CHEAPER THAN INSIDE!"

"FRANKS, PRETZELS!"

Seven day beard, a pony tail and a bandana. Gold chains. Big paunch, must enjoy his products. Hands were clean though, and man, the smell.

Des punched his brother in the arm as they joined the line. Opening day. A tradition for the O'Brien's. His brother had driven up for the day. Braden lived back home, but couldn't miss this.

They had gotten there real early, so parking was less of an issue. Parked close, which was the issue. For both of them. Braden had the family traits.

Ballparks were with the times. Friendly to people with disabilities, complete with not only washroom facilities for the disabled, but also more benches outside. If you were early enough to get one.

It all took planning. Early meant parking close. Shorter walk to the field, but then it wasn't open just yet, so a bench. Broke it up, anyway.

Des pulled his jacket a bit tighter. With his paddy cap jammed on his head, the spring breeze didn't cut quite so badly. "Can you believe this state? Hot, no humidity, my ass!"

"I thought we weren't going to do this," Braden glared. "We talked. Talked about freaking surgery, for heaven's sake. Bypasses, sleeves and bloody elastic bands!"

Des grinned maniacally. "It's cold! We have to wait, there's only a bit of a line and hey, it's a ballgame!"

"Okay. You're right. What's one game? Get me the regular. I'm going to hold the bench." Braden walked back and did the family sprawl. No one else would sit there. Could sit there.

Two people in front. Des looked over the options. Inside the gates, you got the specials. Texas Rangers had the boom stick, 24 inches of frankfurter glory, caramelized onions, peppers, chili, cheese. The Orioles, the mac'n cheese crab dog, which walked like it talked. The Braves, pulled pork on a 12 inch, the Twins wrapped theirs in bacon, then sauerkraut, onions and peppers.

This guy was traditional basic. Oktoberfest sausage, onions, dark brown mustard with seeds. Serious looking buns, had to be to handle that monster. Pretzels close to Frisbee size. But the guy had poutine, with pulled pork! On a cart. Seriously.

Serious cart. Motorcycle tires, thing must've had a muffler. Enough chrome, glaring sun, red, white and blue lettering. Flag draped around the front like bunting, must be breaking some kinda law.

The two little guys in front got 'dogs. Looked pretty good, but seriously. Next to those sausages, pretty measly. Probably couldn't do 'em justice. They did gawk, though. Quality talks. Quality rocks. They appreciated them. But not everybody could do it.

"You?"

A big smile broke over Desmond's face. "Where have you been all my life?"

"Look pretty good, huh? A sausage, man?" Gold chain sported a crescent moon, and a cross.

"Two. One for my brother, over there. And hey, can you put that poutine on top of the works? And two large Peppers."

The guy grinned, "Think that's original? What do you think the poutine is for? Some put the poutine *and* the pulled pork on top! Gotta stand out, if you're standing out here! Gotta be unique! Gotta have a gimmick! Haven't had one of mine before? Here every game."

"Hey man, I got a 110 inch Samsung, a couch, corn dogs in the freezer. Try to pretend."

"Corn dogs! Not even close! This is the Arizona Diamondbacks! D-Bat dog! If you wanna spend twenty five bucks! Had one of those? 18" corn dog on a stick, jammed with bacon, cheddar, jalapenos. Not bad, I'm a fan! But give a guy a break! Twenty five bucks! Hear some places you can get bacon on a stick, too. Bacon beer, and bacon sunflower seeds if you want to be healthy. You can't beat this, though. Watch me! I'll make you into a return customer."

Des picked them out, glistening, gorgeous specimens, slowly turning on the grill. Healthy, huh? Oktoberfest sausages were not hotdogs. Hot dogs were full of god knows what. These, these were on a different level. Saliva squirted salaciously. They talked about the team that started it all, the Texas Rangers. Two foot Boomstick. Hotdog, jalapenos, onions, chill, cheese. One dollar more at twenty six and the team with a blue crab mac'n cheese dog. Baltimore. The one they both wanted to try.

"Hey, what kinda buns 'ya got? Looks like more than one kind! What kinda street vendor are you, anyways?"

"Everybody's a health nut now. So, I got my regular, white, or my whole wheat. Want those?"

"Sure, two whole wheat. And what do you put on the poutine?"

"Hey, man, you pick it out. Everybody gets the curds wants poutine, that's poutine, right? But then there's mayo, catsup, even that pulled pork if you want it. Pickles some people, have a guy that likes mustard. Turn my stomach. Mustard? Come on."

Catsup, Ketchup. Sugar. Straight sugar. Glucose/ fructose. Sucrose. Straight into fat. "Pulled pork. Ketchup, that's straight sugar, man." At least pulled pork was protein, straight up.

"What, another health nut? Want the bun?"

"Hell, 'ya. Getting whole wheat, right? And look man, I'm just getting one!"

"You ordered two! Right?"

"One's for my brother, over there."

"So is he all for this health thing, too? Sure he's gonna want whole wheat?"

"Nah, but I've gotta drag him kick'n and scream'n. Gotta look out for my younger brother!"

Des saw Braden look at him, shot him a thumbs up.

"Here you go, man. That's eight bucks. That much inside will get you peanuts. Seriously, in a little bag, whipped at your head!"

"Thanks, man. Here's ten. Keep it. And hey, mind me asking? A cross and a crescent moon?"

The guy grinned, polishing his chrome. "I'm Muslim, actually. But love this country. Freedom. Never take it for granted. Freedom to worship however you want. Or not! I support all religions. Got a yarmulke in the back!" Des flushed a bit, nodded and smiled, and stepped away from the cart, balancing his selections. Made it back without dropping a single solitary fry.

"What the heck is this? Whole wheat?"

"Hey man, like we talked before. I've been doing a lot of reading. Whole wheat is seriously better for you, it's like 25% slower sugar."

"Slower sugar?"

"Yeah man, slower sugar! Weren't 'ya listening? Sugar slaps your pancreas, then insulin comes scream'n out, and then you put the whole thing into fat! Take it from me, bro, with the size of this sausage, we gotta have some strategy! And there's eats inside too, remember? Gotta pace!"

"Okay, okay, and like this poutine looks killer. Good choice, just razzin 'ya. And a small soda. More healthy choices, right?"

"You got it, man. Gotta take steps, make a stand! All that hydrogenated corn syrup, same thing, straight to fat! Less is more, man. Make do with the small pop."

"You got it, Des. Older brother knows best!"

"Hey, did you hear about the reno?"

"What reno?"

"Ya know about Fenway Park? Ever been there? The grandstand section?"

"What of it? And no, never been. Gotta go."

"Well, not to the grandstand section. Oldest seats in the majors. Put in during the depression, or something. Hundred years ago. Things have 17 inch seats!"

"So how big's a regular seat?"

"Nowadays, 18-22 inches. You know, we pick the section, right? We sit stadium seating. Get to spread out, get enough room. Remember that year? Couldn't even freaking sit down!"

"Yeah, don't remind me. So what about the reno?"

"More 22's! Finally, people are listening to the average man!"

Braden looked at him. "Bro, my main man. We are not 22 inch seat average men."

Then, like it was a shared, privileged joke, the two extended their necks, guffawing.

The O'Brien's finished up their pre-game snack and ambled up to the gates, just opened. Throngs approached, but kept a polite distance from them.

Braden grinned at Des. "Seems the old magic still keeps talkin!" They had noticed as boys that together, they were fairly imposing. Even more than alone. Sort of like a cop on a horse. People stood back. People behaved.

They took their time. Floated with the crowd, sort of a huge piece of driftwood amongst the foam. Over to the side, reserved for wheelchairs, no turnstile for them.

"Certain benefits, eh, Braden?"

Braden grinned back and joined him bypassing the turnstile line. Right through.

"Tickets, gentlemen?" Red laser flicked over the bar codes.

"Grandstand seating, Section W, four over on your right."

Crowd didn't quite cut it. An ocean. Bodies, tops of heads bobbing up and down. Thankfully, a bit of room around them.

"The john first Des, then the seats. I don't want to drag myself back down here more than I have to."

They both went, joining a single line this time. Stood, shuffled, stood, shuffled, groaned and congratulated themselves for not being female, their line static. Got in and stood to one side for the stalls. Two disabled stalls, both used.

The brothers O'Brien stood with arms crossed, leaning against the wall. Youngest first.

Des looked around, the ridiculous little porcelain urinals against the wall, fourteen inches apart. Come on. Moved to the sink and rinsed off a bit of BBQ sauce from his fingers.

His turn. Leaned against the wall over the toilet, swung the door shut behind him. Braden hadn't done too badly. Turned, grabbed the bar, aimed and sat. And hoped. Walls so damned tight, disabled stall, like really. Grabbed a wad of paper, pulled the bar and levered himself up. Turned again, one foot up on the bowl, moving his massive pannus to one side with one arm and reached. Sighed.

Not much of a mess. Easily cleaned up. Flushed, suspenders up and then the damned door again. Leaned against the wall over the toilet, swung it open and out.

Washed up at the sink, people parting ways in front of him. Cleared his throat, "Harrumph."

Probably Braden had gone up to the stands. Moved out, pulled his cell out of his pocket and leaned against the wall. Email check. Just a couple of minutes. Pulled the air into his lungs, one, two and three. Okay.

Looked to one side and saw the wall defibrillator. One of the security guards was looking at him, head tilted. Did he look that bad?

Wow, major thirst. Moved to the concession and got a Pepper. Two, because there was the thirst, then you needed something in the stands. And you didn't drink water in the stands. Yesterday read about that floating garbage island between Hawaii and California...another reason. All water bottles. Damned if he was going to contribute to that.

Pepper. Tradition, anyway. Beer, now that was stupid. Alcohol made you pee like a racehorse. Pepper.

Braden was there, a chip off the old block. Nice little radius of space around him. Perfect. Still warming up, sunny.

Assumed his seat and ignored the grumbles. One guy was a bit chirpy. Des leaned over a bit and looked at him, stuck his chin forward, just short of aggressive. More than imposing. Practice since grade school...good at it.

He stood down. Sat down that is, over there. Good riddance.

"Des, have you seen that guy here, the one with the bags of peanuts?"

"Oh, the one that throws them, from like 50 feet away, and always nails the guy?"

"That's the one, and he's over there! Hey!"

"PEANUTS, WHO WANTS PEANUTS!"

This guy was a show unto himself. Three ring circus! Underarm throws, sidearm, and an overhead throw, the guy could probably play given some cleats!

The brothers waved their arms and got noticed. 2 bags each, one in each hand!

"Yeah, the guy's amazing, HEY, GIVE US SOME MORE!"

"Des, I thought we were going easy!"

"Man, this is peanuts. This is great stuff, protein and fat, almost no carb! This stuff is Atkin's, in a bag! Atkins personified, Atkins incarnate!"

Braden grinned, downed them. He had a Pepper, too.

"Good thing we got the Peppers. Gotta think..."

"Yeah man, gotta think. Peanuts are good, but man, the thirst, gotta be ready."

* * *

Despite the spring day the sun was direct, and hot. No shade in that stadium, not in the grandstand seating. Took the heat down with Haagen Dazs. Usually plain ones, always chocolate dip, occasionally with nuts. And Peppers. Because Haagen Dazs simply goes with Peppers. It was like apple pie without ice cream, or pancakes without maple syrup.

A rule.

The home team was just behind. It seemed they would tie it, then be back one again. The crowd was really getting into it, chants, trumpets, screaming, and the wave. Wave after wave.

Braden and Des wouldn't stand, of course. Imagine having these two, stand up all the time? This veritable mountain of flesh, in front of you like a two ton truck on the highway that you just couldn't pass. Imagine how many people wouldn't be able to see! Bad enough the occasional trip to the john, the groans, the leaning back, the muttered comments.

During the sixth, Des was left alone for a while, Braden sauntering off to use the facilities. Thought it was his trick going to the john, then lounging against the wall for a while in the concessions...and having a few. Concessions. Had to forgive the guy though, the obvious solution. Exhaustion plus a walk, plus neighbour's cat calls, plus a nearby concession. May as well just stay down there and pound a few. One year they actually got concession tickets where they could just stay up there and forage. That was a year. Still wasn't back. Started to worry a bit...a whole inning? Thought of that defibrillator. If he had heart problems that meant Braden's risk was higher.

Braden was back for the seventh, though. Had to see this, runners at second, third, and their favourite at bat. Couldn't stay in the concession for that!

"Sorry man, some nachos."

"Yeah, I know, hard to resist, but look who's up!"

It was a hit, and suddenly they were ahead. Absolute pandemonium. Things thrown in the air, hats, bags, beach balls (where did they come from?), popcorn and even pop. Soda, all over. Soda from behind.

"Hey!"

The O'Brien's turned around and sought out the launching source, face to face. Continued to stand as the rest sat, the end of the play.

"Hey guys, please sit down! We can't see!"

Des threw a little wave, then turned and sat down, pulling down his little brother.

"Hey, you know we get to stand up, too." hissed Braden.

"I know, I know, little brother. Look, seventh inning stretch coming, just wait and you can get all your pent up energy out."

And stretch they did, much to the consternation to all involved around them, the loudest stage whisper the, "I wish people like that just wouldn't go out in public."

* * *

Des collapsed into his chair and put his legs up.

Well, that was opening day done. Thank God. Never again. His feet were purple, swollen, numb. Bagged.

Utterly knackered.

Grabbed his iPad. Doc said to do the calorie count when off the reservation. He knew it. He was.

Oktoberfest sausage on a bun...cheese and onions...no poutine, say 887 calories. Poutine, small, 700 calories. Pulled pork: 5 oz, 260, let's say 2 oz, let's say 100 calories. Peppers...9 x 150 cal, or 1350 cal. Peanuts, 6 bags. Let's say a couple of ounces per bag...6 x 320 cal, or 1920 cal. D-Bat dog...who knows. Google....3000 calories!!!!!!!!

Haagen Daz...3 x 290 = 870

Grand total...what, 9000 cal?

Doc said a farmer did 4000 calories more per day, than he. A graphics designer. 4000. Sat back. And he had restrained himself. Easily would have eaten more. At least nachos, cheese sauce, pizza. Looked those up.

Nachos...350? 2 slices at least...pizza...270 per slice...or another 1200-1300 calories?

Then there was the Venom Dog, sausage, black beans, guacamole, Pico de Gallo, sour cream. Almost did that one. The Sonoran. Dog with bacon and Pico, beans, mayo. Managed to restrain himself there. Maybe it was the money. But he had done it. Just the corn dog this time...

Well, could look at it a couple of different ways. It's what he ate, or what he could have. The next biggest loser was certainly not him. Sighed. Seems he was doing a lot of that.

Grabbed his paper. The thing that had started this all off.

Obesity in our Society

The study of human behaviour is interesting. A human being does make individual choices, but does so in an environmental setting. There is the family, the suburb, the town, the province, the nation, the society. Similarly, there is the nuclear family table, the school cafeteria, the work lunchroom, the grocery store, the restaurant, the town facilities, the provincial and national policy and laws, and societal belief systems. In reality, although one makes choices, one's elbow is nudged.

National, societal decisions can have dramatic impact on behaviour change. For example, more transplants happen when a nation allows one to opt out of a standard organ donation policy. Those nations that allow one to opt in have a success rate more than 80% lower (Novak & Brownell, 2012). However, there are substantial political barriers to increasing taxes on unhealthy food, limiting its advertising, changing food labelling, or altering tax subsidies for certain crops and produce. This is nothing compared to changing society's belief that 200lb is a normal weight for a male, or that popcorn must be eaten with movies, or a hotdog with a ball game. These insidious, ingrained, customs and belief systems often seem unnoticed, because so many of us share them.

Ingrained belief systems are a challenge. There is objective fact and there is interpretation of that fact. Every perception by a person is an interpretation, coloured by one's mental landscape. That mental landscape, those mountains that tell us what "good" or "bad" is, what "fit" or "unfit" is, what "tastes good" vs "tastes bad", what is "comfort food", etc., impact our interpretation of what we perceive. Things are immediately labelled, a process which renders something complex into a two dimensional cartoon. As distortional as that is, a judgement is then put upon this cartoon; it's good, or bad, or healthy, etc.

So, that full plate of mac and cheese, despite obviously not being on the diet plan, is a comfort food that causes pain when pushed away. A carrot doesn't seem to quite cut it. Foods, amounts of food, timing of food, as well as movement and exercise all carry emotional baggage. A lot of this is shared socially. Many people eat hot dogs at a baseball game and nowhere else. Popcorn and movies. Champagne with boat launches. A person with overweight or obesity must address all this for success.

Since the mid 1980's, the cost of healthy food has risen dramatically compared to that of carbonated drinks, sugars, fats and oils, perhaps at least somewhat due to national subsidy of commodity crops (Fields, 2004). Introducing local zoning bylaws to prevent fast food outlets to open near schools is unheard of, but would likely be effective to change youth eating habits. Changing school cafeterias to remove vending machines with junk food is easier, more so is control over the family dinner table. There is more impact higher up the ladder, but it's difficult to make happen. It's easier to influence change close to home, but perhaps with less impact. Once one leaves the dinner table and goes for a walk, there's a DQ just standing there, beckoning...

Where national policy has failed to achieve change, private industry has swung in to fill the gap, with less than breathtaking efficacy. There are myriad diet plans and exercise routines out there.

Sat back. Rolled the paper up, elastic, launched the tube towards the bedroom.

Looked out his window. Moon this time. His room illuminated by the Sky dome view, droning, on because that's what he did. In the door, Wrigley Field went on. Job one. Routine. Pools of darkness behind remaining piles of pizza boxes. Was going to clean those up.

Could see himself reflected in the balcony window. Really saw. Dark room, massive wall mount illumination.

And a huge guy on a couch.

Him. Massive.

Saw the building next door, looking down Sumac Street. No sumac as far as he knew, some scrawny maples imprisoned beside garbage containers, mailboxes, parked cars. Apartments were little Christmas lights scattered across the face of the high rises. Sparkled.

Pulled out his stadium field glasses. Not to be a perv. To count the TVs. Started at the top. Left to right, up to down, every blessed one, every one, a television. Some dimmer apartments a bit dark, fluttering light, probably smaller sets...lots of big screens.

Saw his little buddy padding down the sidewalk. Even from this vantage point, scraggly. Suddenly, he felt like he was seeing the only real thing amongst all the concrete.

Des threw the field glasses on the couch. Guessed that everyone was vegging. Like him.

Heaved himself up on the couch, heaved again and tipped forward. Up to the window. Cars. Streams of cars, red and white sparkles. Cement, shadows. Cement.

He was trapped in a trap, a cement trap. Wrapped up in sparkling lights.

CHAPTER FOURTEEN

Doc pushed back in his chair. Sparse hair, even a bit grey, and as thin as the edge of a razor blade. "A D-Bat dog? Ever had the Sonoran? They're amazing, huh?" Jerk.

Fell off the exam table. Well, not really. That would have been cataclysmic. Epic. Call the paramedics and the Jaws of Life. Let's say, startled. Big time. "Doc, you're skinny as a rail! What the hell! I'm here for some help, and you tell me you eat twenty five dollar hotdogs?"

"What I'm here for, is to not BS you."

Right. Well, honesty. Tried to imagine Doc, outside clinic walls, with a ball cap, eating a mac'n cheese dog. Not quite. Couldn't do it. But...one point for being straight up.

"Ok, Doc. Talk to me."

"There's no such thing, really, as bad food, Des. Well, that's not true. There's processed food. Not the best. Oxidized, and lots of fats. Maybe a bit off...Don't like that rancid word, but the stuff can increase inflammation. It sort of gets into your cell membranes. I guess there is. There is some bad stuff... Did you only have that?"

"Well, no. A few Peppers. And some other stuff..."

"Did you count it up? Do the calorie thing?"

"Yeah, Doc. It was a lot."

"A lot?"

"More than that farmer burns daily, let's just say that."

Doc rocked off his chair and stood up, stretching his back. "Did I tell you I got a standing workstation? Hate sitting. Kills my back. But there's no such thing as bad food, Des. There's what you eat, in relation to what you burn. Simple as that. Thermodynamics. You eat more than you burn. I think, by the sounds of it, way more."

Went rummaging through some papers, probably looking for that damned BMI chart again.

"I know, I know. The palm of my hand." Des looked down and shook his head. The last time he ate that little, well, he was little. Littler. Probably never little. Size is in relation to everyone else, but also in relation to what you label yourself. "I don't think I can do this."

"Tell me." Leaned against the desk, arms folded. Classic Doc pose. Probably learned that in his first year of med school.

"It's just everything, Doc. It's not just the decision to eat less. That's just one thing. It's what everyone else does, how society is, what everyone else expects, traditions, the whole big fishing net I'm caught in. It's what I'm used to doing, what I always do, what my buds do, what my brother does, what the person beside me on the grandstand bench says, expects, does. It's a net, a virtual spider web of situations and expectations, things that force you to act in old ways.

"I did some real changes there. Believe it or not, that intake was lower than normal. I chose whole wheat and overall ate less. Never counted it all up before. Quite a smack between the eyes." Des spread his hands. Massive, pink hands. Oktoberfest sausage fingers. Looked at his palms.

"Were you able to start some new behaviours, or deflect old ones?"

"Sure, the whole wheat bun, at least was whole wheat! Still a bun, but different. Yeah, I know bread is bread. Got it. Emphasized a few more peanuts. Tried to drink smaller Peppers. Most of the time." Shoulders slumped.

FAT

"You need a battle plan." My General. Three stars, on his helmet, he could just see them.

"Huh?"

"They're called implementation intentions. Basically, you take a piece of paper and write down situations that can come up, times when you think you'd be forced to act in ways that would be in conflict with your decisions, your goals. Some people call them *If, Then Statements*. If, for example, you see a hot dog vendor, then you will immediately do behaviour x, y, or z. Sounds like you had a bit of one there, or did you?"

"No, I just saw that he had some whole wheat buns and took those instead of the regular. No big plan. Frankly underneath, I was looking forward to the baseball game, sort of like an off the books special event. No rules."

"Rules are a bummer, aren't they?" A Doc joke. Ha.

"I've just started to become aware of them. Ball game, pig out. Haagen Dazs, Pepper. Actually anything sticky, or greasy, or actually...good, Pepper. Have a Pepper on hand in case you get thirsty. Peanuts, Pepper. Concession, nachos. At least, that's my brother. TV, pizza. Pizza, beer. Beer, nuts and chips. Upset, beer. Upset, freaking anything that isn't nailed down."

"There you go. There's the start of *implementation intentions*, or *If, Then Statements*. Situation A begets reaction B. Ball game, pig out. There's also, tired, sit down. Or lie down. That one most people have. Standard ones in relation to obesity also include, bored, eat. Or upset, eat. Or even more basic, hungry, eat."

"Ok, Doc, you've lost me." Didn't this guy have a couple of dozen strep throats out there? Where was this going?

"Simple stimulus, response. Stimulus A, gives response B. In your past, in your present. A lot of it is a trained response. You learn that if you cry, as an infant, your mother will give you milk. It all gets tied up, hunger, agitation, the love and warmth and closeness of your mother. Learned response. Essential for survival! I'm not knocking it. But it doesn't do you much good now, when you're a 37 year old graphic designer."

"Are you saying when I'm upset, I want my mother's teat?"

Doc and Des looked at each other, then both broke out laughing. "Right. But some of that response remains. As you live your life, that mental mountain does change a bit. Right now, it's upset, eat. It would help you with your weight problem if you could break that up."

"Break what up? The upset, eat, the association?"

"Heard of Pavlov's dog?"

"Nope, neither Pavlov nor his dog."

"Russian physiologist, who investigated conditioned responses. He trained his dog to salivate at the tone of a bell."

"Wha...How did he do that?"

"That was the response of people when they first saw this. How was it possible? Impossible, people said. I actually heard somewhere that people paid to see it! All he did was restrain his hungry dog and show him food while ringing a bell. Did that ten times, then went up on stage and showed his dog, drooling after he rang the bell. The dog had learned to associate the bell tone with food."

"Oh... so no big deal. Bell meant food was coming, so he drooled. Got it."

"No big deal, huh? Listen to this one. Mid-seventies. A researcher conditioned mice to drop their immune response to a flavour."

"Now, you've got to explain that one! Drooling, I sorta get. Immune response? You mean antibody levels, like on a blood test?"

"Actually, proven in human trials now, five or six times. Once I remember in the mid-nineties, with MS patients. Dropped their immune responses to a flavour. So help me. Just paired an immune suppressing drug with a flavour a dozen times, then took the drug away. The flavour alone was enough. The antibodies dropped."

"How? How the heck?"

"Well, beats me all to... heck." Doc had that all knowing, beats us all to heck expression. Sort of brows up, shrug.

"You don't know?"

"Nope. Don't think anybody does. Brain's an amazing thing. Probably the biggest last frontier in medicine. All closed up in a box, you know."

"Okay, now we're way out in left field, talking baseball. Where the heck are we? I want to stop jamming food in my face!"

"On course. We're on course, hang in. You need to disrupt the conditioning. Years of conditioning. If Pavlov had rung a different bell, played a different tone for his dog, if Adler had used a somewhat different flavour of whatever, cheese, there would have been less drooling, less of an immune response drop in those lab rats."

"So give me examples. Get concrete."

"Anything can help. Wearing different clothes, sitting in a different area, doing something backwards, hanging with a different friend with different habits. That's changing the tone of the bell."

"You mean if I hadn't gone to the game with Braden, if I had gone with... my neighbour, then I wouldn't have eaten so much?"

"I bet. Or at least, it would have been easier to restrain yourself. You usually go to opening day with your brother?"

"Wouldn't be the same." The thought, actually upsetting.

"That's my point. Wouldn't be the same. Would have felt weird. Different path. Different planet. Less likely to eat a blue crab mac 'n cheese dog on Pluto."

"So this is your implementation intention stuff?"

"Nope!"

"Then what are you talking about?"

"Well, it's sort of the same thing. I was talking about disrupting your triggers. An implementation intention is a plan. Identify your usual trigger and your typical response. Then, develop a plan ahead of time, a strategy to deal with it."

"So there's deciding to change, or avoid the trigger, and that's a bit different. An implementation intention is a plan, a coping strategy when the trigger occurs, or likely to occur."

"There you go. You can deflect your response, or minimize it, for example. You can plan to do something that will take you completely away from that behaviour, or you can manage to change your response to be more in line with your goals."

"Huh?"

"Deflecting would be doing something to prevent you from eating the blue crab dog, but minimizing would be having...I don't know, a ballpark frank and mustard, instead of the mac'n cheese."

"Where do I start?"

"Start with big behaviours that are really destructive, ones you do all the time."

"OK, help me here. Minimize apple pie and ice cream. Major problem."

"You're on, buddy. How many calories, you're learning them, I know you are. One eighth of a pie, a reasonable scoop of ice cream..."

"Six hundred, eight the way I make it, or, guess I should say, double that. Because I don't eat no eighth of a pie. Now come on."

"Okay, you would eat half a pie? A few scoops?"

"Yeah, probably. So that's what, 1500-2000?"

"Okay, minimization. I'll give you my favourite breakfast, or one of them. A cup of slow cooked oatmeal, with shredded apple and cinnamon. Dollop of low fat Greek yogurt on top. Could pick vanilla. Bet that's...probably 200, 250."

"That's still a lot!"

"Excuse me, Mr. 2000?"

"Okay, ok, I get the minimization. Have the oatmeal thing instead of a piece of pie and ice cream. Doesn't sound quite so satisfying."

"Know what, you may be surprised. That Greek yogurt has protein. It helps kill hunger, longer. It'll fill you in a way pie can't. Mind you, it can't stand up to half a pie comparison. That's a lot more food volume. You're going to have to shrink that stomach a bit, or half jam it with celery, or something."

"Got it. Okay. Deflection example, please. Blue crab 'n cheese dog, at the park."

"Deflection, the best deflection, would incorporate synergy."

"Doc, you keep talking in riddles. First it's immune response, then it's synergy, which is what the heck anyway."

"2 + 2 = 5. Synergy. Remember your goal. Weight loss."

"Okay. To get even more mileage than not eating it...so that would mean exercise. Or vomiting what you already ate." Like really.

"I don't recommend vomiting! That's another kind of pathology! But sure, go for a walk, or do ten push ups."

"Doc, I can't remember a push up. But thanks, I get it. Think I should write down implementation intentions every day?"

"You'll find that you have regular habits, every day. You won't have to keep rewriting them, gotta learn the new responses. Doing them again and again helps develop new, more adaptive learned responses. Your chosen deflection, or minimization, will become a more normal behaviour pattern. You could even write down a deflection and a minimization, for each difficult trigger. So if you're feeling weak, you can stay strong by picking the ball park frank! But sure, if you're going into a high risk environment that you haven't worked out the plans for yet, sure, do it."

"High risk...I guess I've got to start thinking like that. I'm a young guy, with a heart problem. Time to get more serious. You actually eat that for breakfast?"

"I'm not trying to stress you, but you've simply got to get that weight off, Des. Yes, sometimes I eat that, more usually with cottage cheese though. And nuts. And berries. And a piece of fruit."

"Cottage cheese, yesch!"

"Great protein hit, man. Try it with berries, you'll be surprised. Used to have a "heart healthy" breakfast of a bagel, no butter, but with jam and a half a grapefruit. Old thinking, faulty thinking, old theory. Ravenous by 10 am. No kidding. Straight sugar breakfast, spank the pancreas, insulin overshoot, sugar crash. Protein with every meal. I can cruise right through the morning, now. Protein! I use low fat cottage cheese, put cinnamon on it, no sugar. Going Med full on? Do the Greek Yogurt!"

"No sugar?"

"Another rule, right?"

Transom windows allowed a peek at the blue sky, a little ray of sun breaking into the room. Looked at life. Without pie. Apple pie. Songs written about it. Mom and country. The very flag. Birthdays, Sunday evening dinners after pot roast. Dad and Braden, sitting at the kitchen table waiting for a piece, straight out of the oven, mom with oven mitts, a little blush, so proud. Flakey crust, melt in your mouth, salivate at the very scent, apple pie. With sharp cheddar, contrast. Or ice cream, vanilla bean. French vanilla. And coffee. Rich, earthy, dark, black coffee...

Try to deflect that one, with freaking oatmeal.

Twit.

* * *

Blinds closed, fairly dark, illuminated numbers shone 0830, and under the duvet. Still.

0831. A finger of sun slipped between the slats of the blinds.

Des wasn't asleep. Watched the sunbeam slowly move, delineating his landscape almost like a sci fi laser, traversing from plains near the edge of the bed, then mounting the foothills of his left leg, bent up at a ninety degree angle, across his thigh, climbing to the precipice.

He was a landscape unto himself, a geographic entity, a freaking mountain with a nocturnal oxygen mask, and he knew it. Mount Des. As if anyone could, or ever would. At least as a kid there was Braden, next bed over. Mom and Dad down the hall.

Four walls and Des. And the video screen. Screens. Can't forget Wrigley Field on the wall. At least that one had a name. Oh, and windows. Yes he could, and did quite often thank you, look outside.

Rocked back and forth. Counted under his breath, one, two, three...rock and up, the bed groaning with each wave.

"You want me up, I'm up," talking to the laser beam. He opened the slats and saw that little dog, trotting down the sidewalk. A bit ratty, but a bounce in his step, head held up. He wasn't letting life get him down. All that concrete, not a speck of grass to roll in and still springy.

Dogs. Dogs were either stupid, or some of the most remarkable creatures on this planet. Didn't he know he was in a concrete prison, just like his? Maybe didn't know better, what a field of green looked like. Where did he do his business, right on the sidewalk? Wondered about the last time the little guy ran, on actual grass. Must not know what he was missing.

He did. Des knew. Life was pretty paper thin, paper dry, paper boring.

So Doc wanted him to plan. To do these implementation intentions, or so he called them. As if something so incredibly simple would actually work.

Flipped on the net and Googled them. Looked up implementation intentions. Okay, okay. Figured. Evidence. One article, a few and on obesity. There was a big performance difference between groups...women, but what the heck.

Fat is fat.

So having this plan, this intention, having these implementation intentions, has actually helped people. But writing up a plan was different from having the intention. Two different things. And certainly wasn't the same as a new behaviour. That was a whole different planet.

So why the 0830 up time? Usually got up at seven, or half after. Hiding under the blankets for what? Sometimes it was easier to just not do anything. To just not. To put it off. To not decide. To stay in the comfortable rut. Easier to just not.

Change.

Commitment. Not just frontal lobe but deep kernel, innermost essence, heart myofibril stuff. Core decision, getting to the very pith. Sure, a planned behaviour would help. But without commitment, without that passionate grip, that fire, well, kiss it goodbye.

That's what was missing here. That's what was missing with Desmond O'Brien. Him. Lots of good information out there, swimming around on the Internet. Moreover, a lot of that information actually existed between his ears caught in some kind of neural net. Added to the catch was a new fish, this new awareness of a fairly simple tool named implementation intentions, but without that deep commitment nothing had changed, or ever would.

Remembered old Mr. Shankar, letting him off the hook with that frog. Introductory science, down at State. Doing muscle neurophysiology experiments and just couldn't pith the thing. Experimental protocol was to grab the slimy little amphibian and ram an ice pick into his brain. Science. They called it pithing.

As if he could do that. Ever. Poor little thing, plucked from his watery home, only to have his last moments fluorescently lit, until the big grab and stab. Right between the eyes. Or where ever. Didn't watch. Couldn't.

Was that what he had to do? Pith himself this time? Metaphorically ram some implementation intention between his eyeballs into his frontal cortex? Was this what it was going to take to get him to commit? If he couldn't do it to a frog, how was he going to do it to his own psyche? Would he have to destroy all his thoughts, all his loves, all his behaviours, in order to do this?

Is that what it was? Is that what Doc was proposing? Wonton destruction, the self-inflicted frontal lobe ice pick, so that new thoughts could come? What did it say about all those fond memories, the twinkle in mom's eye as she brought that mouth-watering apple pie out of the oven? Those wonderful, visceral associations, the aroma, the salivation, the togetherness. The love, the desire, the family, the hunger, the satiation, all woven together into a beautiful thing. Did he need to destroy that?

Des sat at his coffee table. The chip and dip, nuts, pizza, beer, pecan pie and ice cream table. Looked at the rings on the wood grain. Turned, looked out the glass at the cement bars on his cage, the high rises across the street, the little piece of sapphire blue sky between the bars...

It was there. Beyond, behind and above those bars, the sky was there. The same one that was over everywhere else, too. Over the Sahara. Over the ocean. Over the rainforest. If those sunbeams could penetrate into his cell, maybe, just perhaps, there was a way out.

He wasn't jammed. Boxed in. A particle of sawdust glued into particleboard. The only lock on the door fitted the key in his pocket.

Sat back and thought about not committing. Not changing. He knew he wasn't stupid. He knew calories in, calories out. It was just so difficult, the web he was in. Maybe there was some glue. Particleboard? Maybe. Expectations, routine, habits. Of not just himself, but everybody else. The whole society he was in, from his family up. Community, city, state, the whole enchilada.

The whole world had apple pie problems. Well, maybe not. He remembered those Oxfam kids from TV and the grins on their faces when presented with a clean bucket of water.

Des wondered how they'd get him out. Desmond O'Brien. When that day came. How would they physically, actually, achieve the extrication? Looked at the bottles lined up for his morning breakfast. Ramipril, metformin, aspirin. And that was just what he took now, his morning doses. Rosuvastatin at night. How was it going to end?

When?

Networks showed a guy being lifted out of his home the other day, by some freaking piece of construction equipment, some kind of excavator. Extricator. Had to knock down a wall and pick him up with the shovel. Paramedics couldn't lift the guy, or get him through a door. Had been jammed into his La-Z-Boy for weeks apparently, unable to get up. Had to bury him in a piano, or some kind of boxcar, probably.

Thought of his mom watching that.

Right. Not him.

Pithing? Not pithing, but something else. Remembered Shanker with his test tube continuing to dump, what was it? Sugar, in and that supersaturated solution. Couldn't believe how much dissolved sugar he got into it, still liquid. Test tube dancing over the Bunsen burner flame, clear liquid swirling at the bottom.

Then that one introduced crystal. And wham, solid.

Was it that TV news story? The forklift or whatever? What did it? Doc with his stupid implementation intentions?

Or that image of himself buried in a piano. Wondered what kind of music that would make.

Whatever.

Decided to do it. This wasn't pithing, but crystallization. Growth, not destruction. Breaking up some learned behaviours that were destroying him did not mean he didn't love his mom, for Pete's sake. In fact, this wasn't tearing up the old him. It was evolving him. He could use that fabric, that life, that existence, that behavioural, thinking and emotional weave. It was a platform he could stand upon, his starting point, a launching point. He wasn't getting rid of it, but building a new structure, weaving a new cloth from it. And he could even help, maybe. Braden. His folks, friends. He was a thread in their existence, their fabric, too.

He could help them.

Old school, he was going to do this the traditional way. All those memories, all that past. A computer word processor just didn't seem to fit. A few pieces of copy paper came to hand, easily fished out of the inkjet. A glitchy Bic found, hiding in the back of the junk drawer.

Ground up some dark roast and flicked on the pot.

First thing the goal. Washboard abs! In spite of himself, Des had to choke down a chuckle. Washboard abs indeed! As if! Survival first. First, he needed to plan for continued existence.

His.

Freaking pill bottles first, the physical manifestation of his illness. The visual, tactile, gustatory representation of what had gone wrong. Brightly coloured, each species in their little terrariums, sitting there, decorating his apartment. They screamed illness. Disease. Deterioration and physical slide. Just like the song, six feet down suddenly seemed not so far away. Those, those pills, he wanted gone.

General goal: life. Well, too general. But not really! Fat affected everything.

Sat back, set his teeth, looked out the window, the little sapphire glimpse, and sipped his coffee. Hot.

It was always hot. Fat made it hot. Like wearing arctic tundra gear, 24/7. Full blast A/C, hot. Sweat, often dripping off his very nose, towels, changing clothes. Rank. Sweat. Sitting in front of the fridge, not just because of what was inside, but because with the door open it was a bit cooler. Watching the big screen with a floor fan forcing air full blast, turning up the volume.

Looked at his sweat. His sweats. Practically all he wore.

Clothes you'd have to order off the Internet, because stores never had the size. Stupid styles, muumuus not so great for guys. Des laughed. His shirts were muumuus. He imagined Kit, or rather that lab girl, Sunshine, what was he thinking, Kit was his friend, married, with kids, trying on one of his...

Images, memories crowded his brain, spilled.

Sweatshirts and sweatpants, and everyone knowing that's all that would fit. Could get big athletic shoes, but the laces were a pain. Some geriatric brands with Velcro were okay, sandals the best. Underwear rolling up into a tube. Suspenders, because belts were a royal pain. Putting them through the belt loops before the pants went on, because any other way was just impossible, physically undoable. Couldn't reach. Too much of a pain and never seemed to work, anyway.

And having to take some off to use the toilet. Clothes, literally off. Maybe the worst thing was having to use a public stall and stand waiting for the disabled one. Hang stuff on the hook, aim and hope to make it on target, then putting a foot up on the toilet. Rotating the knee laterally, forcing it over with an arm, stretching that inner thigh a few times to loosen it up, trying to ignore the zits. Big, sore, too often pus-filled, thigh zits. Pannus dead lift and shift aside, wishing there was an additional arm available, diving under and super stretch to reach target number two. That was wipe one. Then there was number two, and doing the whole maneuver again.

Could anything be worse than that? Things came close.

Getting into a car. Out of a car. Out of bed. Picking something off the floor, having to get down on all fours, then struggling back up. Kicking his newspaper through the front door.

Sitting on furniture, trying to imitate the soft descent of a humming bird, gently lighting on a chair to test its capacity. He'd broken more than one. At restaurants, bad enough. They should be prepared. But pretty embarrassing at a friend's. Was that why he didn't go? Probably both ways, fear of inviting from the inviter, too.

Elevators, and the look on people's faces.

Which is a whole topic on its own. People's faces. When he just had a few minutes for breakfast and just ran in for a doughnut. Well, not run. But he was in line with a bunch of others doing the same thing! The looks! When he was out for a walk, which he did sometimes. Couldn't he use the sidewalk? Didn't he have a right to be there, too?

Which he seldom did of course, because it was freaking exhausting. And hurt his knees. And feet. And back. And almost every other Goddamned thing else. Including not being able to breathe. If he didn't get chest pain.

Which of course would prevent him from even calling to enquire about skydiving. No cardiac patients doing that, of course.

Not to talk about the weight limit! Wait, there's a weight limit! Want to do x, y, or z, watch for the weight limit! Horseback riding. Magnetic resonance imaging. Step on a ladder.

Or on a freaking scale! Weight limits for scales!

Sat back and gulped some Java. At least he took that black.

That's right. He wasn't a complete disaster. Not everything he did was wrong. Hadn't he cleaned up some of those pizza boxes? Hadn't he actually gone grocery shopping? Wasn't he visiting Doc, looking at his problems squarely in the face, intending to do some intentions?

Got up and took out his package of slow oatmeal and a pot. Actually had a couple, cast offs from mom. Bit of a loose handle, but what the hey. Poured a bit in, added hot water, flicked on the stovetop. Grated in an apple. Dumped in some cinnamon.

Apple pie, sure. Didn't smell bad, though...Sipped coffee.

More water, stirred, looked like it was done. Okay, one palmful. Poured the amount into a bowl and looked at the tiny serving.

Intention, or behaviour. Poured the rest of the pot in the garbage. Protein! Grabbed his cottage cheese, pulled off the tinfoil and dumped in another palmful. Now that started to look like some food. Dumped a small handful of nuts on top.

Okay. Day one, breakfast one. Beyond intention, to doing.

Des fully opened the blinds, brought his bowl to the table, and set it down. Grabbed the paper and started to think...

He had duly imagined, clarified and illuminated his current life, and even trajectory. Where he was going. Looked at the bowl in front of him. Well, a bit of a jar to that image, but it was pretty clear.

He could see it on his gut, feel the fat move on his arms, his legs rub together, hear it in the way he breathed. 3D, clear, Technicolor, Disney vibrate your seat and spray water in your face reality. He had seen someone eerily like himself get extricated from his lazy boy by heavy equipment operators, not paramedics. Graphic, movement, colour, right there on his Wrigley Field.

How could he fight that? Was that the basic problem? The wiener in the hot dog? Somehow he had the awful feeling that all these emotions, the warm fuzzies he got when he thought of apple pie were of stronger impact on his behaviour and his choices, than any information. Worse, he was becoming certain in his most prominent gut, that imagination beat willpower every time.

And he had just imagined being extricated from his apartment. Him. Desmond O'Brien. By heavy equipment operators. No pine box, but a piano.

He had even heard the piano strings.

Des felt had almost felt the spade full of dirt biting down on his lid.

How could he fight that? He had seen his path. There it was laid out in front of him, in juicy techno feel, techno sound, technicolour.

Had a bite of oatmeal, crunched up a few nuts. How did that guy have his coffee? Did that guy, that poor guy stuffed into the piano have oatmeal with that coffee, or apple pie?

He sat back in his chair and let the sunlight warm his eyelids. Orange.

Visualized. Crowded it out. If imagination could stick him on a path, he was going to choose it, and pick one that didn't end up being jammed into a piano, not just drift along. End point.

142

Thought of himself, his family, the people around him when he was…ninety nine. Fit, strong, tall, sure, grey hair… a belt, no suspenders. Playing…soccer…with grandkids…and Sunshine, setting, but there…the muscles on his arm. Shorts, muscles on his legs…the power, he could feel it!

Half way back. Imagined himself at retirement. The things he had accomplished professionally, interpersonally. People he had encouraged, maybe someone he had saved…Braden? The gym, his vegetable garden, his…log cabin…

Half the way back again. Teenagers? Wondered…sports? Schools? Worried about cars, what they were doing? Exercise. Finishing a marathon…

Half way back again. Uncomfortably close. No. Not an effort. Try didn't exist, just like Yoda said… Sunshine…always a part of this. Building that cabin…? But strong, throwing out clothes, pill bottles hitting the garbage, perfect blood work…

Months from now. Shiver went up the back. What…where… struggled with greys, shadows…couldn't quite see.

Tomorrow. Probably later today, and every day. He was going to make his new internal world push out this life, shatter some walls. Paper. Set to work.

At the top, he wrote down an image of his goal, the life he wanted. No weight restricted access, no wait for the disabled stall in a public bathroom. No pill bottles, as if that would ever happen. Nice to think that, though. Maybe less. Damn it! No! Able to go up and down the stairs. All the stairs. Breathing. Less sweating. Actual clothes.

And some sunshine. Sunshine. Maybe. If he had the guts to ever talk to her.

Good thing it wasn't a pencil. Would have shattered at that one. Who needs enemies when you could just use yourself? She talked to him, first.

On the left, Des wrote down situations he considered to be most risk prone. Baseball games, home openers. Hanging with Braden. Television ballgames. So many situations. Working at the computer. Emotional upset. Family events. Occasions. Things that linked up to other behaviours, like the simple coffee in his hand, so often leading to dessert. Like apple pie.

Looked at his bowl. Bit of a crunch, a creaminess in his mouth. Warm cinnamon apples. Not bad.

Started with his coffee. Realized and remembered. Black coffee, for him, made him think of sweet. More specifically and quite often, apple pie.

So on the left of the page, in his column of at risk situations, or triggers, he found the word, COFFEE. Middle of the page, started a new column, what did Doc call it? Deflection? Minimization? Didn't matter, called it, "LESS". On the right another column, called it, "SYNERGY", liked that one.

Maybe...another column. Right beside the trigger, a way to alter that trigger. Change it up, change the tone of the bell. Try that...

Tasted the tang of cinnamon in his mouth...could put that in the coffee and change the flavour. Might remind him now of this new breakfast choice, but that was a few hundred calories less than dessert. Put cinnamon in that column right beside the word, "coffee".

Under the word, "LESS", put his breakfast he was eating right now. No rule that he couldn't have that any time of day, not just morning. Better than pie!

Under the word, "SYNERGY", put...what could he put? Exercise. But what?

Looked about his room, at Wrigley Field. Amphitheatre. Computer screen.

Had to work. Couldn't get around that one. Computer was here to stay...what did that mean...? Grabbed some boxes, duct tape...he could get the actual gadget on line, but what would that take, weeks? He'd had enough reading about standing work stations. Time for action, now.

Soon the computer was up. Yes, up on boxes. Stupid boxes. Not adjustable, up or down, just up. If he wanted to sit during his work, he'd have to go somewhere and sit. Fine.

Amphitheatre would have to go. But that set, Wrigley...a fortune. Didn't he want to watch the ballgame? Was it wrong to watch the stupid thing?

Hands on hips...or at least as close as he could get them. To where he figured they may be...

The television. A lot of his sedentary behaviour, his lack of movement and his binge eating were all built around that device. Television, rest, television, veg, TV, binge. It was probably his biggest trigger and he knew it. The pink elephant. Biggest thing in the room that he couldn't talk about. Think about changing. What else would he do? What else was there?

Right there. Less than fifteen feet from his kitchen. Right there. Huge proximity to risk. So easy. That little beverage fridge, right beside the sofa.

Kicked that over. Kicked the plug, right out of the wall, sparks, smoke, brilliant, all the lights off, and the stupid fire alarm. Opened the windows, waved air at the thing till it stopped blaring out that piercing noise, cracked open the door, no neighbours. That was just so stupid. A decision though, and action. Clear action. Pulled the cord out of the outlet. Wondered if he would need an electrician.

The frying pan came easily to hand, a practised, routine, well-coordinated maneuver. Six strips of bacon, half the package. Gritted his teeth. Knew how to do this, a pro. Right temperature, flipped, nice caramelization, perfect...dripped the grease into a coffee mug, just like always.

But not like always, dabbed the fat off with a paper towel, wrapped the bacon up in some Saran and flicked it in the fridge.

"Wrigley. Buddy. You, more than anything else, have made me what I am today." Stood right in front, eyes moving, TV set to coffee cup. Of grease.

"Set on, fat on. I think that's the link..."

Sat down at the table and finished his oatmeal, colder now, but cold apple pie was just as good.

Looked at the set, dark, silent, a faithful companion, no, a servant awaiting instruction.

A bit of the grease was starting to congeal around the rim of the cup. Stood up to face Wrigley.

Who was really expensive, and thought better of it.

"Listen, bud, I've got to do something that will stick. Television, fat. So, sorry…"

Dabbed, with great precision, a daub of grease all around the screen. Just off the screen, one inch, every couple of inches. A dashed line of grease. Fat.

A wobbly housefly helicoptered around his head, then slowly landed on the set.

"Right. It's going to attract flies. Great." But maybe that would help.

Set the beverage fridge back upright and looked at the scorch on the wall. Opened the fridge and took out a Pepper, cold in his hand. Cracked it open and smelled it.

Des walked over to the sink and poured it down. Looked at the cup of bacon grease, only warm now, and poured it sloppily into the now empty bottle, some of the fat dripping down the edge of the bottle.

"Now, that is gross."

That's what it was, though. Soda, fat. When he drank it, straight on his gut. And everywhere else.

Put it to his lips and tilted the bottle. He could smell the bacon fat. That smell, in the past, so welcoming, that aroma, associated with Dad at the stove and weekend mornings…just didn't seem the same coming out of the Pepper bottle. Some of the smell of the pop was discernible, right around the edges, but not just on the periphery, merging with the bacon fat.

Put it to his lips. Almost watched himself, tilting the bottle more, a timid movement at first, then a swig. Grease slid over his tongue. Swirled the fat around his mouth. Felt it, that gastrointestinal reverse gear kick in. Went to the bathroom, swallowed.

And vomited into the toilet.

CHAPTER FIFTEEN

*T*he bus pulled up with all its stench. Clouds of dense black putrid exhaust, cough. He was there again. The big guy.

Perked his head up, tail subconsciously activated. Didn't get up, no reserves. None at all.

He stood there, looking at him. Huge male. Immense. A leader. But where was his pack? Always alone.

And he turned. Went into that building, through those doors. Slumped. Nose on paws, tail still. Stay still. Stay small.

More big people, and little people, a gaggle, talk, so much talk. The bunch from the bus. Didn't smell as bad as that big thing, that monster, that hard, shiny, dirty stinking thing that had shrieked to a stop in front of him. No familiar scent. Looking at those little black things in their hands, not even looking, big feet, some work boots, but safe in his cubby, a painted over basement window. Little girl...?

"Mommy, a dawgy!" *Little pig tails, pink ribbons, a sparkly ball. Shiny black, scuffed shoes, shirt half tucked in. Freckles, spaces between her teeth.*

"Doris, come this way. Dirty. Dirty dog."

"Oh mommy, he's just a doggy! You're so mean!"

Doris blew him a kiss as she was dragged away. People called him things. Probably Dawg was the most common. Heard Dirty quite a lot. Usually with a funny voice tone. Didn't like that word.

Sun was getting warmer.

So dry.

The man came back out of the doors. Perked head back up... tail. Tail, tail, tail...carrying something, coming over! Got up on trembling legs, turned head a bit...

He was so hot, the man, could smell...but he was talking...

"Hey, Bud...you look real thirsty..." *He had trouble putting the dish down. Had to lean on the wall, breathing hard...some spilled. But almost full, clean, clear, beautiful water.*

People would throw a crust. The vendor would almost hand him a wiener. A whole wiener. But water. Water, he was never given. Water. Water came out of puddles, sand, pebbles, weeds, oily scum...

This was water. Clean, clear, beautiful water.

He was still standing there. Looked up, brushed head against his leg, and drank. Oh, what relief. Cough, choke. Too fast, slow... slow...oh what glorious relief. He could feel it trickling down to his stomach, almost felt it in his very paws.

"Good boy, look, after you finish that, it's not much, sorry, all I got..." *and dropped a crust, bit of dry cheese on the side. Tail, tail, tail....The big man touched him gently between the ears, the neck, the back.*

"Good Lord, boy, you're all bones!" *The crust went down pretty fast, crunched it up, some teeth a bit sore, but so good. Water. Gave water. Looked up. Maybe...maybe...he wanted a pack.*

The man looked down. Way down. His shoulders moved up and down. He was hot, too.

"Bud, I think it's against the rules but some rules are straight bad. If you want, you're with me. Come on."

Shook his head, ears flop. Left a bit sore, but stretch. Strretchhh...

The big man walked to the doors. Looked behind, and stopped.

"Well, come on!"

Knew that word. Knew dawg, dirty and come on. Going inside? Never happened. Legs were a bit shaky, but knew where they were going. With him.

* * *

Des muttered, "...now what have I done..."

He looked down at the dog, and then into the lobby. No one. Sliding through the doors, he walked into an amazingly open elevator. The dog trotted right in and walked behind his legs. Doors closed.

Dog looked at himself in the elevator doors. Looked up at Des. Quite the pair. Looked down. Pair of legs! Mastiff kind of a guy.

Doors opened, miracle two, nobody. Down the hall. *Curry, fish. Sniffed the floor, the walls, that greenish stain on the carpet.*

"Bud! Come on!" Nudged with his toe, just to break the trance. Got to the door, brass key already in hand. "Come on, come on!"

Lots of smells in here. Pizza, old beer cans, man smell. Put his nose up to appreciate, to remember. This was an event.

"Gotta get some actual food for you...pizza crust! As if dogs eat bread. Dogs must be carnivores, I guess like wolves." Des pulled open the cupboard and looked at the canned supplies.

Stew. Irish stew. Potatoes, some carrots, but meat. Gravy. Mucked around in the cabinet for a can opener. Gotta be here somewhere. Dog just sat there. Looking up, tail brushing the floor.

Des remembered stories of the poor third world kids, swollen tummies, desperate for food, any food. Remembered something about their stomachs exploding. Or was that what his mom used to say to make him finish every last crumb, every scrap on his plate? It didn't look like dog had a big swollen tummy.

But decided to just give a bit of food, anyway. Wondered if he would throw up and how he'd clean it. Certainly had a smell. Looked at his coat. That poor dog hadn't had a loving hand in a long time. Des suddenly realized how alone he had been for so long, and how now his Wrigley Field crash pad office seemed a bit more real, more alive. Didn't know whether or not to zap it. The stew. He stood there, bowl in hand at the microwave, pondering...

Looked down at the little guy, ribs so evident, right through the straggly fur. Probably didn't care. Pushed the button for a quick minute but took it out at 10 seconds. That tail, a virtual blur.

Of course. Getting it on the ground. That was going to be an issue. Had managed it with the water, a miracle. Leftover ice cream tubs were good for something. That's recycling, right? Reduce, reuse, recycle. Reused. And dog might need that again.

He'd try to keep it full of water.

Got a soup ladle out of the bucket and put the stew in that. Leaned over, holding it for dog.

Didn't last long, that stew! One little ladle scoop, gone. One more little one.

Dog looked up at Des. This man, was feeding him by hand. By hand.

"You don't bark, do you? I might even be able to pull this off." Thoughts had started to crystalize in his head. The lady on third had a dog. It wasn't impossible. There was a bit of a kerfuffle about it, couple of years ago. He remembered signing a petition, supporting her. Dogs had never bugged him.

How was he going to do this? He had trouble taking care of himself, even showering, much less taking care of a dog.

Showering. He needed a bath. A bath, and Des had trouble showering himself. Well, he had a detachable showerhead. Suppose he could dribble some shampoo down, maybe use…maybe use the ladle, or something like it. Towels all over the floor, just like when he had a shower. Just rinse him down.

"Come here, you. Come with me."

Des put the ladle in the sink and went to the bathroom. Had lots of towels, big white ones. Big guy, big towels and threw them on the floor. Dog had come right along, already less shaky on his paws. Closed the bathroom door after them as he moved to the shower.

"Come here, in you go."

Dog sat there, looked up and turned his head. *Tail, tail, tail.*

"In the shower, go on…" Des gently pushed the dog with the inside of his foot, gentle firm pressure. He seemed to understand, got up and walked tentatively to the edge of the stall, looked up…

"In you go, we're going to wash you up a bit. You've got a bit of a smell…don't look at me like that, it's ok, you've been living on the street! Hey, I've got a smell too, don't look so insulted!"

150

Des gave another gentle nudge and dog finally got in, lifting one paw, then the other, then the last two, over that ledge.

Des held the nozzle in his hand, pointing at the wall, and turned on the water. Not too hot, not cold, moved the handle, probably just right, not too strong. Pointed the nozzle down, not right on dog, but beside.

"Want a little shower, Dog? I'll let you decide. Want a shower?"

Dog looked up through the spray. The water was warm, could feel it on his bottom, on his paws, splashing up onto his chest from below. Distant, faint memories floated up, the water sensation, the warmth, the feel of a distant master's hand on his back, a painful sweet thing, images and touches and moved under the water. Warm fingers, gentle watery fingers worked into his fur, the water around his feet turning brown.

"Wow, maybe we won't need soap! Look at that dirt run off you!" Des worked the water back and forth, slowly realizing Dog was a chocolate. Bedraggled became less stray looking and more like...his. His dog. He hoped. An odd feeling in his chest...nitro on the counter...but not anginal. Something weird, something fragile, growing. Suddenly he hoped, dare he hope. Hope that dog would stay. With him.

All at once it wasn't Des. Just Des. Des in the apartment. Des secluded, going to the odd ball game with Braden. There was no window in that shower, but the light actually seemed to change. Colours seemed a bit less watercolour. If that was possible in a shower.

Change was no longer an option, but a choice, a door opened and passed through. At least mentally. He'd change. He had to. For him. For his little bud.

"How am I going to do this?"

The water continued down the drain, a bit less brown. And Des realized he didn't mean the shampoo application, but meant taking the dog out to do his business. Take the elevator? He'd have to. He'd only managed a couple of flights so far. Maybe go down the back stairs, pop out the fire escape door and hang out until he could do that elevator again. It meant taking him for walks. Giving him a proper bath, cleaning those ears. Taking him to the vet. Carrying up dog food.

He had trouble enough with his own groceries. Maybe Kit could help, or maybe, their bigger kid.

But he was his dog. If he'd have him. People usually picked up their pet's poop. This was not going to be easy. Des squirted some soap down and gently worked it in as well as he could with his ladle.

Which didn't work at all. Dog flinched away from the pressure, gamely staying in the shower though. Had a metal pull up bar on one side of the shower. If he held onto that, and eased himself down to his knees...

Which he hadn't done in freaking years. On his knees. Des O'Brien, on his knees. Heaved his chest and looked at dog, in the eyes. If he was going to get bitten, this was it. What were the signs of rabies again? Drooling...

Oh, come on. Dog didn't have rabies! He turned his head and seemed to smile, water dripping off his ears.

Des took some shampoo in his hands and worked it into dog's neck, gently moving the skin over his ribs. Didn't seem to be have any sores.

Or at least too many. Dog flinched again, but gamely hung in there. Took the shower head and more dirt, water brown again, swirling down the drain. Leaned over to do his back, his haunches.

And felt a tongue on his neck. Their eyes met. Des put massive hands on either side of dog's head.

"I can't keep calling you Dog. What's your name? As if you can tell me...

"Chocolate lab, eh? We should call you a chocolate name, like Black Magic. But you're brown...Brownie, Godiva...but that's for girls. Milky Way! But that's stupid. Hershey! What about that, boy? Wanna be called Hershey?"

Tail, tail, tail, and another wet tongue, this time right across his face. Des finished up with the shower head and leaned in to smack the control off. Dragged a towel up from the floor and tousled Hershey's head, gently rubbing his coat, avoiding that sore. Ears seemed a bit tender, too. Wondered what to do about that.

Probably just needed food. Regular food and somewhere safe.

And took a deep breath. Braced his left hand on the counter, reached up to grab the metal bar to the side of the shower, and heaved. Heart hammered, one foot up, pushed, pushed, and up she rose. Just like the Titanic.

Smiled. Had to find out if they actually did raise that boat. Something about that movie he saw. Did they do it? Smiled. That was a first. Up from the knees. At least a first, in a long, long time.

Hershey still didn't bark, sat there and looked up, wagging.

"Maybe I should have called you Wagster!"

Des kicked the towels together and into the bedroom, with the others. A pile in the corner. To complement the piles of pizza boxes he still hadn't gotten around to. Things were going to have to change. Had a roomy now.

He hoped.

Hershey walked over to the door and sat down, looking at the door handle. Interesting behaviour, they both realized. *Hersh sensed some old memories, some dusty behaviours that seemed to fit. No business in the den. That was for outside, not inside. A huge thing for masters. Huge.*

Des finished with his towel shovelling and leaned against the wall. "You have to go outside, don't cha?" *Tail, tail.*

"Who needs a stand up desk when they live with a lab, eh?" Des shifted, something didn't fit. And it was a lack of a collar. And a leash.

And the lack of a plan. Brazenly go down the elevator again? And he had a couple of plastic grocery bags...But he realized he'd have to go right down on the ground to pick it up. Madly searched his mind for a solution and could find nothing. A ladle? His food ladle? He had always despised dog owners that would just let their dog poop on the sidewalk, only to walk away. That wasn't going to be him.

Come on, think. He was an apartment dweller. A hoe, a hoe would have worked. Strode over to the closet and looked at the vacuum and the associated tools. No.

Hershey yawned loudly, and shuffled at the door. There wasn't time.

Des moved to the door, jamming a grocery bag in his back pocket. Grabbed the potato masher out of his utensil bucket. "Let's go."

Had to cut the odds. That woman with the petition, she was the exception. That was made clear. Hadn't really looked into the legislation. Des had a feeling that this no pet thing wouldn't stand up in court, but he didn't want to push it. The stairs were down the hall, to the right. Big breath, teeth gritted with determination. Nitro in his pocket, never used. He would go down, all the way. Had only done two flights thus far.

But this was down. Down. Come on, it was controlled falling. Who couldn't do that? Des tried to imagine it in his head as he walked down the hall. Just had to make it down. Four flights, then out the door and Hershman could relieve himself.

Des gripped the doorknob with determination and swung the door open. He relied on Hershey to follow and concentrated on the task at hand. Leaned heavily on the rail and just tried to keep the feet moving, realizing that a slip would be a disaster. Heh, heh, heh, laughed under his breath and imagined the scene. They'd never get him on a stretcher. Would have to drag him down by the ankles, or roll him down, flight by flight.

Step, grab, step, slide the hand along and grab, concentrate, and breathe. Sweat dripped and rolled down his sides, down his face. Garish light from incandescents, painted cinderblock, cigarette butts, wrappers, cobwebs and centipedes. Stains.

What on earth could that have been? At least the filth was distracting.

Hershey didn't seem to care and kept right beside him, just a little behind. Heart thrashed in his chest and sweat rolled into his eyes, but this was for Hershey. He had to get outside. Had to prove he could do this. If he couldn't do this, well, if he couldn't at least take his freaking dog outside to poop…

Almost down. The last flight was dim, incandescents taken out by something, projectile, spear, bat, something. Heh, heh.

At least he could laugh, joints screaming with pain, right hand rubbed raw from the metal railing. Two more steps. He looked forward to the door and slipped, sensing his left heel slide forward. His heart gave way within, slipped along with his heel...

Swung his body harshly to the right, never letting go of the rail with his right and grabbed on with his left. The railing heaved, groaned. Cement bolts held...most of them. A couple at the bottom shattered, the end of the rail loosening but held.

Des hung on and breathed. Breathed. Wondered what he looked like. Purple. Blood vessels standing out on his neck, his forehead, pounding pulsations. Drenched, absolutely, literally, drenched.

"Woof!" Hershey sat by the door. *Come on, you didn't fall, get over it...*

"Did I say that, or did you say that?" Des moved to the door, swung it open, and walked into a pool of streetlight. Hersh trotted over to the light post and lifted a leg.

Certainly seemed less shaky. Wonder what a ladle full of stew will do and proceeded with number two. Right there on the sidewalk.

Which was about all he could do. Des looked up and down the street, concrete walk, curb, asphalt road, brick, cement buildings. Little trees in their metal cages. And a brown pile, right there in front of him. The potato masher, jammed into his belt, had somehow survived the journey.

Looked at the dog. Sitting there, wagging. Looking right at him. Felt his screaming muscles, drenched shirt, his pounding feet, his twisted back. Pulse slowly returned to normal. Looked at his hand, some early bruises, a few bleeding abrasions. Wondered about his tetanus status.

Looked at the dog. At the exertion. The actual cardiac risk, the risk of actually dying simply taking the dog out for a poop, the nitro in his pocket. The pain. The incredible amount of bother, of real work, this was all going to be.

He'd have to get a glove for next time.

"Somehow, Hersh, I don't think mashed potatoes will ever be the same..."

Des picked it up, plopped the poop into his garbage bag and stood looking at his ladle. Put that in the bag and tied the top. He'd have to take the whole thing back up, take out the ladle and ... flush. That's what he'd do.

Starving. Hershey hadn't eaten in ages, he was sure. And had made it. Days? Had he gone days without eating? Or only just a scrap?

Thought of the kids. Infomercials. The tiny little ones, big brown eyes staring at the lens. Wrapped up in rags.

This dog. Thought of him begging, hiding, going through garbage. To just live. Going for possibly days without eating.

Days. And wondered just how long he, Desmond O'Brien, could go without putting food in his mouth. Des held Hershey's head in his hands and felt it. Felt it inside. Suddenly just knew, he could do this.

Hershey sat down, looking up at the big man. No, no collar. No leash. But he knew when he had a good deal.

CHAPTER SIXTEEN

Des tuned in intentionally this time. The Chronobiology of Fat, Part 2, with Dr. Bill Hu. Wondered if Doc knew him. Right. Like if you're from New York City, must know Mary Sue, on 5th. Stay tuned, commercial after commercial, be there or be square. Hersh was zoned beside him on the couch, nose buried in the cushions. Black coffee, no pie. After all, you had to watch something before Letterman. Vegging with a purpose. Purposeful vegging. Sort of like PPV. Pay per view. Pay per veg.

Pay to veg?

Finally. Sci-pop music enveloped the opening credits. Professional, but playful. Clearly some thought had gone into that theme music. No fireplace and hot chocolate tonight. It appeared that the interviewer and his victim were walking. Forest scene, mid-day. Dappled sunlight on the path, a cyclist bobbing by. Clearly in the can.

The interviewer seemed to be caught putting his hands through his mane, clearly proud of it. Startled a bit, he flourished the mike. Flourishing while flustered. Maybe proactive and good for your empowerment, but bad TV. He would have edited that out.

"Dr. Hu, thanks for making it back tonight. We've had a lot of great feedback about your last talk, lots of interest in this chronobiology idea. Welcome back! Though I guess this forest really isn't mine to welcome you to!"

The scene, generally pretty steady in this post gyroscopically stabilized camera era, wobbled a bit. Clearly the path wasn't clear.

"Whoa, careful, you okay?" said Hu, clearly breaking protocol and acknowledging the presence of the cameraman. Gone was the tweed jacket, in its place a dark blue track suit and...Pumas? With the shock of ink black hair and hawk like face to complement it, Des was just waiting for him to trip himself.

Maybe not in the can...another time zone? Image stabilized.

"Dr. Hu? Thanks for getting us back to the chronobiology theme."

"Chronobiology, what a word. Time, biology, stick 'em together and shake it up."

"Pardon me, Dr. Hu?"

"You ever seen it?"

"Pardon...?" Flustered again. Maybe good hair, but...

"Dr. Who. You know, the time traveller? Had to watch it. Started during my internship year. How could I not? Everybody was asking me. Not only did I have a last name that sounded like him, I had his first initial."

"I thought Dr. Who had no name, sort of part of the whole plot thing?"

"No, on one episode he let his first name slip. Basel. Lots of nerds in university. So, I was sunk."

"Interesting, interesting. You were making a point?"

"The most interesting thing for me, is how no matter where or when he was, do you know what the time was? Really?"

"Dr. Hu...?"

"The time was, really, now. Not centuries ahead, or ten minutes ago, but now. We must recognize that there is only one time during which we lead our lives. We, especially in the west, live in the future most of the time, letting our lives slip away as a string passes through the eye of a needle. Pretty soon it's gone. Now. We live in the now."

"Chronobiology of adipose..."

"Now, now. I'm on point. Listen to me. I'm trying to make a point. Did you just see what happened to our cameraman? He almost fell. Where was your head? In the now, tending to the poor chap, or wondering what's going to happen to your ratings?"

"Dr. Hu...," fluster didn't come close now. Flummox? No, more like gobsmacked but angry. Angrily gobsmacked. Gobsmackily angry.

"No, no. I'm not criticizing. I get the whole thing. Cameramen are truly behind the scene, meant to be invisible. No acknowledgement, I get it. But I was trying to demonstrate that your head wasn't in the now. You want to know the chronobiology of eating, of adipose deposition, of exercise. I understand. You want to be able to plan. To live in the future."

Dr. Hu turned to the audience and pointed. "Who amongst you right now, and I'm going to guess a fair number of you are overweight or obese as more than half our population is, who among you is actually standing, or walking, or watching this on a treadmill video screen? Who is eating right now, inappropriately, not because of hunger, or energy deficit, but sheer boredom and habit?

"The biggest answer to this question, this so mysterious question, is eat less all the time, and move more all the time. Every now. All the time. We need to flip our sick societal paradigm on its head. We book time to exercise. And sit all the rest of the time. We need to book time to rest! And not diet in the future, tomorrow, the next meal. NOW. And all the time!" Dr. Hu gesticulated wildly. "I'm sorry, this is so aggravating for me. The Paleo diet is such the rage. But it originated in times that were so different. It's working for people. I'm a little vexed that people are following this before we get good outcome data, like we have for the Mediterranean diet. Remember, only the DASH and Mediterranean have outcome data. All these other diets, these other religions, millions following them, have no outcome data. Me, it's Med all the way. I just hope our paleo followers are doing the right thing. We just don't know. And hope they're being as active as our ancient relatives were."

"They were really active?"

"Hunter gatherers. And remember other, larger animals were trying to gather them! So, they were not only chasing prey, but prey themselves. I bet they were active. Half the time running for their lives!"

"There's no particular time at which exercise is more powerful, or eating more likely to put on fat, then?" The interviewer was truly looking vexed, likely wondering how much of a show they could stretch out of this.

Dr. Hu leaned against a tree and looked up into the branches, as if to find an answer. "Sure. Some studies indicate, for example, that if you burn substantial calories before breakfast that a fat burning state ensues that lasts all day. Early morning exercise done prior to breakfast appears to be the only time where exercise achieves increased 24 hour fat oxidation (Iwayama, Kurihara, Nabekura et al, 2015) suggesting it may be the best time to induce weight loss. Before breakfast, the body is in a carbohydrate depleted state. Similarly, Chomistek et al (2015) found that morning exercise appeared to correlate with a lower risk of obesity. Women who completed less than 39% of their exercise in the morning had a 26% greater risk of having obesity compared to those with greater than 54% of their movement in the morning."

Dr. Hu turned and pointed his hooked nose into the camera, "But exercise at any time simply helps, period. Exercise in the morning leads to getting to sleep easier and if you exercise later in the day, but not in the three hours prior to bed, that decreases awakenings when you're in bed. There's clear evidence that eating within three hours of bed tends to put weight on. Some studies on diabetics show that anaerobic, or weight lifting type exercise, after a meal can really pull down sugars (Heden, Winn, & Mari, 2015). While exercise both prior and after eating dropped sugar, exercise post meals dropped triglycerides as well."

"The issue of fasting itself need be addressed and probably comes under this topic of *chronobiology*. Look at the evidence for morning exercise and at the effect of evening eating. Early morning exercise is a proven fat burner. Eating in the evening, within 3 hours of bed, is associated with putting fat on. Think about it.

"Basically, morning exercise is at the end of a fast. And, it's eating in the evening which breaks a fast. Look at the word, "breakfast." How many of us do?

"Fast?

"It takes 9 to 12 hours, if not 15, to burn up all your sugar stores. That's a fast. Burning up all your rapid access sugar, to enable you to burn your stores.

"Your adipose. Fat.

"Eating that piece of pie and ice cream at 9 pm and then going to bed at 11, up at 7 for breakfast does get you 10 hours. I suggest it's not enough, not nearly enough. Want that weight off? I suggest nothing after dinner at all but water, clear tea or black coffee. If you can tolerate the caffeine!"

"...and when do you eat? You are inferring the need for a longer interval, one certainly longer than 10 hours."

"Good question. Who knows. Studies are ongoing and should be out in a couple of years. Currently fasting styles are either starving for a couple of separated days a week, perhaps eating only 5 or 600 calories all day, or jamming all your eating into a small time window. Suffice it to say, try to go a longer interval without eating and get some movement in during that time."

"...so staying in bed for 15 hours isn't going to do it, huh?" Grin.

"...well, lying in bed does burn some calories. More if you're not alone!"

"Doc, was that a joke?"

"Oh never, you know me! But seriously, this fasting epidemic we're now experiencing has some truth in it. Where there's smoke, there's usually some fire. Fasting starts a cascade of events in the body. Basically, the body needs energy.

"Where does it get it? Stores, like that adipose we all want to get rid of, and garbage. Things that just may make us all sick."

"...hold on, Doc. You're suggesting that fasting may help clean up our bodies?"

"Sure. Basically. A recently published 25 year study of monkeys may have just tied up the whole thing."

"Doc, you've lost me."

"Monkeys, Watson, monkeys. We've proven that in everything from simple organisms like yeast, all the way to lab rats and now up to primates, that excess food kills. Well, or at least that caloric restriction leads to longer life. And less disease."

"Okay, Doc. Spill it."

"25 years. We'll never have another study like this one. Monkeys that were restricted in energy intake, that's calories, but not nutritionally deprived lived substantially longer and better. Less sick, with a longer life. (Coleman et al, 2014)."

"So that means..."

"Eat less. Live longer. Better. Now, that study was on calorie restriction. That's sort of the grandfather for this intermittent fasting idea. Sort of the same, sort of different. Intermittent fasting advocates feel that the refeeding stage is essential in their goal to clean up that body garbage and create healthier tissue. Sort of makes sense, right? Fast, the body uses body stores including sludge and possibly, even less healthy tissue. Refeed and the body recreates the tissue. Fascinating stuff. Again, let me stress...no outcome data here. May come though. Lots of theory. You could look at intermittent fasting as a good way of eating less. Of living your life, exercising, in a glucose depleted state. And a way of still enjoying food. Which I love!"

Hu was walking again, the interviewer following with his microphone. "But overall, the emphasis we need to address today is exercise. We talked about diet last time. There's two ends of the stick in weight control. One is diet and the other, activity."

The interviewer was looking a bit relieved. "Activity. You mean exercise. So, how about Exercise and Adipose? How about that for a new title, theme for the show today?"

"Sure...but about that stick. Society is holding it. That's what we're forgetting and probably why we're all stuck. There's the stick, but we have to get unstuck!"

With serendipitous good luck, the cameraman had found a dog, yanking with all his might on an enormous tree branch several times his weight. Zoomed right in, the strain, the determination, paws dug in, tug, tug, tug…

"I don't think we can address all of society in this interview." The camera moved back to the irked anchor.

"No, you're right! But a reflection of what I'm talking about was your correction of me. I said activity and you said, you mean exercise. But, one thing at a time. Let's talk exercise. This word to many people carries a lot of emotional baggage, perhaps more than mac' n cheese, or even BBQ. Exercise is defined as an activity requiring physical effort, carried out especially to sustain or improve health and fitness. The definition is courtesy of Google, looked it up this morning. But that's not it, really. Exercise has become something that requires a time commitment, something that one plans to do and make time for in a busy day. It's something that requires garments by Nike or Under Armour. It's done in a gym, with music. It's supervised by instructors and it's not pleasant. Not one little bit!

"Total global health club industry revenues as reported by Statistic Brain Research Institute (www.statisticbrain.com) amount to more than 75 billion. Interestingly, 67% of people never use their gym membership, 25 % of Americans are inactive, and less than 20% of high school students are active more than 20 minutes a day. However, 96 % of adults engage in leisure daily, men and women both averaging more than 5 hours."

"Five hours of leisure activity? Doing what, for heaven's sake? Five hours? Give me five hours and I'll show you what I can do with it!" The interviewer just grinned, shaking his mane.

"9 out of 10 older adults watch television in the USA, for an average of almost 5 hours daily. This behaviour has been associated with increased death rates. The lowest death rates were found with those people that had less than three hours of television, and who reported consistent activity (Keadle, Arem &, Moore, 2015). All screen time is associated with obesity (Foulds, Rodgers & Duncan et al, 2016). When comparing other quiet leisure activities such as reading or even using a computer, television watching was most highly correlated with obesity, so much so that one extra hour watched appeared to correlate with an extra 2 centimeters on the waist size (Heinonen, Helajarvi, & Pahkala, et al, 2013)."

"Hold on, hold on. You're saying that if people watch this show every day that they'll put on 2 centimeters on their waist?" Now that was a couple of good goose eggs for eyeballs.

"I guess I am, sorry. Most people veg when they watch TV. I think it would be different if they watched TV on their treadmills. Met a guy the other day who had a TV bolted onto his barbecue! These things should be bolted onto exercise equipment.

"Uh...televisions, not barbecues. If you bolt a barbecue on your exercise equipment...well, that would be interesting!"

The interviewer shared a dutiful laugh. Nationwide programming this was not.

"Evidence supporting the use of regular exercise is overwhelming. A mere 30 minutes of walking a day is equivalent to a physiotherapy program for back pain (Hurley, Tully & Lonsdale et al, 2015), the use of an antidepressant for mood disorders (Craft & Perna, 2004; Blumenthal, Babyak & Moore et al, 1999), and improves diabetic patients (Colberg, Sighal & Fernhall et al, 2010). 30-40 minutes of exercise aimed at maintaining a target heart rate, when combined with cardiovascular care, can actually help clear arteries of plaque (Kurose, Iwaska, & Tsutsumi, 2015). It appears that the human body simply needs daily exercise, and at least 30 minutes of it. Many physicians feel that 30 min can be broken down into 10 minute segments."

"So how long should we exercise for?"

"Of those few people that actually do this thing called exercise, the average caloric expenditure is about 100 calories a day (Levine, 2002). It's really not all that much when one looks at the entire day's metabolic work. Metabolism are those complex chemical processes that go into maintaining a body. It's a word that's often used popularly, and even (often wrongly) in obesity counselling. The thin person that can eat a whole pizza is said to have a fast metabolism. The overweight person is said to be

CHAPTER SIXTEEN

able to gain a pound even looking at a donut, a victim of a slow metabolism. It's that black box within which the calories in, calories burned equations lie. Women that are sedentary tend to burn about 1800 calories a day, the most active 2200. Men burn about 400 more."

"So that's the average calorie burn?"

"Interestingly though, there can be a huge swing in the amount of calories burned in people of similar sizes, even up to 2000 calories daily. (Levine, 2002). Basal metabolic rate is the amount of energy a resting, non-eating body uses just in self-maintenance. This number is basically dependent on body size, larger people having a higher BMR. It makes up about 60% of metabolism in the resting body. 10% of a person's metabolism comes from food processing, and is fairly stable person to person, despite lay wisdom to the contrary. What varies is everything else, the calories burned in formal exercise plus those used in day to day activities."

"So we need to exercise, you said...30 minutes a day?"

"If people would do that, it would largely put me out of business. Yes. A lot of things get better. However, this show is on weight loss. The 30 minute a day advice for metabolic improvements and diabetes care seldom achieves weight loss, as calories burned can be easily replaced. Longer term studies of those that do lose weight and keep it off with only exercise suggest that at least an hour a day is needed of moderate to vigorous exercise, burning 2000-2500 kcal weekly (Colberg, Sighal & Fernhall et al, 2010)."

"So who can do that? Exercise for a whole hour, daily?" Arms widely separated, as if to plead his case.

"I hear you, and that's the normal response. Occupation therefore matters a great deal. A lumberjack will burn more than a computer programmer. That person watching television burns no more than 30 calories an hour, compared to someone cutting the grass at ten times that amount. These calories burned outside of formal at the gym exercise constitute the bulk of the variability between persons. Not the gym time. It's called Non Exercise Activity Thermogenesis (Levine, 2002).

"Generally, people can't do an hour's worth of vigorous exercise daily. It's the energy that is burned during life activities outside the gym that can make the difference. That person consuming the same amount of food, but burning less in day to day activities than someone else, can slowly, inexorably, put on adipose, simply by staying consistently in a positive energy balance. Those that do lose weight are much more likely to keep that weight off by having a higher "leisure-time physical activity index" (van Baak, van Mil & Astrup et al, 2003)."

"So Tom, our cameraman, see, staying in the now! Can eat an entire sub for a snack, and he's skinny as a rail! How come? Is he that more active than me?"

"Karl, he's talking about you! Don't worry, I'll help you tie him up with duct tape after the interview. But sorry, in regards the activity, probably! Yes, Tom is likely more active. That slender person able to scarf down an entire pizza and not gain an ounce of weight, likely burns a great deal of energy during the day. Often at the gym, yes. But everywhere and every when else, too."

"Okay Doc, I think I get it. We've been set up to put weight on."

"Expound, student..." Hu looked positively Who-like.

"The human body is setup to retain calories, to live in a hunter gatherer, scarce food environment. We moved all the time, out of necessity. Now, we have easy access to food, some of it not that healthy, and simply too much of it. Combined with that, we sit around. All the time!"

Hu looked pleased. "That in itself is probably partly genetic, too. Part of the body's way of holding on to calories. So, if we want to entertain ourselves and eat more, or eat junk, we'd all better move it, move it!"

"Is it the junk Doc, or is it just the amount of food?"

Hu's shoulders slumped. "I know. This is hard to get. Listen, you can gain weight eating too much of almost anything. Well. Kinda hard with broccoli. But you know what I'm trying to say. Overeating, consuming more energy than your system needs is easier with junk food, which is very usually higher in calories.

And full of fat, sugar, and other nasties. So it's the amount yes, and it's the junk yes, and it's because of the setting, which is that of rest. The default position, the usual state of most human beings, is to be at rest now. Rest was meant to recover your body to move again, and to miserly hold on to energy stores.

"The world's changed. Human bodies haven't changed much, at least so we think, from prehistoric times. We have bodies made to move and keep moving, and to hold onto energy reserves. That's how we're made. But that's not how the world is anymore."

"So that's the other factor. You were talking about both ends of the stick, but then that stick is held by society, or something like that."

"Yes. That stick is stuck in the ground. On Fifth and Main. We can't understand the whole problem until we look at that."

The interviewer beamed. "It's official! A miniseries! Roots, watch out. Dr. Hu, would you be able to do just one more interview, next week? On the Fifth and Main issue? Society, and its impact on obesity?"

Hu smiled, and turned to the camera. "Sure. But please, out there. Do me a favour. Those of you not disabled, can you please just stand up?"

With this, Hu shook hands with his interviewer and jogged down the path.

CHAPTER SEVENTEEN

The dog's arrival was catalytic. Transformation struck the O'Brien apartment. Pizza boxes, beer cans, assorted clutter, gone. The stand-up workstation arrived, delivered by professionals that unbelievably helped him install the stupid thing. Des actually started paying attention to the screen beacon, the little flashy pop-up that reminded him to stand. It seemed that simply having a gadget, one that enabled him to stand and pull up his work surface to continue working, facilitated the behaviour change.

Hershey would sleep right beside, if not on, his foot. At night, he would lie right at the foot of his bed and would know how to scramble out of the way. Thunderstorms, and often when it was perfectly clear, brought him right on top of him, snuggled in close.

Odd, but it felt like a family. He started actually living his life differently. The stairs, once that dreaded option, became regular egress for them. Downstairs was still a significant chore, but amazingly easier. They'd stall outside and wait for opportunities to dart, as much as Des could dart, back up the elevator. So far luck had been with them.

Hershey's hair started to shine and grew back in over that sore spot. Regular, real dog food. Ribs became less easy to see. Always proud, but now a zing. Des would sometimes wait at the bottom of the stairs as Hersh would run up and down the road at almost a berserker pace, always to come back, breathless at his feet.

Which routinely prompted good natured expletives about the free demonstration of how to make time for real exercise.

CHAPTER EIGHTEEN

D es stood at his computer, and Googled, "Diet plans." Over 23 million hits. Right. He needed to get some responsible summary, somewhere. Some university site, or famous clinic perhaps.

Found an article...

Some diet plans that actually have some basis in scientific research include the DASH, the low caloric DASH, the Mediterranean diet, the Low Glycemic Index diet, the currently ever so popular Paleo Diet, the Gluten free diet, Atkins, the Diabetes Associations diet, Weight Watchers, the ketogenic diet, the Vegan and vegetarian diets, the No Added Salt diet and the cardiovascular diet.

Of all these diets, though they all sport research papers, only the DASH and the Mediterranean have abundant research of a certain type: papers that report outcome *data. That's end points. Large numbers of patients studied. Death and event (such as heart attack) rates. All these diets can get weight off. However, we just don't know outcome data for the others.*

Oddly, obese and overweight patients are often relatively mal-nourished. Vitamin and mineral deficiencies, etc., are quite common. One expects to see vitamin A, multiple B and D deficiency, Zinc, magnesium and essential fatty acids depleted. Many of the foods chosen by these patients are simply high in calories, but low in nutrients. When a nutritious food is chosen, often it is in a fibre poor state, which increases its glycemic load, or sugar hit. Compare a glass of carrot juice, which certainly is nutritious, to eating the carrots themselves, which have all the fibre.

There is no "Fibre Diet", but perhaps a name such as this would draw attention. Choosing to pick higher fibre foods is good for gut flora and thereby general health. The fibre itself works to lower the effect of the sugar in the product.

DASH stands for Dietary Approaches to Stop Hypertension (Mayo Clinic, May 2013) and has evolved over the years. Initially out in the 90's, DASH now has less emphasis on grains, but has demonstrated continued success in lowering blood pressure. It encompasses theory from the No Added Salt diet: mere salt restriction can lower blood pressure. However, by adding foods rich in nutrients such as magnesium, calcium and potassium, and restricting portion size, this diet has been shown to be as effective as a blood pressure medication, lowering BP in the range of 7-12 mmHg. The portion restriction and food choices often lead to weight loss, especially in those with overweight and obesity (Soltani, Shirani, & Chitsazi et al, 2016).

The Mediterranean diet (for example, Mayo Clinic, June 2013), one rich in plant foods and whole grains, which replaces butter with olive oil and herbs instead of salt, is associated with a reduced risk of heart disease (about double that one expects from the use of a cholesterol lowering drug), some cancers, Parkinson's disease, depression, diabetes, obesity, autoimmune disease and dementia. Its main features are a move from butter and other vegetable or nut oils to olive oil with its mono-unsaturated fats. There is a preponderance of fruit, legumes (beans, lentils) and vegetables. Processed meats play a very small role in this diet, as actually do all meats. Fish (again, a source of polyunsaturated fats) is emphasized. Dairy appears mainly as yogurt and cheese. Sugar and sweeteners are used very little. Grains appear usually whole and pasta is small portioned, al dente (which appears to lower the glycemic index).

A light to moderate use of red wine is often seen in the Mediterranean countries. A two year study on a mere 224 patients has shown some improvement in type 2 diabetic patients with a light use of red wine which is, "...apparently safe and modestly decreases cardio metabolic risk" (Gepner, Golan & Harman-Boehm et al, 2015). Perhaps this issue in this diet, more than any other, illustrates the problem of differentiating between the statistical phenomena of association, versus causation, even for scientists. Studies such as the one just mentioned move from shown association and inappropriately suggest causation far too early. The association of the Mediterranean diet, which may include red wine, with some cancer reduction should not be taken as reason to consume alcohol, a substance proven to cause, *not just be* associated with *cancer (WHO, 1998). There may be, however, differences amongst alcohol choices. Beer in itself has been shown to be associated with significant glycemic load (Sluik, Atkinson, Brand-Miller et al, 2016). The cancer reduction and other health effects of the Mediterranean diet may have absolutely nothing to do with red wine consumption.*

In any diet, even with a diet as well substantiated as the Mediterranean diet, it behooves one to think carefully and adapt a strategy to personalize an approach. Here is where the advice of a health care provider can be so helpful.

The Gluten free diet is for those with wheat allergy (quite rare, approximately 0.1% of the population), celiac disease, or gluten related disorders, which amount to possibly 6-7% of the population. Most of the people in this group are actually suffering from non-celiac gluten sensitivity, perhaps a manifestation of cell mediated immunity. They do not have a clear antibody to gluten, but their suffering can be clear and substantial. Celiac syndrome itself is not clearly associated with low body mass, interestingly enough. Some with celiac are underweight, but not all (Capriati, Francavilla, & Ferretti, et al, 2016), as they suffer from malabsorption when the intestine is inflamed. Celiac patients (about 1% of the population) have antibodies to gluten, which is a family of proteins found in the endosperm of wheat, rye and barley (separate from the wheat germ and the husk of the wheat grain. Those with gluten related problems should avoid wheat germ also). These antibodies attack the bowel and create typical pathological findings on biopsy. Those without antibodies while consuming gluten do not have celiac disease, but non celiac gluten sensitivity is a real thing. This medical diagnosis has been associated loosely to many conditions, ranging from schizophrenia to autism to irritable bowel syndrome (Catassi, Bai & Bonaz et al, 2013). Research is ongoing and more clarity will come to this issue. Suffice it to say that most people, certainly more than 90% of people, can eat gluten safely. Avoidance of gluten will not lead to weight loss in itself, a recent study from Chicago showing a prevalence of 38% for overweight and obesity (Stein, Liao, & Paski et al, 2015) amongst those with celiac disease.

The Glycemic Index, or low glycemic load diet is based on eating carbohydrates that release sugars slowly into the system. Simple sugars (candy canes and all day suckers) release sugar into the system very quickly, inducing a quick insulin response often greater than is needed. This relative over release of insulin then leads to low blood sugar, called hypoglycemia. Low sugars lead to hunger and more eating. The classic glycemic index diet has no portion size direction. Literature reviews found in the Cochrane database show limited evidence as yet for the use of this diet in coronary heart disease or in gestational (pregnancy related) diabetes. However, in studies of obese and overweight people, this diet was associated with more weight loss and improvement in lipid levels compared to other diets (Thomas, Elliott, & Baur, 2007). Another review in 2008 found that the low GI diet was associated with better control in diabetes, with less hypoglycemia, compared to standard diets (Thomas, & Elliott, 2009). A comparison of high and low carbohydrate equivalent calorie diets in diabetes type 2 showed fairly equivalent weight loss, but better control and less medication in the low carbohydrate arm of the trial (Tay, Luscombe-Marsh, & Thompson et al, 2015).

The Paleo diet is all the rage, possibly one of the most popular diets, and is accumulating more scientific data. This diet, which limits grains, dairy, salt and processed foods, has been shown to be associated with improvements in metabolic syndrome (a pre-diabetes, pre-cardiac condition): weight, blood sugar, lipids and blood pressure improve (Manheimer, van Zuuren & Fedorowicz et al, 2015). Emphasizing lean meat, vegetables, roots, fruit and nuts, this diet also shows improvements in insulin sensitivity (Masharani, Sherchan

& Schloetter et al, 2015) and a possible reduction in non-alcoholic fatty liver (Tarantino, Citro & Finelli, 2015). It also appears to be more satiating on a calorie by calorie basis than a typical diabetic diet (Jonsson, Granfeldt & Lindeberg, et al 2013).

The Canadian Diabetes Association diets direct portion control and avoidance of simple sugars. One quarter plate is said to be palm sized. In each meal, the diabetic patient takes one palm's worth of starch (potatoes, or grain products including noodles, etc.), a similar amount of meat or alternatives including beans or lentils and two palms of varied vegetables. (Canadian Diabetes Association, 2016). One fruit can be added to each meal, as well as a glass of milk. The diabetic diet is associated with improved sugar control when compared to ad lib diets and weight loss in many patients.

The 2016 American Diabetes Association standards of care position statement has moved away from this and acknowledges that there is "no one size fits all eating pattern" for those with diabetes. The ADA's position is that the same calorie restriction with meals of different components (fat, protein, carbohydrate) yield the same weight loss. However, things are changing. They do recommend lower glycemic load carbohydrates that have higher fiber and recognize that ingested protein can increase insulin response. A bow is also given to the Mediterranean, that diet rich in monounsaturated fats, which may improve cardiac risk and sugar metabolism. (Omega 3 supplements, however, they report as having no evidence and are not recommended.) At least a 5% weight loss in overweight and obesity has been advised to achieve metabolic improvements; intensive medical follow up has been advised. A daily calorie deficit has been directed, usually in the range of 500-750 calories, with 200-300 minutes per week of physical activity. The ADA diet provides room for more aggressive calorie restriction with close medical follow up.

Well, there was too much information. Remembered Doc's visit, with some Washington Apple thing and catheters in a vein, and sugar. Donnie's Paleo. And his fifty freaking pounds. He could use some of that action. He'd have to pump Donnie tonight, guy's night meal then the game, on good old Bacon Wrigley. Maybe he could get through a game without jamming himself full of crap, move from intending and actually start implementing some new behaviour, forming some new traditions.

It was going to be all Kit, although she couldn't come. Salmon, he'd practiced and could do it reasonably. Olive oil on the electric fry pan at 300. Some lemon herb spice he'd found and some pepper. Avocado salad. Asparagus. Eggplant and yes, it wasn't half bad.

Took a big sigh. A guest with no dessert planned. Really bothered him. Dinner without dessert was becoming more normal for him, but this was a guest. Doesn't guest mean dessert? So it was fruit.

Which didn't feel right.

Had some pears, apples and some berries. Grocery shopping had become a weekly event with Des, sometimes with Kit, and sometimes without. Had discovered that not only did Kit naturally move more, she ate different things. Bought bananas, but not the melons, or pineapples. She did buy some junk, but it had KIDSTUFF written all over it, usually. And not much.

Hersh sprawled at his feet as he Googled fruit recipes. All had sugar, or chocolate sauce...and closed the computer down in frustration.

"What do you think, little guy, I'll just cut some up I guess."

His dog, and it was pretty clear that they were together now, turned his head and thumped his tail.

"Right. You knew all along, right?" Des reached down to rub his head, realizing that this simple movement was now a lot easier. He loved petting Hershey and did it often now, usually not even aware he was doing a full flexion at the hips each time. Was avoiding the scale, almost not wanting to put a number on it. Things felt looser around his waist, though and the stairs were less anxiety provoking.

Pizza boxes were all gone, now. He had actually vacuumed and tidied up the place. Bric-a-brac balcony was still an eyesore but hey, one thing at a time. Cobwebs of some substance were now gone, gummy circles rubbed off the crap table and cupboards held new communities of foodstuff. Olive oil was his mainstay, but couldn't do it all. Discovered that peanut oil had a higher heat tolerance than olive oil, sometimes better for frying. Lived together, along with the vegetable oil, vinegar and butter. Yup, he used it. At least it wasn't margarine. Choices. Had learned how to make his own salad dressing, so vinegar was a tolerated immigrant, and hey, fat was fat.

Natural peanut butter, salsa, and an assortment of spices were on another shelf. Had discovered spices instead of salt and was in an experimental state with curry. For a month had practically eaten curry for breakfast, until he felt he was actually sweating the stuff out his pores. Too much. Was living at the back of the cupboard now.

Going overboard, one of his tendencies. Oh well. Two edges to that sword. Realized that it had got him into trouble. Was now using it to help. Cleaning was now his thing. Regular event. The corner cobwebs had entirely grossed him out. Beverage fridge was gone, the wall neatly painted behind. Proud about that one. Had done it himself, from paint purchase to roller, to clean up.

Put his hands on his hips, which he could actually now feel, and realized he had a lot less veg time. Well, a lot more vegetables, but less vegging. Weird, inappropriate word, that.

Avocado salad was done, hours ago. Kit said something about letting the flavours meld. Meld. Interesting foodie word. They'd see. Lime juice, tomatoes, onions. Fish he'd cook just before, only took minutes. Had let that sit out to come to room temp. Asparagus and eggplant were ready to go under the broiler. Brown rice. Donnie probably wouldn't eat it.

Intercom bleated.

Hersh stood up, tail, tail.

"Yup, that's Donnie. Want to meet a new buddy? Let's go to meet him at the elevator."

The neighbours were 100% pro Hershman. They had seen the Des makeover and approved. Besides, little guy never seemed to bark and was Mr. Sociable. All the kids loved him, and would actually come and ask to take him out.

He had a collar now, an official tag, both license and name. Hershey, and his phone number. His dog. Sometimes he wondered though, who was rescuing who.

Usually carried the leash. Hersh didn't mind it, but a lifetime on the streets, independent, had made him prefer the off leash experience. Probably like most dogs, Des considered. But unlike most dogs, this guy stuck right by and didn't go tearing down the street. Only put the leash on when a threat type of situation occurred, like a tottering old man with a cane. Or some gang bangers, who usually gave Des a wide berth anyway.

Because massive talks.

So, left the leash hanging by the door and ambled down the hall to the elevator, Hersh by his heels. Stood with arms folded on his chest and considered that walk.

Used to be a big, big deal. He had just, without even thinking, taken a walk. And it was no big deal at all. Life was changing.

The door at the end of the hall under the fire escape sign opened with a flourish, and Donnie stepped through.

"Donnie! Down here!" Des started to walk down as Hersh looked up, almost in inquiry.

"Oh, go ahead if you want. I'm not going to run. Would be unseemly."

Hershey tore down the hall to greet Donnie.

"Well, who are you?" Donnie crouched down and tousled the chocolate's ears, provoking a bit of a whimper, but no withdrawal.

Des shook Donnie's hand. "This is Hershey. Well, that's what I called him. Remember him from the bus? Don't know if you saw him. Would always seem to appear when I was out. A stray, I guess you'd say. Or street kid. Dog. Whatever. Stays with me now. Should take him to a vet about that ear. I think it's a bit sore."

"Think he'd let me look? I have a dog, at home."

"Don't know. Probably. Let's go back to the apartment."

"Sure. Never been in this building before, rode by it lots."

The three went down the hall, as Des discussed the building. "Fifteen floors, say there's a pool outside, if you call it that. Built in the 40's, I think. More of a puddle."

Des swung the door open. "Went up the stairs, huh?"

Donnie was still breathing hard, but beamed. "Yup, new record. All the way up. You know, kinda addictive."

"What, stairs?"

"No, life change. Weird. You live in sort of a rut, you know? Same thing, every day. Get up the same, eat the same, do the same things. But when you start changing, that can be your new normal. It sort of feels right to push myself all the time, to challenge myself to do new things, or old things in a new way."

"Well Donnie, you've dropped a ton. Two tons. Congrats."

"Want to play ball. Like you. Followed you at state. Really something, man. I can't believe it, sometimes. The ROLL. Man, you don't know how famous you were." Donnie started to turn red, as if he'd really put his foot in it.

"It's okay, man. Long time ago. Hear about my heart attack?"

"Yeah, was big news. You okay?"

"Yeah, thanks. Take pills. Handfuls of freaking pills, but working on that. I'm feeling a lot better, recently. Wasn't doing myself any favours."

"Hey man, like your place! Look at that big screen!" Nice move, topic change, hot topic for anybody.

"Yup, meet Wrigley. My main man. Or at least before Hersh. Able to stay for the game tonight?"

"Sure, at least part. Have some homework. Hey, what's that stuff on it?"

"You able to see that?"

Donnie was pushing his finger into the grease down one side of the set. "Hey man, you spilled something! Looks like...bacon grease? What is this?"

Now the big man turned red. "Yup, that's Bacon Wrigley, his new name. Sort of freaked out one day, realized that stupid thing was the core of a lot of my problems. Sort of knighted him with bacon grease. Sir Bacon, I dub thee. Helps me remember."

Donnie looked at him a bit funny. "You a psychology major? How'd you come up with that? Does it work? Watching less TV?"

"Don't know if it's that, or if it's Hershey. I start watching the thing, and Hersh stands there, right in front of me and barks. Never barks, unless I sit down and watch Wrigley. As if he knows I'm vegging and shouldn't. Don't want to bug the neighbours, so I usually turn it off, and take him for a walk. This guy is my new coach." Rubbed his head.

"Hey, let me look at his ears. Labs have big floppy ears. Sometimes they get a bit of an infection. Gotta try to clean them a bit. Come here, Hershey."

Donnie sat down, right on the floor and pulled him over. Hersh was game, and licked his face.

"Looks like you have a new buddy, there."

"Think you're right."

"I'll leave you to it and start the fish. Cooks fast, hungry?"

"Hey man, always. Hunger's my bud, too. Having a bit...of hunger...means I'm burning. Getting less, though. Easier and easier to take. Funny how it all changes. Makes me wonder if my actual brain is changing! After we play a bit, I'll check his ears for 'ya."

Electric pan to 300, and some olive oil. Like rehearsal. Sizzle, some lemon pepper on top. Flip. Broiler was hot, asparagus and eggplant in. Rice in the ricer, good name for that gadget, in the zapper.

Donnie appeared around the fridge. "Has a bit of an ear infection, some drops should help. Can get them at the drugstore."

"Thanks man, write it down, will 'ya? Thanks."

"Des, hope you don't mind, still trying to do this paleo thing. Probably won't eat that rice. But brought you something!"

Des had noticed the plastic bag but hadn't mentioned it, guy style. Out came a tub of Greek yogurt and something called dextrose syrup.

"What's this?"

"Dessert! Have some fruit?"

"Actually, yes! Was going to have that for dessert, but seemed kinda boring...What's the idea?"

"Was in Greece last year with the fam. Amazing. Cruised to Santorini and rode a mule up this hill to the top. Seen postcards, or pictures? Blue, blue sky. White roofs everywhere, windmills from centuries ago. Amazing views of the ocean. And a killer local restaurant at the top. Wanted a traditional Greek dessert. Had this."

"Dextrose syrup?"

Donnie cracked up. "No, right. Dextrose syrup is not traditional Greek. They used honey. Now this, this is real, fantastic Greek yogurt." Hefted it in his hand.

"Neat. Can't say I've tried it. Have had the fruit bottom light Greek. Not this."

"Well this man, is an experience. The Greeks cut the fruit up and sort of have it around the edge of the plate. Pile of yogurt in the middle and drizzle honey over it all."

"I thought you were Paleo. You won't eat rice! And you're eating honey? Or, what is this stuff?"

"Honey substitute. Sort of the same. Less sweet. Better for us Paleo's when we're gonna cheat."

"Dextrose. I used to know this. That's just straight glucose, right? No fructose."

"Yeah man, right! Know this stuff?"

"Trying to read. Actually, just before you came over. Trying to understand these different diets. Understand what you mean about changing, getting sort of in the rut of change. I've talked to my doc about diet, and Kit. Remember her? Have changed a lot of things, but still mixed up. So talk to me about this dextrose."

"Just breaks down to glucose, like you said. No fructose. Less sugar hit. And hey, you use it like a spice, just dribble some on, not gob it on like a layer of goop."

Hershey grabbed one of his toys and squeak squeak squeaked, rolled on his back.

"Quite the attention getter, huh?" Donnie said, leaning over to rub his tummy.

"Loves that. I think you have a buddy." Des remembered his speech. Sugar, as a spice. Imagine that coming off Donnie's lips. Maybe he had something else to shop for. Had to be careful with that one.

* * *

Dinner went better than expected. Practice had helped. The salmon was actually good and cooked properly. He was starting to actually do this thing called cooking. Donnie appreciated the Avocado salad and even tried some rice.

"Haven't eaten this in a while."

"So why not? What's the big deal about rice?"

"Trying to stay away from anything that'll kick up insulin and store fat. But this is slow cooked black rice, probably the best of all the starches. And you know, you can actually cook. No kidding, not bad."

Compliments. From something other than his graphic art work. Amazing. Weird feeling, that one. But definitely a good one.

Dessert was actually stellar. Des couldn't remember anything quite like it. Cut up slices of dipped apple, pears, berries on a spoon and yogurt. He'd have to remember that one.

Ate it during the first inning, right off the crap table. Probably first time it had supported anything that healthy.

Between hits, foul balls and grounders the two discussed the Paleo diet. Donnie almost waxed religiously on the topic, obviously well read. Dairy he had decided to leave in. No milk, cheese? Too hard ball for him. He'd have fruit and his Greek yogurt for breakfast, cheese and fruit for snacks, veggies and meat for other meals. Des pushed back a bit, discussed his Med diet. Fish, instead of meat. Took Donnie a lot of planning. Would sometimes take a spinach salad to school, with a hardboiled egg, and blue cheese dressing. Apparently his family was being supportive, his father actually starting to follow his lead a bit.

"Yeah, it's hard. You've got traditions, you know? Like popcorn with movies. Chips with ballgames. Hey, have you had one of those eighteen inch cheese and corn dogs at the games?"

"Listen you, you're supposed to be Mr. Paleo, Mr. Life Change. What are you talking about? Of course I've had those things, look at me! Do you eat those?"

"Well, the batter's a problem. The coating on the thing. And the fries. Actually the whole thing's a problem, as I'm not supposed to eat processed foods. Sort of sacrilegious. Paleo's, at least strict ones, don't eat processed food. Luncheon meats, sausage, stuff like that. But they're amazing, huh?"

Des took a deep breath, and let his shoulders fall. "Yes."

"Know what? Had one last week. Thought I was going to barf."

"What?"

"Yup, couldn't believe it. Haven't broken step with my diet in months. Had a moment of weakness, always loved those dogs. Almost barfed."

"What are you saying? Why? Was it bad?"

"Well, yes it's bad! My system I guess just changed, couldn't take it anymore. Destroyed the whole game for me. Never again. But, I was just bringing it up as an example of a tradition. You know, ball game, eighteen inch 3000 calorie corn dog."

"Oh, I get it. The rut. What you're used to doing. What everyone else is doing? What everyone else expects you to do? I get it. Big time."

"Look, lets the two of us go to a game. And do it different. No crab'n cheese dogs. No eighteen inch corn dogs. You know? Start a new thing!"

"You're on."

CHAPTER NINETEEN

"120/80, Des. The books say I've got to keep you on a bit of an ACE inhibitor, but not bad. We can talk about that. I'm torn, myself. Impressed with the weight loss, too. See, comes off pretty fast for many people, at least in the beginning."

Des was meeting with Doc every month or so, tinkering the meds down to match his lifestyle and body changes. He'd stopped doing finger prick sugars, as they were all normal. Now, he had another lab requisition in hand. Hopefully more pills would drop.

"Doc, I never did get that. I understand the exercise bit. If you're really out of shape, really heavy, then a bit of exertion is huge exercise. I get that. Makes sense. But what about this diet stuff? If thermodynamics is king here, I mean calories in and calories out, how is a few extra calories so awful when you're big? Obese? Morbidly fat? Isn't it all the same? Wouldn't a hundred extra calories nail you the same whether you're a trim athlete, or someone like me?"

Doc tilted his stool back, a maneuver that usually ended up in him almost tipping over. Seemed to persist at it though, sort of like the kid at school just determined to balance a spoon on his forehead.

"I see you're still labelling yourself." Which was not an answer to the question.

"Doc, I call it square. Or oblong. Or spherical. It is what it is. I am what I am. Fat."

"A lot less adipose than before, Desmond. You are still calling yourself fat."

"Isn't that what I am, morbidly obese? Right there on your chart?"

Doc swung the monitor around to show Des his problem list. Jabbed a finger at the line. Obesity III. "What does that say?"

"Obesity class three. Morbidly obese."

"Des, we need to find a way to not only note the problem, but quantify the risk. You're really close to dropping to class two. Remember, diagnoses are not meant to be labels, but are given in an effort to find a possible treatment and to clarify risk. It's not meant to stick a label on your forehead. Start wearing a label and you become it. You fulfill it. You make it true. You've had some real success. But you've got to get that self-definition of Fat out of your head."

"Okay Doc, you're beating a dead horse. Got it. I've been in an excess storage situation for, well, a lifetime. By moving more and eating less I've been able to use up some of those stores. Any better? But I still want to know about that little thermodynamic question you've nicely ignored."

"Sorry, Des. Adipose, body fat, is in itself an organ, with certain functions. It's actually an endocrine organ that secretes hormones. When you get too much of it, it starts acting differently. In a distorted way. Some things we understand and some we don't. It's a lot easier for a person with excess storage of energy, as you call it, to put on more fat. It could be those EDC's I've talked about before, those chemicals from the environment that are fat soluble and accumulate in fat, or other more well-known factors. For example, fat secretes estrogen. Know that?"

"My fat is releasing, into my system, a female hormone…"

"Right. Estrogen. And guess what estrogen does?"

"Increase breast cancer risk. Stroke, blood clots. It's been in the news."

"Right. Hormone replacement therapy, estrogen plus proges-
terone. That's probably some of the reason behind the increased
health risk from obesity. But guess what else estrogen does, to fat?"

"Doc, don't know. Stop the grilling."

"Sorry, usually a conversation like that is easier to remember.
Just trying to help you walk away with something here. Estrogen
holds onto fat!"

"So, that's the reason. If a skinny bony person eats those 100
calories you spoke of, compared to the obese patient with a huge
adipose store, the overweight person may be more likely to turn
it into stores. And won't be able to get rid of it as easily, due to
estrogen holding it, sort of like quicksand."

"Well, sort of. You've got the essential elements. There are a
lot more hormones involved that combine in their effect to hold
onto adipose and distort the body's metabolism and physiology,
including blood pressure. Might be one reason your pressure's
dropping, better hormones."

"And that estrogen, sucking on to fat. Which secretes more
estrogen!"

"Sure, that's part of it. And, for some reason leptin, a hormone
sort of like insulin that has an opposite action, doesn't work properly in obesity. When insulin goes up, leptin, that hormone that
helps stop eating, is supposed to go down. Doesn't in obesity. No
one knows why; research continues. It's all complicated. But as
the fat comes off, the organ starts behaving again. Hormones start
acting more normally. Behaving better. For some reason a lot of
people, but certainly not everybody, can really make that weight
come off in the first few months. Then, they get a bit frustrated
as the weight loss slows. Don't be one of them. You see, the basal
metabolic rate is higher for bigger people. As the weight comes
off, your furnace cools down a bit. But don't get discouraged!
Keep the goalposts in sight and keep driving towards them!"

"Any other factors?"

"Oh sure, lots. Haven't even talked about muscle. You burn
more calories on a treadmill than lifting weights, but the weight
lifter will continue to burn calories for days, just to repair muscle.

Good to combine aerobic and anaerobic, the treadmill type exercise, and the weight lifting. Then there's testosterone that increases muscle, burns fat. Another factor. Trying to pin down one factor, one reason, for obesity is a fool's errand. It's a big, complicated system. Like blaming one kind of food, kinda stupid."

"My buddy has lost a ton, doing Paleo."

"We talked about diet, right?"

"Well, kinda scratched the surface. Didn't talk about DASH, or even the Mediterranean much…"

"Well, well. Reading, huh? Dr. Google?"

"Why not?"

"Good Lord Des, don't mind you reading. I try to follow the Mediterranean as much as possible, myself. Great long term data for disease reduction. Lots of good ideas in those other diets, too. They're sort of formal styles of eating. I sort of think of them like religions. Or styles of swimming. They'll all get you across the pool."

"A religion?"

"Sure, a lot of people following these diets are pretty dogmatic. Most have pretty rigid rules. Like the Paleo diet for example. These people are trying to eat like our ancient ancestors did, the cavemen before us. One of their rules is to eat nothing that's been refined, which is generally smart. That means flour, for example. They don't touch anything with flour in it."

"Think that's one way Donnie lost weight, cutting out all breads, buns, pasta."

"Yup, all of those are starches, complex sugars. They call bread the staff of life for a reason."

"Huh?"

"Staff of life. Biblical reference. Listen, if this was post-apocalyptic planet Earth and someone gave you a loaf of bread, you'd take it. Quick energy and body stores. Our bodies were meant to be used in a nutrient deficient environment, life. Not with refrigerators packed with TV dinners. Bread would keep you going."

"I thought it was all crap?"

"Bread made from refined flour, despite being enriched as
people call it with vitamins and what have you, yes, is basically
sugar. Whole grain breads can be a different story, with 100%
whole wheat being just that. Whole grain breads, maybe yes,
maybe no. Often a lot of white flour. Things like rye bread can
have in essence half as much sugar effect at white bread, if you
can find one that is actually 100% non white flour. If you take
the gluten out of bread, you get rid of most of the non-sugar
nutrients."

"Isn't gluten bad? Look at all those gluten free diets out there!"

"There are a lot of people that have gluten problems. There's
celiac disease at about 1% of the population, wheat allergy at
perhaps 0.1%, and gluten sensitivity, at about 5-6%. Lots. Sure,
they shouldn't eat it. But you can. Just watch the proportion,
watch the dinner plate like I told you. One palm is for starches,
and if you want to use some bread, okay. I'd pick the better breads,
though. And the idea to avoid processed foods is a good one. But
just be smart. There's a difference, for example, between regular
and natural peanut butter."

"Isn't peanut butter peanut butter?"

"Look at the labels, Des. Regular is full of icing sugar. And
other stuff. Look at the natural peanut butter label. Just peanuts.
Sure, it would be better to eat peanuts. Your body would have to
chew it up and that would eat up some calories. Some Paleo's also
don't eat much dairy either, claiming that ancient man wouldn't
eat cheese. Or have yogurt. Or drink milk, from domesticated
animals. But if I was a caveman, practically starving as usual, and
brought down an animal that had milk, I'd drink it. Research also
is suggesting that grains did play a role in ancient diets. Again,
use some common sense. We're waxing on here way too much
on these little religions. Remember the big data. Mediterranean,
right? Heavy veg and fruit. Olive oil, not butter. Fish, legumes.
Yogurt. Not much sugar. Can't knock that diet for almost any
indication, including obesity. But we can steal ideas from other
sources, right? We took some ideas from that Washington Apple
diet, remember? The celery?"

"Oh yeah, did that for a while. Thanks for the reminder. Cheaper than a bag of salad, I guess."

"Exercising, right?"

"Suppose I could do more. Got a dog. Spend a lot of time with him, walking him, you know. Not much gym time sometimes. Actually, no gym yet...," Des confessed.

"The gym isn't the big thing. There's too much emphasis on that, another religion. The gym is great and gives some people the opportunity to really get their heart rates up. A lot of people in this society, never have to run. No saber tooth tigers around! That's good for your heart. But remember the NEAT thermodynamics thing!"

"What's that again?"

"Non Exercise Activity Thermogenesis. The calories that you burn not doing formal exercise. Remember, most people that exercise only burn 100 calories a day in formal exercise. There's way too much emphasis on it. Yes, you need 30 minutes or so of elevated heart rate, for heart health. Every day. But where the emphasis should be is on moving. Just moving. Unfortunately, we humans now have very sedentary lives. We lie down to sleep, sit to eat breakfast, drive to work, sit to work, sit on breaks, sit at lunch, sit at work, drive home, sit to eat, then sit and watch television, or game. Occasionally we have a short gym break. Then we do it all again."

"We just sit too much."

"Yup. Our bodies are made to be constantly moving. That's what the Paleo devotees have forgotten. This isn't the ancient world, or should I say prehistoric world. We're not hunter gatherers any more, but video screen watchers. Our lives are also markedly longer. Cavemen didn't live into their seventies. They're trying to impose a diet, which they're not even very sure about, on a different time and place. Besides which, our planet can't support everyone living on that diet. Impossible. We frankly need grains, for people to live."

"So it's more important to just keep moving all the time..."

"Just like that farmer I told you about. 4000 calories more than a sedentary worker. 4000 more calories burned, daily, than a computer graphics worker..."

"...Without a dog..."

"Right. That changes everything, doesn't it? Take this lab requisition. Let's see where you are. Maybe more pills can go. See you in a few weeks."

CHAPTER TWENTY

The last of the dishes stood on the drying rack. Fry pan, one dish, couple of forks, knives. A cooking spoon, a pot. Looked at the phone on the wall and considered past habits. Most had just cell phones now, but he was a die hard. Family tradition. Couldn't quite wrap his head around a home without a number. Probably some day would give it up... paying twice, after all.

Would usually grab the thing and order. Fifteen seconds. Then, sit and wait for delivery. Would buzz the guy up and grumble about walking to the door. Open the box, sit and eat.

Now, it wasn't quite farming, but had to at least go to the store to buy the stuff. Bring it home and store it. Decide what to cook, sure, that was video screen time. Peel, scrub, open cans, boil or whatever. Stand to do it. Then there was clean up.

Used to just pitch the pizza box on a nearby pile.

Even eating this way was burning more calories. And healthier stuff...

Hersh had helped with that endeavour. Licked the plates clean, or darn near. Probably not ideal dog food, but he had to help with chores, right? Heh, heh...

"Come on, you, let's go." Des walked over to the leash hook, and popped on Hershey's collar.

The trip to the stairwell was a routine, no longer the imposing traverse. Down was no longer much of a problem. Up was still another matter. Working on that.

It would come. Was coming.

Thought about Sunshine, and that morning's blood test. Was pretty shocked. Struck up a conversation, and even had coffee, was her break time apparently. Or so she said. Seemed a bit early. They'd been on contact on Facebook, but that was nothing. Electrons and glass screens. Had to watch this line of thinking.

"Come on Hersh, you know the way." Cracked the door open and Hersh charged through. Tried to make it a race to the bottom. As if. Would normally charge down to one landing, sit there and thump his tail till Des joined him. Same thing next flight. The stairs game.

Des had taken matters into his own hand one day and brought a broom. And light bulbs. Funnily enough some neighbours were also now using the stairs regularly. Used to be his personal work out facility. Should have membership cards.

"Hi, Des!" Kit came storming up the stairs, followed by her brood.

"Kit! How're you doing? Let me help you with that bag." Des grabbed the grocery bag, turned and went up a flight to their floor, Hershey playing with the kids behind.

"Des, look at you. Not only down, but up. Look at that!"

Des flushed around his ears. He had confessed his stairs secret to his neighbour one day in a fit of openness. Felt like AA, or must be. Stand up and tell it like it is. Found out the support was massive. Actually now had it on his Facebook page, called it the stair counter. People chimed in to say congrats and leave encouragement. His goal was up the stairs in four more weeks. Right there, written down, pants pulled down.

No wiggle room in that one.

"Working on it, Kit, you know that. And thanks for the encouragement, you're my biggest cheerleader. You, and Sunshine."

"Oh, your lab girl. What's going on with you two, anyway?"

"Nothing, nothing. Just coffee. Black coffee."

"No sugar, huh?"

"Not even as a spice." Des laughed and handed her the bag at her door. "Hersh, leave those kids alone."

"I think it's the kids, not Hershey. Come here, you."

Hersh came over and thumped his tail. Kit always seemed to have a biscuit in her pocket.

"Kit, how do you do that? You don't even have a dog!"

"No, but my kids do. He's a chocolate lab. And he's kinda cute," rubbing his ears.

Des laughed and pulled the dog away.

"Come on, it's business time."

They made their way to the stairwell and started down again. As they descended, Des looked at his hand, still able to make out the scars from that first day. No glove needed now.

Noticed the sweat. Still there, probably always would. But not dripping off his face, nose. Things were changing.

Flights passed with little notice. Used to be a big deal, one, then two, then three. Sort of like the up direction was, now. Out the door at the bottom, and took a big breath. Stars peeked out behind cloud cover. Between cement skyscrapers. Felt the sidewalk underneath as he took a turn with his dog.

Wondered what it was like.

Before it all.

Just before.

* * *

Set the alarm at 0630. As if he needed that. Hersh normally got him up. Already on the bed, the rascal. He'd long got over that one. Dogs. Pack animals. That's how they slept.

Remembered the sleep-ins, the flex time Petticoat Junction, Bond in the afternoon. As his life had grown, the time in bed had shrunk, as had the television time. Funny, the sleep seemed even better. Wondered what Uncle Jed had been up to, or if Jethro had ever finished that bowl of cornflakes.

Turned the clock around so he couldn't see it. Basic sleep hygiene. Light off, right to bed. Never had trouble falling asleep any more. And since the increase in exercise, wake ups were uncommon, brief events.

Tonight was different. No sugar in his coffee. That one just bugged him. Bugged him like a brown recluse, usually hiding but now right out there, crawling neuron to neuron, spinning a web through his frontal cortex. Little drops of poison just glistened along the axons.

Hersh put his head on his leg, which he was wont to do, but couldn't sleep like that, pushed him off. Still struggled with the heat. Getting lighter, but still had that non-factory issue, owner installed, subcutaneous deep freeze sleeping bag. Felt his pannus, smaller but still there. As if. His two favourite words. Like really.

Felt the pillow under his head, the softness of the sheets. Kept the bedroom pretty cool, but that street dog, so used to sleeping on concrete and now addicted to King Size Serta, was a real space heater. Sleep slowly drifted in. Thoughts warped, fractured off, and spun away. Images of colours, distortions…

…the stars above.

And the club in his hand, gnarled, dirty, sinewy.

Big stick, really. Little branches on the side rubbed off with a stone. Fit his hand well, a favourite tool. Bare feet beneath, toes splayed like his hand, callused, and moving quickly. Ran with a rhythm, easily, loping, a natural, well-practiced oscillation. Branches reached out and dug fingernails across his skin, barely noticed.

He'd been moving for days, weeks. The herd of which they'd been following at the periphery was moving, in search of water and leaf. Terrible drought. The sun beat down with a sledge, unremitting, unforgiving, leathery gliders turning above, biding their time. Des looked up, irritated, then fought down the hunger tearing at his belly with a handful of berries and a few leaves. Mouth desert dry. He took a sip from the gourd at his side, carefully safeguarding the rest, pushing a brown, wizened root into the hole.

Could feel the movement, see the twisting motion of his hand, feel the impatience, feel the hunger. The awful, burning hunger. Sun battered skin. Scratches, scabs, bruises, insect bites.

Scars from old conflicts, bites, burns. Survivor. So few of them now, scattered in a loose line behind him.

A tree. Ideal. Fern like fronds largely consumed by herbivores, had a welcoming, graceful branch much too high for sabretooth. If only. If only he could rest. For just a moment. Looked behind at the others, leaning on him.

Infants swaddled around the neck. If the herd moved, they moved. Comfortable cave left behind, even they seemed in pursuit. Little ones, faces painted with soot to mimic their elders, little sticks in their hands, quietly keeping up, mothers looking ahead, looking back, looking ahead, occasionally cuffing one in the ear, dragging another along. No cries, no screams, a silent loose association of early Homo sapiens well aware of the importance of stealth. And community. Some dodged to one side to pick a berry, or dig a root. Others behind, big males, clubs in hand largely attending to their rear, watching for their predators.

Straggler. Older, previous injuries made him trot at a different kind of rhythm, on the edge of the pack. Weaker, older, but imposing, a mass of flesh, woolly fur patchy at best. Every day the animal was a bit slower. The humans followed and waited. Day after day, they followed, sometimes breaking contact, only to find the trail and follow again.

Finally a stumble. Pack mates startled and separated. It was the end. They let him fall, unattended. The pack moved on, an inertia not to be stopped by an aging, failing, senior.

Des held up his arm and sank to the ground. Behind him, he knew the others were doing the same. The old beast struggled to his feet, shook his fur, bleated in fury and started again, only to fall, a massive impact, taking the last breath.

Beckoned the others forward, but turned to the back, joining the others at the rear to put up a periphery, a loose cordon of human flesh to protect, or at least warn the others. Envisioned what he'd seen too few times before, the group approaching the beast with stony knives, the little ones eagerly awaiting.

Crouched down behind sparse vegetation and swept the horizon...

...Alarm bleated, had been going on for a few minutes, by the look of it. Sunlight poked between the slats, poking Hershey in the eyes, on his back as usual.

"Whatcha doing, sleeping in or something?" Des rubbed the dog's chest and stood up.

And recognized he hadn't rocked back and forth to do it. Had just sat up, swung his legs over and stood.

"Well, what do you know?" Stretched, grabbed his sweats, third new pair in as many months, downed the glass of water at his bedside and walked to the leash hook.

"Well, come on, you."

Hershey jumped down from the bed, pushed out on his front paws, bum straight in the air, classic dog Tai chi. Stood up and shook, fur moving opposite in direction to his rotation. Scampered up for the leash.

"So, that's what it was like, eh, boy. Short little intervals of rest, the rest of the time chasing the woolly mammoth. Or getting chased. Or trying to find a berry. Should make a website, intervalsofrest.com, or what about the lie? The big lie we're all living? The one we, you and I, are actually dealing with? Defy-the-lie.com? What do you think?"

Hersh was a good yes man. He agreed. Defythelie.com it was. It was so much more than just exercise, or just diet. It was the brain effect, the labelling. Routines. Society. That intervals of rest idea though...couldn't let go of that one...that would stick in his brain...

* * *

Intervals of rest, indeed. He was a far way from that.

Des grabbed the door handle and pushed it open. His apartment had evolved. Gone was the train set landscape of pizza boxes, beer and Pepper cans. This was a place he could invite friends to see, to come over, for a meal, for a game. The bachelor pad was gone, despite no other humanoids. Looked at Hersh. A home.

Closed the door with authority. Hersh looked up, a bit of a change in rhythm there.

"Hersh, I've got work to do." Wondered how many dog owners talked to their dogs. Probably all. Because they weren't dogs, really. Family. And you talk to family.

Des stood in the middle of his living room, a surveyor on site. Wrigley, or Big Bacon as he was now affectionately called, centre stage. And that's what it was, an amphitheatre.

Well, that was waxing poetic. Ancient Greek poetry. Hardly amphitheatre. No rising seats around the edge, but there really was a circle. Circle of seats. The whole focus of his living room, and probably his apartment, was that television. At least that beverage fridge was gone.

In its place, new paint on the wall. Latex antique lace.

"Hersh, I think this place needs more than new paint."

Wrigley was big, and was going nowhere. If he were to make a house...but that wasn't the situation. Started up Google on his iMac.

"Time, Hersh, to spend some of that money I've been sitting on." As if he had piles. Those two words again. And he probably did.

Have piles.

Started laughing to himself, and looked for second hand exercise equipment. Exercise bikes...probably pushing it. Images of that red bike, his speech, whirled through his head. He had actually never ridden the thing. Sat in his garage, just so Brownstone couldn't get his hands on it, the putz. Flush flickered at his ears as he surfed over to bicycles, racing, touring, big fat wheel versions for snow or sand.

And had another image. Touring through France. On a bike. Saddles with a nice partial round of cheese, and what the heck, he was biking, a baguette. Could see himself moving the pedals, feel the breeze in his hair whistling down his collar as he passed a vineyard, a country manse in the distance.

"And that, Hersh, is a goal. Not a daydream." Hersh was lying in the sun, totally oblivious. Thumped his tail a bit at his name.

Opened up his Facebook page and updated his stair count He was right on track. Thanked a few of his buddies for encouragement and put up a new goal. Bike tour France. Could feel his heart thump. Subconsciously felt for the nitro in his pocket and took a deep breath. No heaviness. Hadn't felt that, ever. Kept the thing with him ever since his MI. Took it out of his pocket and glared at it. Excitement, not cardiac...Fear, perhaps.

He was not being stupid. Was not. Touring France he would. And that stupid bottle would stay in his pants. This was no fairy tail. Looked at Hersh. Tale! Right beside that cheese would be some pill bottles, and he knew it.

Accept the past and move on. Finished it off and put a date. Year from today. Right there. Bike tour La France, one year, today. Thought of the food...those little portions would be just right.

And took a deep breath, again. Posted a picture of that bike to Instagram. There.

Back to the exercise equipment. Looked around his room. If he was going to take a few hours off to watch a movie, or a game, and he liked watching the game, then he didn't have to veg. Well, maybe eat veg. But not be one. Right in front, that's where it was going. Treadmill first, exercise bike later, say...six months. First, he'd have to stop those thighs from rubbing together. Couch could go there, and the chair there, crap table...

Which should be renamed. Veg table!

Appreciated his head start, his formal monitor stand, where he could move it from sitting to standing. Remembered getting rid of his memento pile of pizza boxes, and duct tape. He had already started, was on the path. Thought of his caveman self, running, moving constantly to just survive. Probably took a brief rest in a tree, for a few minutes, before running again. Short intervals of rest.

Felt his whole paradigm start to shift, and started moving his feet, as he was typing. Why not? Going to throw him in the looney bin?

His living area was going to reflect the new reality, his new philosophy of having intervals of rest, not exercise. His new stance. To Defy-The-Lie.

CHAPTER TWENTY-ONE

Sunshine had not only encouraged the Tour de France, but bet him a bike.

Right there on the Facebook page, a challenge. "You do this, and so help me, I'll buy you the bike. And you can even have it red."

He had shared that story, one day. Hershey and he had taken longer and longer walks, one now being to the lab. Every day the two slowly pushed the distance, now encompassing much of his end of town. To his surprise, there were a couple of small parks, tucked away out of the bus line's direct routes. One abutted the lab. The things you find walking! Somehow, they often appeared there at lunch, or coffee break time. Weird, dog had taken right to her. Like some long lost relative. He'd heard of cat people, people that cats were just drawn to. Guessed she was a dog person.

Des picked up his phone and broke a habit. Actually dialled. No texting this time.

"You're going to get me a red one. So help me. That's a rude one!"

"Not kidding, Des. You make those flight arrangements and you'll have that bike. Graphite. Red. Whatever. I know what they cost. Not kidding. It's right there, in black and white. You not only made a public commitment, so did I. Not kidding!"

Des swallowed hard. Thought of all he had accomplished. He was getting used to breaking ruts. But this was the biggest one. Isolation. Sure, he had friends. Donnie. Kit and the kids. Hersh. But this was something he didn't even want to look at. The ROLL he may have been. The ROLL he would always be.

"Look, want to go out sometime? Sorry, that came out awkward. Maybe should have done that over coffee, at the park. But maybe couldn't have gotten it out. Anyway, it is what it is! Awkward or not, interested?"

"Well it's about time, buddy! What've you been waiting for? Did I have to hit you on the head with a stick or something?"

Des thought of his dream the night before. Hopefully not that one.

"I, uh...sorry..."

"Forget it. My place, Saturday night. I cook. You come. And bring Hershman, he can run around."

* * *

Dirty yellow checkered cab. Bent antenna, dent on the back left fender. But big enough. Big old Chevy. Des breathed a sigh of relief. Driver was a vet, bald guy with a flag tattooed on the back of his head, dog tags.

Turned out she had a trailer off the interstate, at the foot of the mountains. The taxi driver had taken the piece of paper out of his hand, had a look at the address, shook his head, frowned and punched it into his GPS.

"Bud, you know how much this is gonna cost you? And there's a charge for the dog. Some of my buddies, hey, most of my buddies, only service dogs. But got one myself. Had a fight with the boss and actually won it. I'll take your dog, but it's another ten. Had to clean up last week, couldn't believe it, guy got out of the cab and didn't even tell me. You'll fit better up front."

Des waved him off. "Hersh is a champ. He won't. But believe me, if he did, I'd clean it. He's my bud, my dog, my job, not yours. Thanks for taking us and you can have twenty for the dog, not ten. Thanks, man."

Guy code, let him open the door himself. Hersh looked anxious, as if he'd be left on the sidewalk.

"Think I'm going to let you sit here till I get back, Doofus? You're with me, remember? In the back, big guy!" Opened the door, throwing in the leash emblazoned with poop bags and a small bag of kibble. Hersh jumped in and sat up in the back.

"Should really have a safety belt for the dog. Can get them where you buy dog food, usually. He's cute! Been with you long?"

The two men buckled in, the driver rubbing Hershey's head.

"Saved me a few months ago. A stray. Seems happy to be with me."

"Saved you or saved him?" Dark gaps between yellow teeth, a big grin.

"Well, I guess we saved each other. No kidding. Should 'a seen me a few months ago. Could never have fit in here. No way."

"Good on ya, man. Sit tight. Going over to the Circle Bar ranch, huh?"

"What?"

"That address. It's a horse ranch. Biggest in the county. Sit tight. It's a nice drive. Take about thirty, once we hit the interstate."

Des looked at the address again and scratched his head. Should 'a Googled it. But figured downtown worker, town address.

The big Chevy rolled down the street, taking routes Des had never seen. Slowly the garbage seemed to diminish, at about the same rate as the buildings shortened and spread apart. A bit more vegetation, but what did you expect in this state. Signage became more disperse.

Hersh seemed fascinated, staring out the window, first the left, then the right. Miles clicked by and Des felt his muscles start to loosen.

"Beautiful country, this. Used to live out here as a boy, before I was deployed."

Des nodded, the road curving between hillocks and now masses of foliage. Ahead he could make out a typical ranch entrance way, two telephone poles on guard on either side, Circle Bar Ranch between.

Sunshine was just inside, astride a big speckled mare slowly chewing some cud. Must have maneuvered so the sun was behind her. All a scheme. Seemed radiant, the sunbeams refracting through her hair.

Mind you, the cud thing really didn't fit.

"Hi Des! Hey, I know you, aren't you from around here?"

"Yes sir, miss, used to be one of your neighbours, but that was a long time ago. Just down the way, a little cabin. Maybe you remember Judd and the boys. I was one of 'em! Luke!"

"Well, welcome to the ranch! My trailer is just down there." And pointed the way to a little two wheeler, off the main driveway.

Luke drove down to the trailer, rolling to a stop in front of a little picket fence, a whimsical thing probably twenty feet from its front door. Odd, a little postage stamp in the middle of acres of open space. Roses poked through the pickets. Des could see a garden, tomatoes, peppers as he levered out of his chair, only to see Luke standing in front of Sunshine, hands on his hips.

"You wouldn't be Missy, would you? Did they call you Missy?"

"My Lord, yes! That was my nickname!"

"Well, come on down off that horse, and let me take a look at you!"

Hersh was observing this whole exchange from inside the car, head turning curiously.

"Hey, Sunshine. Can I let Hershey out of the car? Okay with the horse?" Her name was something more formal, with some kind of a south western belle ring to it, but it never seemed to catch on with Des. Didn't mind. Maybe even preferred Sunshine. Maybe used to nicknames.

"Sure, Des. We actually breed dogs here. Actually Labs! The horses are all used to them. Remember, they're bigger than your dog!"

While Missy and the cabdriver were talking, Des opened the door for Hersh. "Now listen you, behave...Whoa!"

Hershey bolted out of the cab and tore around Sunshine/ Missy in concentric circles. The horse gave a bit of a snort, raising its head more out of reflex than anything, but then just seemed bemused.

"Des, I think he likes it here!"

"Well, doesn't really get a chance to run. Sometimes he goes on a tear in the apartment, you know, wall to wall to wall, but tires out pretty quick with all the body slams. You know, sort of does a side spin and a hip check against the boards to stop. Wow, look at him run!"

All of a sudden Hersh was running up the little hill next to the trailer, then lapping the trailer. A couple times, then came to an abrupt stop in front of the cab, where Luke and Des were leaning watching the performance. Tongue hanging out, tail thumping, a vision of canine happiness.

"Luke, I know this sounds kinda weird, you bringing a fare up here and all, but like to go up to the main house? Like to see if anyone's around from before?"

"Missy, that I would like."

The two men got back in the cab and slowly rumbled up the curving road to the house, quite a goodly distance from the road. Missy led the way on her horse, cantering gently ahead with Hershey at the horse's heels, as if he knew exactly where to place himself in the procession. Would look at the horse, then up at the rider... Odd.

"Des, if this isn't the damnedest thing. So help me, looks like that dog belongs here. Fits right in, don't he?"

Des grunted, keeping his thoughts to himself, slowly kneading his leather leash in his massive hand. Sweat dropped off his nose, unnoticed, as he watched *Missy come Sunshine come whatever that other name was* dismount, and flip her reins over the rail in front of the house.

Hershey bounded right over and jumped at her, paws versus thighs.

"Hersh! Sunshine, sorry..." Missy grinned over her shoulder and rubbed his ears.

"It's ok, we're buds, right bud?" And rubbed him vigorously between the ears.

Ranch, so ranch style home, massive cedar timbers. Fieldstone walkway, pillars. Broad, welcoming porch, complete with fireplace and rocking chairs, one complete with a rocker. Cedar shake roof, a bit of green mossy like growth along the edges.

As Des levered himself out of the car, remarking to himself subconsciously that it was an easier procedure, he saw Sunshine waving him over.

"...and this is Desmond O'Brien, remember me telling you about him? And guess who the cab driver is?"

"Luke? Is that you, from next door? You've lost all your hair! And got a tattoo! What did you go doing that for, ya goof?"

Luke didn't seem to mind and literally ran over to hug the old lady. Little round spectacles, little red cheeks with a brush of flour on one and an apron busy with daisies. Ninety at least. But then, Des wasn't really that good at guessing these things. Better keep his guess to himself.

"And you, are you the one Beatrice calls the Roll? What kind of name is that, young man?"

By this time Des had ambled up to the porch, sidestepping Hershey who had made himself at home in front of the welcome mat.

"Hello, ma'am, Desmond O'Brien. They used to call me that in college. Football. I think Sunshine, I mean Beatrice, used to see me play once in a while."

"Des! You were the whole team! There were banners everywhere! The Roll!"

"Well, young man, what happened to 'ya?"

"Uh, pardon me, ma'am?"

"'Ya don't look like Mr. All American, now do 'ya? What happened?"

"Grandma!" Beatrice/ Missy/ Sunshine positively petrified.

"It's ok, don't worry. She's right. Grandma, can I call you that? I had some health problems and sort of lost my way. But actually, right now I'm better than I've been in years! That little dog over there has got me chasing him all over the city, up and down the stairs. Day after day, I'm coming back to my old self. If I was ever there! Certainly, I feel better."

"Wha' do 'ya mean, Damien over there? How is he helping you?" Grandma gestured at Hershey.

"...Dddamien?" Stuttered Des. Confounded, he saw Hershman's head pop up at the name.

"Haven't seen him for a couple years! Took off after that grey mare, what was her name? Poopsy? That one that kept escaping, wandering down the interstate more than once, stupid thing. State police brought her back more than once, cost your Dad more than one nuisance charge. Almost sold her, he did."

"Poopsy, what?" Des looked completely confused.

"Grandma, you must be mixed up. Hershey's a stray. Found in the city. Des found him a few months ago and he's been living with him."

"Who's calling me demented, Beatrice? And who's mixed up? Don't ever forget one of my dogs. Been breeding them for years. 'Specially the chocolates! Yellows, blacks, sure, they're the poster-dogs for working, they're the ones they want to train for the blind, sure, they're smart and calm. Love them, I do. But a special place in my heart for the chocolates, the crazy ones. Don't forget those, no way at all!"

As if understanding this was all about him, Hershey looked from person to person, thumping his tail. Tail, tail.

"Damien, come." Grandma dropped one of her hands to her side and rubbed her fingers together.

Hershey walked over to Grandma and sat, looking up. Licked the hand that rubbed his ears.

"Yup, Damien."

Des let out a sigh. Could stop the sound, but air always told the tale. "Hersh, you've found your home!"

Hershey trotted over to the big man and jumped at his legs. Des rubbed his head.

"Hmmm, well, maybe not. Never been wrong before, though. Should show him the horse," Grandma mused.

"Poopsy? She's in the barn, isn't she?" Sunshine was looking from Grandma, to Des.

"Yes, we don't let her roam around much anymore, right? Probably gets more rides than any other horse, because of that. Show him Poopsy, sure! And this, I've got to see. Help me up, big guy."

Des disengaged from the dog and leant a big arm, a massive tree branch that Grandma seized upon for support. Tiny woman, spidery spindly legs, but pretty steady once she started down the path.

"See, your horse, he'll just stand there, Beatrice. Poopsy, like a dog. Like some of my chocolates. Got to be with people, a bit nuts. She, she would be trying to follow. Crazy horse…"

Grandma narrated the relatively short walk to the barn, a stereotypical affair with Circle Bar Horses on the front. White horse fencing.

An older man was in front, forking hay off a truck. "Grandma, what's this?"

"Jed, remember Damien?"

"Who?"

Beatrice ran up to the man and kissed him on the cheek. "Dad, this is Des, remember I told you?"

The man put down the pitch fork and walked over. "Desmond O'Brien. The Roll. My God, nice to meet you. Great ball player."

The two shook hands. Sunshine's father, older and tanned but not weather beaten. Muscles that Desmond could appreciate. Sparkle in his eye, just like her.

"Nice to meet you, sir. You've got quite the talented girl. A sharp needler!"

"Yeah, got to pay the bills for that horse, don't she? But I think that's more something on the side. Her heart, I think, is in this ranch. Maybe a bit of a more reliable income stream than what she gets here…me and her practically run this thing now, huh Missy? And you, don't I know you?" This time Jed was looking at Luke, who had tagged along.

"Hi, sir. Been a while." Luke and Jed shook this time.

"Yes, yes yes, we're here for Poopsy!" Grandma interjected. "She in there?"

"Yup, don't let her out unless I can be right on her. Funny, great with the kids, will follow the trails just perfect. Let her out of sight of a human being, and she's off. Sometimes put her in that paddock, she's ok in there. Can't let her wander like the others. Like a dog, so help me. Need a leash, or something. In the barn."

Jed ambled over to the barn doors, sliding open the one on the left, a heavy affair on rollers. "So why do you want Poopsy?"

"It's a test, Jed! See the dog?" Grandma pointed.

"One of ours?"

"Think so, but believe it or not, not sure! Me! But the horse'll tell."

The loose group walked into the barn, well illuminated by incandescents and an open window hay bale up above. Most of the stalls were open, save a couple, one clearly Poopsy, as the dog demonstrated.

Hershey had run right over, paws up on the door to the stall.

Poops gave a whinny, and leaned her neck over.

"Man, should put that on YouTube," interjected Luke, watching as the two touched noses. "Or maybe a beer commercial."

"Damien! See?" Grandma was clearly delighted.

Hersh squeezed under the bottom rail and back, in and out, looking up at the horse.

"I guess we can let her out, now. We're all here, and that dog will keep her around. I hope. Didn't work that one day. Remember?" Jed looked at Grandma.

"Yep, that was the day. Couple of years ago. Haven't seen Damien since. Poops got out and I guess Damien tried to find her. And here he is, the brown sheep!"

Des, standing at the back of the circle watching the proceedings, cleared his throat, and swallowed. Sunshine danced over and put her hand on his arm.

"Ever seen anything like that?"

"Nope, certainly not," shaking his head.

Jed was letting the horse out, putting on a bridle, just in case, as he said. Sunshine rubbed the horse's head, and led her out, Damien come Hershey literally at her heels. Somehow they seemed to walk perfectly in tandem, despite Des' concern about a misplaced hoof.

Sunshine brought the horse out to the paddock, took off her bridle and stroked her neck, rubbed her nose. Got a nibble behind the ear it seemed, then with a slap on her flank trotted about the enclosure, the dog also stretching his legs, seeming to measure the space, darting from one corner to another.

"Well, I'll be damned. To think of all the weird coincidences. Like some stupid Harlequin romance, from the girl meets guy, to the dog, to the freaking cab driver, to a horse named Poopsy, and now this dog, poor long lost dog, gets home!" Luke stood with Sunshine, both wearing goofy grins.

"Guess there's more to this world than we know, huh?" Sunshine turned to go back into the barn, and gestured to Des to follow. "Luke, I wanna talk to Des for a second. Meet you back at the trailer? Hey, you wanna stay for dinner? Would that be ok, Des?"

Des gave a nonplussed, sort of Des look, which Beatrice / Missy took for acquiescence, and it was a plan. Luke clamoured back into the cab and rolled down towards the trailer.

"Des, it's all downhill."

"Yeah, yeah, by God, Sunshine, think I can't walk that?"

Sunshine scrunched up her nose, somehow raising her eyebrows at the same time.

"Hey, how'd you do that?"

"What, train Poopsy? Invite a total stranger for dinner? Hey, I invited you, didn't I? And how well do we know each other? Huh?"

"No no, I mean the eyebrows thing."

"What?"

"Oh, never mind. What did you want to talk to me about?" They were back in the barn now, walking to a stall at the end.

"Ever want to ride a horse?"

"Oh, sure. Never did though. I did tell you about the red bike, right? Well, no bike, no horse."

"Come over here." There, on the wall, was a beam scale.

"Sunshine, really, I love you to bits, but..."

"You love me? It is a Harlequin romance!" As Sunshine threw her arms about him, scrunched up her nose again, and pinched his ear. "Listen, goofball, I'd like to ride with you, but you're too heavy."

"Yeah, I know. Too heavy for glider lessons. Too heavy for lawn chairs. I get it."

"No, you don't. You're not listening. From the first time I met you, you've lost a ton of weight."

"Yeah, uh, thanks. Yup. Basically was Hershey...uh, Damien. I think. But thanks."

"I can even see your jawline, here." Sunshine traced it with her finger, bringing out a flush like she was rolling open a rheostat switch.

"What are you saying?"

"This is my biggest horse, King. Sort of a dog's name. We've got Hobo, Care Bear, Poopsy. They're more horse names. Somehow nothing else would fit this guy."

King stood 19 hands, weighing in at 2000 pounds. Jet black, he towered over little Missy, which was a much more diminutive name and seemed to fit the situation. Seemed to look Des right in the eye.

"He's huge!"

"So are you, Des. But even he, a Clydesdale, can only carry at most, including tack, that's the saddle and everything, 20% of his weight. What's twenty percent of 2000?"

"That's, um. Four hundred pounds. Are Clydesdales black? And how much does tack weigh?"

"Well, for a horse like this, and a person like you, we're looking at upwards of fifty pounds. And yes, some Clydesdales are black. He is, right? See the white socks? You're right, usually there's a white mark on the face. Not King. But that weight. That puts you off the horse, doesn't it, little buddy?"

"Well, um, uh…"

"Yes. It does. Don't BS a BS'er. I got into all the horse competitions lying about my age. You lie about your weight and hurt my horse, so help me Desmond O'Brien, Roll or no Roll, mark my words, I will take you down. Down hard." And by the look on her face, she meant business.

"But don't take that the wrong way. I'd say the same thing to my 'Da, or my brothers. No one hurts my animals. Nobody. So. I've got a scale over there. I don't want you on it. But when you say you're ready, and you want to ride, I'm going to be a jerk and check, and I'm sorry. I want to have it right out in the open, right now. Got it?"

Des gestured her over. "Sunshine."

"Yes, Desmond O'Brien?"

"Watch this. I'm going to go over there, and you're going to weigh me. We're then going to take a picture of myself, with King, with that Polaroid camera I see sitting there. Then you're going to give that to me. I'm going to write a date on it. At which time, you better have tack that will fit me. 'Cause I'm gonna ride that horse. With you."

Sunshine flushed and took his hand, leading him over to the beam scale.

"Hey, this one is better than Doc's! Mind if I pop by here once in a while, you know, just to check?" Des fiddled with the slide weights.

"Come on, come on, let's take this picture! I've got to make dinner, you know?"

Des made careful mental note, and walked slowly over to King. Massive dark brown eyes, huge quivering nostrils. Des rubbed the animal between the eyes, making a mental promise to himself, and the horse. Funny, King seemed to bob his head right then.

"Well, that's it then. By the end of tonight, I'll give you a date. And you'll write it on that picture, okay?" Des turned and put his head by King's. Sunshine snapped the picture, contract sealed.

"Come on, I want to show you something. And, like fried chicken?"

FAT

"Sunshine, now who you asking? Now look what we've done right now. Got to be careful, right? All the time. Including tonight...and show me what?"

The two left the barn and turned around back. There, beneath a majestic tree, was a little stone structure. The sun, setting behind it, cast long shadows towards them. The windows sparkled.

"It's a pretty special place, Des. Come take a look."

Sunshine held his hand and led him through the door. Wooden benches on either side of a central aisle.

"Sunshine. This is a church! On your property!"

"Surprised?"

"Can't say as I've ever seen the like. Do people have private churches? You a movie star or something?"

Sunshine laughed. "No, grandma may think she is. Her folks used to come here every day just to talk to God, they say. Grandma still does."

"Is she okay? Sick or something?" Des was suddenly flustered. For the fifteenth time in one day.

"Des! People don't talk to God to just ask for stuff! But no, she isn't sick, far as we know. Pretty ancient, yes. Sick, no."

"Funny what people used to do..."

"Hey, I said I come here, too!" Sunshine took a bench on the right and looked up at him.

"Sorry, sorry. I guess I've had some bad experiences. No offence."

"Des, you've got to make some big changes. To just...survive. You've really started, and I'm proud of you. But don't you think it's time you pulled in the big guns?"

"Guns?" Des looked around and grinned down at her.

"Right, right. I'm quite the linguist. You know what I mean."

Des looked down and put a hand on her shoulder. "I know what you mean. Sometimes I feel pretty alone. I wish I had your faith."

"Stick around, Des. It rubs off." Sunshine punched his shoulder.

"Hey, do you punch people in church? And what is it with you females, anyway? I thought you were expert communicators! What's all this punching?"

Des made a great show of rubbing his arm as she led him out, under that majestic tree. Could just see the branches move. God may have been asleep in the stones of that structure...but was alive in that tree. A leaf, right in his path, came to hand. The sparkling glass windows were nice. But under that ancient tree...Des could almost feel it. For probably the first time. Was he imagining it? No. Him. Something stirred inside. Suddenly he knew he could. That he would. That he was. That He was. Beneath all the lies, his and those of society. That new life that he ached for, was stretching for, was actually NOW. His life was what he DID.

Somehow he knew he'd never look at trees the same. Or at stones, or chipmunks for that matter. The walk looked pretty far. Downhill it was, but still pretty far. On loose gravel.

Somehow that helped. Des had fond memories of gravel, not only in his knees, but being ground into his forehead. Sort of made him what he was. Tough. Or, at least, tougher. And now this. A five hundred meter walk, loose gravel, uneven ground. With Sunshine.

Gauntlet thrown. Again. Probably, she hadn't realized the distance, or his capacity. Wouldn't have challenged, sure. That understanding, that realization that Sunshine had assumed he could walk it, spurred him on.

And besides, somehow it all looked different. Felt different. He folded the leaf, gently, thoughtfully. It was going to be OK. .

Because beside that nitro in his pocket there now rested something else.

* * *

Dinner was a grand affair, served on tin foil plates, paper plates, and some Corel. On the picnic table in front of the trailer and on TV dinner tables, scattered about the tiny yard. Hershey took turns sitting by almost everyone, dutifully pre-cleaning dinner plates and begging for scraps.

Des had scrupulously stuck to the palm plate and did not go back to the trough, though sorely tempted. Was he imagining it, or was Sunshine looking out the corner of her eye at him? Imagination. Runs wild.

Volunteered to do dishes. He, out of the corner of *his* eye, watched Damien sit by Grandma. She had come down for dinner, as well as Jed and a couple of stable hands. The joke was that it was *Beatrice's soup kitchen*, or *Beatrice's Beeline*, or Des' invention, *Sunshine's downpour*. Because there was so much food. Hard to believe it could come out of that trailer.

Little tiny skinny stable hands wolfed down shares that were hugely higher than their four palms plate. Several times. An exponentially larger plate. Des remembered Doc talking about farmers and how they can burn thousands of more calories per day than an office worker.

"Hey, do you guys eat like this all the time?" Des sparked.

"Hey, listen, man. Know what we make? Gotta eat when it's available, man! But sure, we chow down heavy. Sometimes go to the diner, you know, meatloaf, mashed potatoes, a stack. Pie. Ice cream. Hey, you make a pie, Missy?"

Des had a small piece, taking solace in the fact he had skipped the potatoes, trying to prepare for this eventuality, this certainty of dessert with a dinner out. It was like cake without ice cream, oatmeal without sugar, coffee without a cup. Imagine, dinner out without dessert.

A lie. Simply another one. It was a boat launch without champagne.

Well, seems everyone else was on that page, too. So, no potatoes meant he could, although he shouldn't, but then he'd hurt Sunshine's feelings, right? Des stood back and looked at the thoughts roll through his head.

Really, he was the Roll. Wasn't he? The ROLL! And he was going to get on that horse if...

"Des, call it a night? My shift's almost over, and you're my only fare!" Luke was up, wiping his hands on a dishcloth and kissing Sunshine on the cheek goodbye.

"Right, right." Des walked over to Sunshine and peeked around at Jed, the stable hands, and grandma. Hershey at her feet. "Big changes tonight. Make it three months, from today."

"Des! I don't want you to hurt yourself! Come on!"

"Actually Sunshine, I've done pretty well and it's, forgive me, rolling off! So I think I can do it. But don't worry. If I'm short, and I've never been short, I'll be honest and we can see a movie or something. Okay?"

"And you come up here anytime for that weigh in. And talk to King." Sunshine looked down at Hershey. Looked up at Des, uncomfortable.

"Hey, I'm happy for little guy. He did his job. Probably saved my life. Glad he's home, found Grandma. And Poopsy. And hey, I can visit him, too!"

Sunshine grabbed his arm and pulled him down for a kiss. "You're a sweet guy. And I can see a couple of tears in those eyes, and it's that dog and I know it. You're sweet to let him stay. Really sweet." Sunshine gave a little cough and kissed him on the ear again, before running into the trailer, door clattering behind her.

Looked at Luke. Who shrugged. "Gotta go."

Des nodded, walked to the trailer and gently hit the door with the palm of his hand. "Thanks again, Sunshine. I'll call you tomorrow."

"'Bye…" Clearly blowing her nose. Des shook his head a bit to clear it. Didn't work. And walked towards the cab.

Hershey got up from Grandma's side and walked over to Des. For a moment…but he was home. And it was ok. Des rubbed his head, got down on one heel, a relatively new maneuver for him, and whispered in his ear. Hershey licked his, and trotted back to Grandma.

"Well, easy come…" Des walked back to the cab, Luke strumming the wheel.

"All set, man? All your goodbyes?"

"Hey, how about yours? Old timer's reunion, or what?"

"Can you believe it?" Luke grinned and rubbed his stomach. "Fares, or fried chicken? Fried chicken, any day."

The cab backed up, did a lazy three point turn and started down the drive, slowly, so as the gravel wouldn't chip the thirty year old yellow paint. Or chip some rust off, to expose bare steel. Des rolled the window down and looked up at the stars.

"Man, can you believe the sky up here!"

"Light pollution, man. You know about smog? Well, there's light smog. Light pollution. So much in the city, you never see this. Ain't it something?"

The car rolled gently down towards the road. Luke turned on the signal and banked the car into the curve.

"Well, I'll be damned." Luke was looking in the rear mirror.

"What?"

"It *is* a damned Harlequin romance. Look behind us." Luke pulled the car over to the curb and waited for the chocolate lab to catch up.

Des opened the car door, leveraging himself out. "Hey, do you think I'm lost, like Poopsy? I've got to go home!"

Hershey had clearly other ideas, as he jumped in and made himself comfortable on the back seat. Des choked a bit, suddenly needing to blow his nose before getting back in the cab.

"I think you've got a dog, there, mister Des. Mister Roll!" Luke cracked a big grin and shook the big man's hand.

CHAPTER TWENTY-TWO

Commercial for Lite beer, then for sugar free gum, then for another, sexier slice-o-matic. Sci-pop music, opening credits and our in your face reporter, Gerald Rivers, shaking his mane and gesticulating wildly.

Des had the sound off. Really, the guy was a pain. Wrigley made the guy twice life size, even worse. Held the remote in his hand, standing in the middle of his living room.

Hu came on. Doc Hu. Should have a cape, or something. Like, who is this guy? Where does he live, in what universe, and doctor of what?

"...here in Dr. Hu's home, if you can believe it. That's the barking you can hear in the next room. Mrs. Hu lured him out with a cookie. Dr. Hu! Welcome back! But this is your home, so may I say thank you for inviting us!"

"No problem, Gerry. It's my house, my home, and we're here for a reason. Because we can't just talk about the stick, right? We talked about that the other day, the obesity "stick". It has two ends, diet and movement, but the stick can't be seen in isolation. Society holds it. So here we are, in my home. The nuclear family. The smallest building block of that thing called society."

"So that's it? The problem is with the family?"

"Gerry. I'm so glad you're here, because you very much represent the typical person. That's a compliment...really. That's your job. Gerry, there is no one clear reason, no one single, identifiable factor that has led to the obesity epidemic. We've talked thermodynamics, family doctors talk calories in, calories out, but nothing is changing. I think at least part of the reason here is the setting within which the patient lives. Society."

"Okay Doc, you're on. Give us at least some of the answers, as you see them."

"What is the answer to the obesity problem? A recent review of reviews suggests there is no clear consensus at all and calls for more research (Ross, Flynn & Pate, 2016). Usually in a complex problem, the easiest, most uncomplicated solution is the correct one.

"Eat less, and move more: so thermodynamically, so physiologically correct, and yet a real challenge for most people. This simplest of advice, so sound, so true, has been touted for years with little success. Why does Occam's Razor fall through here? The reasons are becoming clearer.

"People are set up not just by their genetics, family tradition and personal habits, but locally, nationally and socially to eat too much, and not move. Advertising dollars for fast food runs in the billions annually, while advertising for healthy eating is basically dependent on government initiatives, and utterly pales in comparison. Although models on TV sport washboard abs, they appear so consuming items clearly associated with weight gain and health risk, building consumer confusion with clear misinformation."

"So it's the advertising! I thought so!"

"Gerald. It's just a reflection of us. It's not just the commercials. National subsidies on commodity crops combined with inexpensive production and volume sales lower the price of high calorie, energy dense junk food. Snacking has become a social imperative at many events, dinner plates have increased in size to handle burgeoning portion sizes... And milk now comes cold out of a carton instead of warm in a bucket! We lie down to sleep, sit to eat, sit to work, sit to recreate, then do it again. Computer video screens have become our window onto the world, which we observe. And participate in only cognitively, our muscles atrophying beneath burgeoning layers of adipose."

"Ugh, that's an awful picture! Is that me? You called me a representative of society. Am I hiding under burgeoning layers of adipose...fat?"

"No Gerald, I guess I should clarify. You are not the ideal example or representative of society, because if you were, you'd be overweight. You're a TV personality that probably has a fully funded gym membership, and workout time during the day all carved out for you by the network higher ups. Right?"

Gerald raised his eyebrows, shrugging his right shoulder.

Hu continued, "Exercise based workstations and computer prompts to move have yet to be shown to make a sizable dent in the nine to five sitting marathon. Workers using the standing workstations stand approximately 30-120 minutes longer in a work day. Computer prompts to move are often ignored. Policy changes, information counselling, mindfulness training and even active workstations (pedalling, treadmills) have yet to accumulate any supportive evidence for usefulness (Shrestha, Kukkonen-Harjula & Verbeek et al, 2016). These researchers (Shrestha et al, 2016) question the utility of standing workstations as they produce such small calorie burns from the perspective of the whole day."

"Do you have one, Doc? A standing workstation?" Gerry seemed determined to make Hu's delivery more conversational, less didactic.

"Yup. Sure do. There are companies out there that make an arm like device that can elevate your monitor to standing height when needed. When you're done with that position, you can pull it back down again to sit. Myself, I just have my monitor raised to a proper height, a permanent position."

"You mean you don't sit down." Gerry was leaning forward, all ears.

"Well, I often sit with patients. My clinic is set up for a sit down interview, designed that way, just as all our spaces are designed in this society. Lots of sitting options. Furniture is for rest. Look at this room."

"You have a very comfortable living space, Doc."

"Thanks for that, Gerry. But this living space is very typical. One can go from home to home and see the same thing. Different furniture, different carpet or window treatments, but the typical living room is chairs grouped comfortably around a television monitor."

Gerry looked around, taking in the silent screen on the wall, looking at the placement of the chairs. "Well, we're sitting here at a coffee table." Lifted his mug and had a sip.

"Yes, you're right. Prior to the television's invention and quick acceptance, living rooms were arranged with chairs at the fireplace, which you still see, and chairs grouped around a central coffee table, for interaction. We still have coffee tables, but more normally they're placed in front of a television, placed to conveniently hold buckets of popcorn and beverages.

"The obese person is set up to continue to lay down more adipose tissue, despite his best efforts, because of the social structure within which he lives (Hetherington, 2007). The solution to obesity is of course to eat less and move more. This intention, however, is but one tiny gear in a massive machine.

"Health care providers, all too prone to deliver the glib, *Eat Less and Move More* direction, need to recognize all the factors at play. Context. We're missing the context! The best motivational speech is being heard by those within their own frame of reference, from past behaviour, family values and traditions to the very social norm of society. High calorie, energy dense cheap food is easily available. Industrial disease has struck our computer screen workers with some force, producing victims that crave the relief of rest."

"Industrial disease. That's a song, if I remember!" Gerry's eyebrows went up over his coffee mug.

"Yeah, great song. Miss Dire Straits. Real, though. I hear the song and smile. Funny, but real."

"So are we just inherently lazy? Is the human being just a lump?" Gerry put his mug down, leaning forward in challenge.

"Gerry, we're made to survive. The human body is built to store energy and be miserly in its expenditure. We're made for survival of a famine state, made for conservation of hard won calories, made to be able to stay active all day scrounging the last blackberry off the bush while chasing the fuzzy bunny. And all this while keeping one eye open for the charging T Rex and occasionally running for our lives! The rules are changed in modern society. Everything around us has changed, except the built in genetic drive to eat more than enough for our needs! To build adequate stores for that famine that will appear, and rest so we can run when we must.

"Gerry, we're made to rest. To conserve energy. So we do. However, we have no need to run from saber-tooth tigers any more. We have full fridges, full of processed food. The famine doesn't come for most of us. Changing the way one lives within this modern society is the secret and it's just not easy.

"It is, however, easier than inducing entire system changes ad hoc. Whereas one may petition City Hall in regards to the pizza parlour opening next to the school, or write the Minister of Youth for increased gym time in school, seldom do things change that easily. One must keep perspective, and realize that confining efforts and concern to a radius that closely matches one's circle of influence is the most powerful way to leverage for change. Petition for change, yes. Try to change society? Sure. We should. But it really all starts with the individual."

"So, it's up to us. Still up to the individual."

"Stephen Covey, who sadly has left us, was one, is one of my heroes. Wrote some great stuff. Seven Habits of Highly Successful People. Read it?"

"Well, I have a copy. Made it through a few pages, kinda hard to read," Gerry confessed.

"Don't feel bad. Each paragraph hits you like a hammer, right?"

"Let's just say it's not an easy, light read. It's a thinker."

"Have another crack at it, Gerry. Great book. He talked about Circle of Influence. Confining your efforts to within your circle of influence means changing things you can do something about. If your kid is in elementary school, you have a bit of an opportunity to impact that school's activity schedule. A bit. More with your own family. Most with yourself! Next to no impact at all with the high school, and just good luck with the state university."

"So this talk is about society. But it comes back to the individual. Their habits. Their behaviour."

"So yes, diet and exercise. That is the key. However for that overweight, obese person, his friends and family must approach the problem in a textural, complete, fabric kind of way, and not in the isolated thread manner. Individually deciding to go to the gym and eat less seldom works, because we're all jammed in a familial, societal framework. A rut. That person suffering from obesity needs more than emotional encouragement from his family and health care provider. And that fabric need be a rough, coarse, solid garment.

"Starting with the individual and working outwards, there must first be sound diagnosis and medical advice. The essence of which will likely be that, eat less and move more. Certainly, metabolic problems need be defined and ruled out. Pathologies that are incumbent on obesity to evolve must be investigated for."

"Whoa, whoa, Doc. Five dollar words. Network TV, remember?"

"You need to make sure you don't have a thyroid problem, or diabetes, that sort of thing."

"Okay Doc, got it. Just remember we're not medical students!"

"Got it, Gerry. Sorry. But patients need that medical assessment. Patients need the best intervention possible with our current medical knowledge. Medications are coming online that facilitate some weight loss. Surgical procedures have been shown, despite their substantial risk, to cut both morbidity and mortality for the morbidly obese patient. Devices exist currently which facilitate both measurement of calories consumed and movements made. Things measured can be quantified for the obese or overweight person, easing change."

"Let's talk some specifics, here. What technologies? What surgeries?" Gerry fingered his coffee mug, seemed to stretch his legs under the table.

"We've got to be careful here Gerry, if we want to stay on time. That's a miniseries in itself. Suffice it to say that the overweight person should start with his doctor. There is lots of help out there, including lap bands, a plastic ring that goes around the stomach, decreasing the volume of food that can get in there, to gastric bypasses, to medications, to simple diet and exercise advice."

"Surgery. You're talking surgery. And devices? You mentioned devices that can help measure and quantify."

"Surgery, for an important, life threatening medical problem. Valid. Often lifesaving! And…what's that on your wrist, Gerry? What's on mine?"

"A wrist watch on yours. Me, I've got an activity band. This is network television, so I'll just avoid the brand name. It counts the number of steps I take, the floors I climb, distance walked, guesses at calories burned, I suppose. Has my heart rate on it."

"Right. So just think of that. That one little device turns you into a scientist, if you use it properly. All of a sudden, you have measurements on one side of the equation. Have one myself. From a cell phone, you can also plug in if you've done weight lifting, or some activity where you can't use your monitor, like swimming. AND, you can plug in all the foods you've eaten, right?"

"Yeah, have never done that, but sure."

"There's both sides of the equation. It automatically does most of the activity tracking. If one is honest and judges food volume correctly, which many people have trouble with, and put it in to the computer, you've got the whole equation."

"People have trouble judging the amount of food they've eaten."

"Oh, you bet. And when you plug in ribs, for example, you get options from at home with salt and pepper all the way to restaurant dredged in barbecue sauce options. You need to be honest. First goof is the food volume and then it's how it's cooked."

"So how does one do it?"

"I'd advise over judging the volume and picking the saucier presentation. Then you might get closer to accuracy. But hey, there are food scales out there! And labels are getting better. The one advantage to eating out is that the food offerings are fairly standard at the chains."

"Huh?"

"You know pretty well how many calories there are in a Big Mac, for example. A bit tougher at the local burger hut."

"So these devices can help."

"Oh, you bet."

"So, the individual needs to number one, recognize he or she has a problem. Maybe hard to do when more than half of the population is overweight or obese, like what's normal? Maybe those commercials with washboard abs models can help."

"I suppose, if they weren't drinking light beer, or eating fried chicken at the same time."

"Got it, Doc. Mixes up the message, right?"

"Distorted, to be sure."

"So that person should get a medical assessment, get diet and exercise direction. What's next?"

"What's next in the widening circle is the patient's immediate surroundings. This includes his family members and the physical structure, the environment in which he lives. Obese and overweight people tend to come from similar families. There is a certain style to life, a tradition in eating and moving that must be broached. Even with a clear desire to eat less, an aromatic plate full of garlic bread with cheese just sitting there on the kitchen table would be too much for many. Does one need treat the entire nuclear family? Perhaps. Realizing, of course, that that nuclear family is part of a bigger family structure, complete with Friday evening BBQ and Saturday at the movies. That Saturday at the movies is often spent at home, on the comfy couch in front of the big screen, with junk food.

"An easy way to invoke change in a family is to change that family. The addition of an exercise requiring, exercise demanding, beloved family friend can mobilize not just one, but every member of the family. God's gifts to mankind are plentiful, but cherished and often overlooked in this struggle to regain an active lifestyle is the family dog."

"So are you advising we all get dogs? Come on, Doc! Wouldn't get along too well with my Siamese!" Gerry laughed.

"Darn close, Gerry. A long legged, exercise demanding, dog. Can fix the whole thing."

Des looked down at Hershey. And he thought he was rescuing the dog.

"... family lives within a physical environment, the family home. The entire modern home is usually set up for comfort and rest. Gamers have special chairs now, with special forearm supports to prevent tennis elbow and controls built into the arms, necessitating less leaning forward. Deep armchairs use the remote control big screen TV set as a focal point. Like we previously talked about, prior to television, sitting rooms were set up for possibilities of interpersonal interaction, with chairs actually facing each other, mind you, often on either side of the ubiquitous coffee/ cookie table."

Gerry shrugged, nodding.

"Our species has moved from having intervals of rest to having intervals of movement.

"The focus of the family home is often the kitchen, with a middle island ready for the lazy Susan. Our new wealth has brought with it all the embellishments, including the wine fridge, heated floors, central air and gas heat. We don't even have the metabolic challenge any more to withstand temperature swings. Many people, overweight and over insulated, are too hot. Well, turn on the A/C! Which is in itself a huge drain on resources and heats up the planet. Hospitals, clinics, people with chronic health conditions, yes, they need A/C. Do we all really need air conditioning? It's ridiculous! It's that layer of fat, that built in sleeping bag. Of course we're too hot. Food of course is always available, ready to fill the tank after one chops wood, which doesn't happen."

"Do you have A/C, Doc?" Gerry smiled.

"You can see my thermostat, over there. Yes, I've got it on today because of those lights, frankly, and sweating on national television would be embarrassing. See that social net at work? How these little factors start behaviour changes? But ask my wife. It's on 2-3 days a year, and often more for the dog, I think.

If he's lying around, with his tongue out, we usually start it. A few days a year. And we eat outside. On that picnic table. All the time. Do you do that?"

Gerry gave another one of his inscrutable looks and a shoulder shrug. "Remember used to. Don't seem to anymore."

"It's the flies, but more the bother, right? Trucking all that stuff outside, then back inside again. Movement. And the heat. Cooler inside with the A/C on. Tell me, how much did you used to eat, outside, when it was hot?"

"Varied...sometimes outside, a good burger, I could eat more. But usually, in the heat, I eat less."

"There you are. Another factor. It's easier to overeat when it's cool. But anyway, I digress. Again.

"A nuclear family approach to obesity would be to turn all this on its head. Turn off the energy sucking A/C. Removal of the television and computer/ video screens from most of the house would be ideal. Perhaps there can be some return to inter-human interaction, sport, even parlour games, where some movement is involved. When television is watched, or computer games played, a time limit should be observed. Standing during these activities should be considered. Standing can lead to moving. A further progression would be to put an exercise device in front of the monitor, a stationary bike perhaps, or a treadmill. One could then evolve the more than 3 hours the average adult spends in front of the tube at home to an exercise period. Merely standing for three hours, depending on physical fitness and body size, can burn up to 150 calories. Walking on a treadmill can multiply this by a factor of 5 to 8. Really torqueing an exercise bike can burn 1000 calories in an hour."

"Show me your exercise bike, Doc. Not here, in front of your tube."

"No, Gerry, we are. And the cameraman, and the lights. We do have a room, with a television and exercise equipment. It's a really good idea."

"We also need to think about access. To food. Food could be made more inaccessible, not easier. That daily visit to the grocery store for fresh veg would add on a few steps, as would at least walking to the kitchen from the TV room. Any barrier imposed between the fridge and the rest position would help, be it distance or stairs. Fast and easy snack foods should include fruits and vegetables only. Clearing the pantry and cupboards of all temptations should make the local food bank happy."

"Big changes, Doc."

Hu nodded.

"Home maintenance responsibilities could be returned to the family members. Vacuuming or other vigorous cleaning burns about 200 calories an hour, cutting the grass 350 with a power mower, (calories from myfitnesspal.com) and likely more with a push reel mower. Merely using a tractor mower burns 170 calories an hour! Even dusting burns more calories than resting."

"Again, the lazy lump issue."

"Again, the labelling proclivity. Call yourself a lazy lump, really identify yourself like that, and just watch what you choose to do, eat, live. We need however to recognize, and really see what we're doing in order to change it."

"Like you said though, Doc. It's not just the individual. Not just the family. It's the rut. It's everything above and outside that. The whole shebang."

Hu nodded, vigorously. "You always were a quick study, Gerry. You're right. Circles outside the nuclear family home are more difficult to control. Every circle above the individual is more difficult but can have more impact, though. We need to exert effort at these levels. Larger family groups could be probed regarding traditional family activities and preferences. Perhaps family gatherings at a park with access to recreational sport activities could serve to help activate everyone. Family menu planners could decide amongst themselves to shake up Thanksgiving dinner."

"A lot of this is family I guess, and should be, that's the basic societal unit. What else, though, Doc? What about work, etcetera?" Gerry stretched out his arms, emphasizing the breadth of the problem.

"Work needs to be reassessed, re-evaluated, looked at from a different perspective. Sitting at work is resting at work. An individual can have a great impact on his health and fitness with one decision. One decision to request, or even purchase a standing workstation can change energy expenditure during the work day for the rest of an individual's work life. Standing is active, is a progression from sitting, which moves one from a baseline of rest to one of movement. Coworkers may start to get the idea. Exercising, moving more at work may start to seem less bizarre. Perhaps people can go for a walk instead of sitting for a meeting. Remember our last interview? I enjoyed that, in the park! Perhaps with some freer, fresh air, people could actually think better! Dominoes could start to fall.

"Above the family, school boards should be petitioned about vending machines, healthy food choices in the cafeteria and active minutes. City hall should hear from concerned citizens in regards zoning for fast food establishments, the existence of bike paths, and the like. Up the ladder, government should recognize sedentarism and the cost of healthy food as priorities. Perhaps the biggest issue for lawmakers in regards obesity is that of obesogens. We all need a cleaner planet. Maneuvers made by these bigger players could impact all of us positively."

"We all agree with you there, Doc." Gerry looked at the camera. "Green planet. On it."

"But it all starts with the individual. We've talked a lot about the fabric. But really, it starts with one. One person. To decide to eat less and move more."

"There's that phrase again, Doc. Bet we could Google it." Gerry seized his cell phone and made as if to start pushing buttons.

"*Eat less and move more* needs be recognized as a thermodynamically correct principle and personal decision which is applied in a complex social context. Although research is ongoing, and more clarity will come to the issue, there may be no missing piece to the obesity puzzle. Yes, we need to understand the role of obesogens and do more research about that endocrine organ known as adipose. We need to understand the role of gut flora better. Simply better. However, there's a real possibility, perhaps even a likelihood, that apart from the needed paradigm shift that humans need intervals of rest, not intervals of exercise, there are likely no new essential secrets, no discrete factors that will drop from the sky to solve this complex problem. Lasting, sustainable success will be achieved only through addressing the entire framework within which the overweight or obese person lives.

"We live our lives woven into a tapestry of interconnections, with other people, social structures, political systems, the environment. The solution is more in the fabric itself, less so the individual threads. Our very environment is producing obesity.

"This perspective can seem disempowering to the individual suffering with overweight or obesity. One can start to ruminate about all the obesogens, trapped within adipose, reprogramming that metabolically active tissue and perhaps our very beings to retain fat. Changing family traditions, even contemplating personal lifestyle alteration is more than a challenge. It all may seem hopeless, an absolute set up to failure. But one must start with the individual! Less adipose, less toxins. An individual's decision to eat less and move more, combined with a wider perspective, can beat this."

"You've got some hope, there, Doc. You think this is all beatable."

"Decisions must be made and action taken, Gerry. What we clearly can't do is frame all this as an unsolvable puzzle. That's the definition of self defeat. Family defeat, nation defeat, planet defeat. Many can impact other people by changing their lifestyle. The family home must be altered, family interactions and traditions shaken up, leisure time reassessed, the workplace environment changed."

"That's a tall order. What makes you think this is at all doable?"

"Today, this may be more possible rather than less. The standing workstation, sometimes accompanied by treadmill or other exercise equipment, is becoming more commonplace. New technology exists to enable measurement and documentation of both intake and movement. This same technology can facilitate interaction and networking, perhaps enabling a social movement. Ripples here could start to build, perhaps even affecting decision makers at government levels."

"You're trying to throw a rock in the water here, with this show. With your efforts."

"It's not about me. Or what I want. It's just about what must be done. Half of the planet is starving, the other half largely sitting around and eating way too much. It's really a shameful situation, one that we need to task our politicians with. It has to be fixed. All the planet wide inequities. This little guy should be able to get a bowl full of clean water."

Hu demonstrated some photographs, then displayed on the screen. The ones that people don't look at, the ones they surf away from. Des did the human thing and looked at his dog. Hard to watch. Remembered Hershey's little ribs, and feeding him from a potato masher.

"...we can all think and eat better. Think, about our environment and chemical use. Think, about what we classify as healthy and even how we think about rest. We can move from intervals of exercise, to intervals of rest.

"Stand up! And induce change. It really all comes down to that one principle."

"Eat less, move more."

Closing credits. More sci-pop music. Shaking hands.

He had toughed it out to the end...standing. So there. Clicked Wrigley off. Threw the remote on the couch, Hersh opening one eye, raising his head a bit, tail thump.

"Always ready, aren't you, big guy?" More tail thumps.

"Well, I always do take you out at night, come on."

The tall and the short, or the broad and the skinny, both previously malnourished, walked to the door grabbing leash, collar and poop bags along the way. Des pulled out his cell and made a call as he was walking down that stained carpet, steadfast in his desire to not notice the smells.

"Donnie, you must be down for the count, got your machine. Me, Des. Look, you got one of those activity bands? If so, let me know what kind, 'cause I want to start. Hey, we could be buddies on it or something! And, did you know anybody else that is on the thing? Maybe we could create some kind of community or something, you know, encourage each other to get more steps."

CHAPTER TWENTY-THREE

"Nice shot, Des." Polaroid, a bit dog eared. Massive horse, massive rider. And a girl. "Who's the girl? Girlfriend?" Doc turned it over in his hands, trying to appreciate the size of that horse.

"Oh, just a friend. You don't know how much that picture means. I've got a new life, Doc. I'm still heavy, but I can do things. Go places. Do the stairs. Hey, they let me ride King! That's his name. I ride all the time, now. Remember, what we talked about? Life? Well, I've got it. Thanks to you." Des flushed a bit, not used to choking out stuff like that. But hey, ya gotta thank people.

"Me? Are you kidding? Did I do this? Get outta town." Doc got up off his chair, rounded the desk, and soundly punched him on the deltoid. "You, are an idiot. She's a girl. You like her, right? Girlfriend. You, Des. You. You did this. I'm just a pill jockey. Look, talking about that, I want to try you off that blood pressure tab. Sugars have been good, right?"

Quite the segue. His head spun from the girlfriend word, then it was right into pill jockey. Pill jockey?

Des had come off his metformin months ago, after a long conversation. It was certainly controversial. Sugars however, had been spectacular, completely normal, and had stayed that way off meds. One down. The blood pressure pills had slowly come down.

This was a big deal. Another what Doc called a big gun, coming off.

Des nodded. "Sugars great. Do them less often, basically now just two hours after a bigger meal, to really test myself. And some fasting. All good, the numbers you taught me. Think its ok, safe?" Guessed Doc wouldn't do that, but he was so adamant about that pill initially.

"To come off the blood pressure pills? Some people would argue, but look at your numbers! You could go up ten points and still be under the guidelines. Think I'll keep you on that statin, though."

"Lot of stuff about those drugs on the net though, Doc. Supposed to hurt your muscles. And some astronaut lost his memory on them. All sorts of stuff." That was the one pill people thought he should be off of. And to think he'd never come off...?

"Sorry, all sorts of crap. Sorry. Unprofessional word. How can anyone look at what happened to an astronaut, of all people, and then make any kind of extrapolation to what could happen to boring old Earth dwellers. Get it? Try to pick the most atypical human being on the planet, then pick someone who's been off it! Know the biggest side effect of a statin?"

"Muscles?" Yep, muscles. Aching, tight muscles. Usually the calves, read all about it. Blog after blog. But Doc had been so bent up about it. Stayed on them, but always had worried. How could all those people be wrong?

"No, decreased death rate. The biggest side effect of a statin is less people die! Remember what we talked about. Add the statin on to regular daily exercise, thirty to forty minutes aerobic, and the stuff cleans out arteries. That's the game. That's the game changer. The thing that turns back the hands of time. Remember your heart attack? I know you're now Mr. Fitness, Incorporated, but you can't change history. You've got plugs on your blood vessels and a scar on your heart. You do."

"You too, Doc. Right? Plugs? You told me. Everybody."

"Yep, everybody but babies. But you've got proven arterial pathology. Plugs, but more than that. Plugs that have actually hurt you. You've had actual heart muscle damage. You're on a statin, period. That, and aspirin. Remember the Mediterranean diet that boasts improvements even better than a statin. Imagine if you did both! Do both! We'll keep a close eye on the blood pressure and make sure it stays down. Look, a lot of people would disagree with this. Want that cardiologist we talked about? Might be an idea to look at those arteries, see where we are."

"Sure, Doc, let's do that. We can get his opinion on those blood pressure pills, too. I think I'll come off in the meantime though, Doc. Like I said, I am getting a bit woozy when I stand up. Goes away, but I bet it's those pills. If I need 'em, I'll take them, but let's try without."

Doc nodded as he typed. And it was one less pill. Des almost shivered. The big lineup. Down to aspirin and his statin.

Who'd a thunk? And who'd a thunk, of him riding a horse. Going up and down all those stairs. A girl. A dog. Desmond, with a life.

"So it was all thermodynamics, right Doc?"

"You kidding?" Doc screwed up his face and looked at him with one eye.

"Huh? You know, eat less and move more."

"What?"

"Doc! Like you always said!"

"Well, yes. Eat less, less energy into the system. Move more, more energy burned up. If you're in a negative balance, the weight goes down. Period. You're right."

"Well, what are you saying?"

Doc moved to the examining table, rolling on his little wheeled stool. Opened a drawer of gowns and drapes. Selected a green drape, in essence a meter squared piece of cloth, and threw it at him. "That's your life."

"Huh?"

"Metaphor, college grad. Metaphor. That piece of fabric is your life."

"Okay, I get metaphors. Keep going. This cloth is my life."

"Your decision to eat less and move more could be considered a thread. A red thread. Well, maybe two. We'll give you two. Let's say you took that piece of green cloth and wove in that red thread. Threads, whatever. What have you got?"

"A green cloth with a couple of red threads. A green life with red threads. Let me off the hook here, Doc! I don't get it!"

"Let me run with this for a while. Let's say you wove in a red thread. From a distance, what colour would that piece of fabric be?"

"Green. Wouldn't see the thread."

"And if you're really, up close to that cloth. If someone told you to describe that fabric in one word, what would you call it?"

"Drape."

"Ha ha. Work with me here."

"Green, Doc. Don't you have a few hundred patients out in that examining room?"

"Green. Yes, green. That's why people fail at diet and exercise."

"Because of the cloth?"

"Yup. To get the weight off, you need a new cloth. Think about it. Let's say you decide to eat less and move more. The correct decision. But then you do nothing else. You get up at the same time, go to bed at the same time, drive to work as usual, sit at your desk, go for coffee break, meet with friends after work for drinks, go to the baseball game with Braden and eat a blue crab Mac n'cheese eighteen inch corn dog whatever because it's the thing that is simply done at baseball games."

"You mean nothing would change."

"Got it. You achieved this change by living a different life. You've got a red cloth. Tell me. What one thing did this? What two things? Give me one or two things that got this weight off so good it's still coming off, hand over fist."

"Hershey. My dog. And Sunshine. And do you really eat those things?"

"Sunshine? Being outside? And yes, I have. Regretted it after, though. I mean, I can eat a lot of food, but that one was a bit much."

"Sorry, but I guess sort of. Sunshine, that is. Being outside, sort of. That's what I call my girl... my friend."

"Funny, you didn't say diet or exercise, did you?"

"Uh..."

"So give me the number three and four on your list!"

Des started to get it. Started to chuckle. "King. Donnie. Kit. My Fitbit friends. My Facebook circle ... a tree, maybe more than anything, a leaf in my pocket ... I get it, Doc. I've got a new fabric. A new life. I was hoping to get a new life by losing weight. Little did I know..."

"That you lose weight by getting a new life. Right?" Doc rocked his chair, folded his arms, and pointed. At Des. One eye screwed up, as usual. "So it was focusing on taking care of your dog. And being able to ride that horse, and maybe, just maybe, feeling something for that girl you insist on calling your friend. Guiding Donnie and being a role model. Achieving steps and fitness. Interacting, encouraging others and competing with your community, and NOT the scale, not focusing on the pounds... and what was that, a tree? A leaf? You on some kind of herbal?"

"No, Doc. But did I ever tell you how much you irritate me?"

"All the time, Des. You imply it all the time. And it's my goal in life and ultimate reward! So what are you going to do now?"

"Well, Doc. Funny you should ask. I've got that new life, that new fabric... part of it will be to weave a bigger cloth!"

* * *

Septembre. That's how they spelled it.

Paris. The foot of the Arc de Triomphe. Triumph.

They had left their bikes behind the hotel, a little place off Beyan. Seventeenth district, arrondissement. His was red. He had bought Sunshine's, only fair. Purple, to set off her hair. Was going to go for pink, but his deltoids couldn't take it.

They had left their key with the five pound furry key fob with the desk manager. When in France...ten minutes' walk, uphill, to the Arc. Dogs, dogs everywhere. Less cigarettes than expected.

Past that little Italian place they'd leave for last day, chic and modern, tangerine blinds and metal. Down that spoke on the wheel towards the hub, on ancient cobblestone streets, gutters not of poured concrete but angled stones, craftsmen, artists. Pedestrian signals at waist height, and two stages to cross the road. Past the tiny chocolatier shop they had managed to evade, the cafes with chairs angled street wards, the macaroons. They'd have some, but today was triumph day. And here it was, in reality.

"So you did it."

"Huh?"

"Goof! We're standing here, in front of the Arc de Triomphe! In triumph! You did it!"

Des looked down at his tour bus map, then up to the double decker bus. Looked at the top sightseeing level, and knew he'd have to go up a little skinny spiral staircase to get there. And that he now could.

"We."

"Huh?"

"We're standing, Sunshine. We."

The Air...

Primal bloodlust.
Feet beating in time, drum, spittle...
Words screamed, labels.
Ropes burn,
My gag tightens.

Flames flicker, lick
Lookalike alight, figures scream....
The noose above
Gnarled branch,
Chest muscles heave.

But God is here
Awake in the leaves above me.
Asleep below,
Within stone.
Dog barks aloud.

Suddenly see
Understand, and forgive them all.
He thinks in me.
Sudden peace,
The air drifts out.

Focus afar...
Shady hilltop, graceful Willow
Begins to fade
Moves away.
The air drifts in.

CHAPTER TWENTY-THREE

Float up above
Feather light, heaven's own approach
Son, stark shadows.
Body low
Sinking down soft.

The air drifts in
So much at rest, the inner peace
They do not know
Heaven sent
The air drifts out.

In all as well
Bellows of moose, lungs of a shrew
Truly shared.
Air is life.
The air drifts in.

And out, sink deep.
The pain is gone, and God remains
Accept, forgive...
Let it go
And out, find peace.

REFERENCES

American Diabetes Association. (2016). *Standards of Medical Care in Diabetes-2016.*
Retrieved from: http://care.diabetesjournals.org/site/misc/2016-Standards-of-Care.pdf

American Diabetes Association. (2014). *Statistics about Diabetes.* Retrieved from: http://www.diabetes.org/diabetes-basics/statistics/

American Heart Association. (2014). *Atherosclerosis.* Retrieved from: http://www.heart.org/HEARTORG/Conditions/Cholesterol/WhyCholesterolMatters/Atherosclerosis_UCM_305

Barnes, R.D. & Ivezahj, V. (2015). A systematic review of motivational interviewing for weight loss among adults in primary care. *Obes Rev. 16(*4):304-18. doi:10.1111/obr.12264.

Bener, A., Zirie, M., Janahi, I.M., Al-Hamaq, A.O., Musallam, M. & Wareham, N.J. (2009). Prevalence of diagnosed and undiagnosed diabetes mellitus and its risk factors in a population-based study of Qatar. *Diabetes Res Clin Pract. (*84)1:99-106. doi:10.1016/j.diabres.2009.02.003.

Berry, D.C., Stenesen, D., Zeve, D. & Graf, J.M. (2013). The Developmental Origins of Adipose Tissue. *Development. (*140):3939-3949; doi: 10.1242/dev.080549

Blumenthal, J.A., Babyak, M.A., Moore, K.A., Craighead, W.E., Herman, S., Khatri, P., Waugh, R., Napolitano,

M.A., Foreman, L.M., Appelbaum, M., Doraiswamy, P.M. & Krishnan, K.R. (1999). *Arch Intern Med.(159)*19:2349-56.

Booth, A., Magnuson, A., Fouts, F. & Foster, M.T. (2016). Adipose tissue: an endocrine organ playing a role in metabolic regulation. *Horm Mol Biol Clin Investig. (Epub ahead of print).* doi:10.1515/hmbci-2015-0073.

Canadian Diabetes Association. (2016). *Basic Meal Planning.* Retrieved from: http://www.diabetes.ca/diabetes-and-you/ healthy-living-resources/diet-nutrition/basic-meal-planning

Capriati, T., Francavilla, R., Ferretti, F., Castellaneta, S., Ancinelli, M. & Diamanti, A. (2016). The overweight: a rare presentation of celiac disease. *Eur J Clin Nutr. (70)*2:282-4. doi:10.1038/ ejcn.2015.169.

Catassi, C., Bai, J.C., Bonaz, B., Bouma, G., Calabro, A., Carroccio, A., Castillejo, G., Ciacci, C., Cristofori, F., Dolinsek, J., Francavilla, R., Elli, L, Green, P., Holtmeier, W., Koehler, P., Koletzko, S., Meinhold, C., Sanders, D., Schumann, M., Schuppan, D., Ullrich, R., Vecsei, A., Volta, U., Zevallos, V., Sapone, A. & Fasano, A. (2013). Non-Celiac Gluten Sensitivity: The New Frontier of Gluten Related Disorders. (2013). *Nutrients. (5)*10:3839-3853. doi:10.3390/nu5103839.

Chamorro-Garcia, R. & Blumberg, B. (2014). Transgenerational effects of obesogens and the obesity epidemic. *Curr Opin Pharmacol.* 19:153-158. doi:10.1016/j.coph.2014.10.010.

Chomisteck, A.K., Shiroma, E.J. & Lee, I.M. (2015). The Relationship Between Time of Day of Physical Activity and Obesity in Older Women. *J Phys Act Health.* [Epub ahead of print]

Chu, A.H., Ng, S.H., Tan, C.S., Win, A.M., Koh, D. & Muller-Riemenschneider, F. (2016). A systematic review and meta-analysis of workplace intervention strategies to reduce sedentary time in white-collar workers. *Obes Rev.* doi:10.1111/ obr.12388. [Epub ahead of print]

Chung, S., Cuffe, H., Marshall, S.M., McDaniel, A. L., Ha, J.H., Kavanagh, K., Hong, C., Tontonoz, P., Temel, R.E. & Parks, J.S. (2014) Dietary cholesterol promotes adipocyte hypertrophy and adipose tissue inflammation in visceral, but not in subcutaneous, fat in monkeys. *Arterioscler Thromb Vasc Biol. (34)*9:1880-8. doi:10.116/ATVBAHA.114.303896

Colberg, S.R., Sighal, R.J., Fernhall, B., Regensteiner, J.G., Blissmer, B.J., Rubin, R.R., Chasan-Taber, L., Albright, A.L. & Braun, B. (2010). Exercise and Type 2 Diabetes. The American College of Sports Medicine and The American Diabetes Association: joint position statement. *Diabetes Care. (33)*12:e147-e167. doi:10.2337/dc10-9990.

Coleman, R., Beasley, T.M., Kemnitz, J., Johnson, S., Weindruch, R., & Anderson, R. (2014). Caloric restriction reduces age-related and all-cause mortality in rhesus monkeys. *Nature Communications*, 5. doi:10.1038/ncomms4557

Craft, L.L. & Perna, F.M. (2004). The Benefits of Exercise for the Clinically Depressed. *Prim Care Companion J Clin Psychiatry. (6)*:3:104-111.

Dobbs, R., Sawers, C., Thompson, F., Manyika, J., Child, P., McKenna, S. & Spatharou, A. (2014, Nov). *How the world would better fight obesity*. Report, McKinsey Global Institute. Retrieved from http://www.mckinsey.com/industries/healthcare-systems-and-services/our-insights/how-the-world-could-better-fight-obesity

Dover, R.V. & Lambert, E.V. (2016). "Choice Set" for health behavior in choice-constrained settings to frame research and inform policy: examples of food consumption, obesity and food security. *Int J Equity Health. (15)*1:48. doi:10.1186/s12939-016-0336-6.

Fields, S. (2004). The Fat of the Land: Do Agricultural Subsidies Foster Poor Health? *Environ Health Perspect. (112)*14:A820-A823.

Foulds, H.J., Rodgers, C.D., Duncan, V. & Ferguson, L.J. (2016). A systematic review and meta-analysis of screen time behaviour among North American indigenous populations. *Obes Rev.* doi:10.1111/obr.12389.[Epub ahead of print]

Gepner, Y., Golan, R., Harman-Boehm, I., Henkin, Y., Schwarzfuchs, D., Shelef, I., Durst, R., Kovsan, J., Bolotin, A.,

Leitersdorf, E., Shpitzen, S., Balag, S., Shemesh, E., Witkow, S., Tangi-Rosental, O., Chassidim, Y., Liberty, I.F., Sarusi, B., Ben-Avraham, S., Helander, A., Ceglarek, U., Stumvoll, M. Bluher, M., Thiery, J., Rudich, A., Stampfer, M.J. & Shai, I. (2015). Effects of Initiation Moderate Alcohol Intake on Cardiometabolic Risk in Adults with Type 2 Diabetes: A 2-Year Randomized, Controlled Trial. *Ann Intern Med. (163)*8:569-79. doi:10.7326/M14-1650.

Hardy, K., Brand-Miller, J., Brown, K.D., Thomas, M.G. & Copeland, L. (2015). The Importance of Dietary Carbohydrate in Human Evolution. *Q Rev Biol. (90)*3: 251-68.

Heden, T.D., Winn, N.C., Mari, A., Booth, F.W., Rector, R.S., Thyfault, J.P. & Kanaley, J.A.(2015). Post dinner resistance exercise improves postprandial risk factors more effectively than pre dinner resistance exercise in patients with type 2 diabetes. *J Appl Physiol. (118)*5:624-34. doi:10.1152/japplphysiol.00917.2014.

Heinonen, I., Helajarvi, H., Pahkala, K., Heinonen, O.J., Hirvensalo, M., Palve, K., Tammelin, T., Yang, X., Juonala, M., Mikkila, V., Kahonen, M., Lehtimaki, T., Viikari, J. & Raitakari, O.T. (2013). Sedentary behaviours and obesity in adults: the Cardiovascular Risk in Young Finns Study. *BMJ Open. (3)*6. doi:10.1136/bmjopen-2013-002901.

Hetherington, M.M. (2007). Cues to overeat: psychological factors influencing overconsumption. *Proc Nutr Soc. (66)*1:113-23

Hurley, D.A., Tully, M.A., Lonsdale, C., Boreham, C.A., van Mechelen, W., Daly, L., Tynan, A. & McDonough, S.M. (2015). *Pain. (156)*:1:131-47. doi:10.1016/j.pain.0000000000000013

Iwayama, K., Kurihara, R., Nabekura, Y., Kawabuchi, R., Park, I., Kobayashi, M., Ogata, H., Kayaba, M., Satoh, M. & Tokuyama, K. (2015). Exercise Increases 24-h Fat Oxidation Only When It Is Performed Before Breakfast. *EBioMedicine. (2)*:12:2003-9. doi:10.1016/j.ebiom.2015.10.029.

Jonsson, T., Granfeldt, Y., Lindeberg, S. & Hallberg, A.C. (2013). Subjective satiety and other experiences of a Paleolithic diet compared to a diabetes diet in patients with type 2 diabetes. *Nutr J.* 12:105. doi:10.1186/1475-2891-12-105.

Keadle, S.K., Arem, H., Moore, S.C., Sampson, J.N. & Matthews, C.E. (2015). Impact of changes in television viewing time and physical activity on longevity: a prospective cohort study. *Int J Behav Nutr Phys Act. (12)*1:156. doi:10.1186/s12966-015-0.

Kramer, C.K., Zinman, B. & Retnakaran, R. (2013). Are metabolically healthy overweight and obesity benign conditions?: A systematic review and meta-analysis. *Ann Intern Med. (159)*11:758-69. doi:107326/0003-4819-159-11-201312030-00008.

Kurose, S., Iwasaka, J., Tsutsumi, H., Yamanaka, Y., Shinno, H., Fukushima, Y., Higurashi, K., Imai, M., Masuda, I., Takeda, S., Kawai, C. & Kimura, Y. (2015). Effect of exercise-based cardiac rehabilitation on non-culprit mild coronary plaques in the culprit coronary artery of patients with acute coronary syndrome. *Heart Vessels.* 2015 Apr 21. [Epub ahead of print]

Laermans, J. & Depoortere, I. (2016). Chronobesity: role of the circadian system in the obesity epidemic. *Obes Rev. (17)*2:108-25. doi:10.1111/obr.12351.

Lapointe, Joe. (1998, Feb 11). The XVIII Winter Games; Snowboarder Stripped of Gold for Failing Drug Test. *The New York Times.* Retrieved from: http://www.nytimes.com/1998/02/11/sports/the-xviii-winter-games-snowboarder-stripped-of-gold-for-failing-drug-test.html

Levine, J.A. (2002). Non-exercise activity thermogenesis (NEAT). *Best Pract Res Clin Endocrinol Metab. (16)*4:679-702.

Lorts, C. & Ohri-Vachaspati, P. (2016). Eating Behaviors among low-income obese adults in the United States: Does health care provider's advice carry any weight. *Prev Med.* 87:89-94. doi:10.1016/j.ypmed.2016.02.015.

Ludwig, D.S. & Friedman, M.I. (2014). Increasing Adiposity: Consequence or Cause of Overeating? *JAMA. (311)*21:2167-2168. doi:10.1001/jama.2014.4133

Manheimer, E.W., van Zuuren, E.J., Fedorowicz, Z. & Pijl, H. (2015). Paleolithic Nutrition for metabolic syndrome:

systematic review and meta-analysis. *Am J Clin Nutr. (102)*4:922-32. Doi:10.394

Masharani, U., Sherchan, P., Schloetter, M., Stratford, S., Xiao, A., Sebastian, A., Nolte Kennedy, M. & Frassetto, L. (2015). Metabolic and physiologic effects from consuming a hunter-gatherer (Paleolithic)-type diet in type 2 diabetes. *Eur J Clin Nutr.(69*)8:944-8. doi:10.1038/ejcn.2015.39.5/ acjn.115.113613.

Mayo Clinic. (May, 2013). *DASH diet: Healthy eating to lower your blood pressure.* Retrieved from: http://www.mayoclinic. org/healthy-lifestyle/nutrition-and-healthy-eating/in-depth/ dash-diet/art-20048456

Mayo Clinic. (June, 2013). *Choose healthier fats.* Retrieved from: http://www.mayoclinic.org/healthy-lifestyle/ nutrition-and-healthy-eating/in-depth/mediterranean-diet/ art-20047801?pg=2

Millman, Jason. (2015, Feb 4). Americans are ignoring the science and spending billions on dietary supplements. *The Washington Post, Wonkblog.* [Web log post]. Retrieved from: https://www. washingtonpost.com/news/wonk/wp/2015/02/04/americans- are-ignoring-the-science-and-spending-billions-on-dietary- supplements/

Myers, M.G., Cowley, M.A. & Munzberg, H. (2008). Mechanisms of leptin action and leptin resistance. *Annu Rev Physiol.* 70:537-56.

National Institute of Health. (1998). *Clinical Guidelines on the Identification, Evaluation, and Treatment of Overweight and Obesity in Adults.* Retrieved from: http://www.nhlbi.nih.gov/ files/docs/guidelines/ob_gdlns.pdf

Nedergaard, J., Bengtsson, T. & Cannon, B. (2007). Unexpected evidence for active brown adipose tissue in adult humans. *Amer J Physiol. (293)* 2: E444-E452. doi:10.1152/ ajpendo.00691.2006.

Ng, M., Fleming, T., & Robinson, M., et al. (2014). Global, regional, and national prevalence of overweight and obesity in children and adults 1980-2013: A systematic analysis. *Lancet.* *384*(9945): 766-781. doi: 10.1016/S0140-6736(14)60460-8.

Novak, N.L. & Brownell, K.D. (2012). Role of Policy and Government in the Obesity Epidemic. *Circulation.* 126:2345-2352. doi:10.1161/CIRCULATIONAHA.111.037929.

Obesity Rates and Trends. (2015, Sep). *The State of Obesity: Better Policies for a Healthier America.* Retrieved from: http://stateofobesity.org/rates/

Otten, J., Mellberg, C., Ryberg, M., Sandberg, S., Kullberg, J., Lindahl, B., Larsson, C., Hauksson, J. & Olsson, T. (2016). Strong and persistent effect on liver fat with a Paleolithic diet during a two-year intervention. *Int J Obes (Lond).* doi:10138/ijo.2016.4.[Epub ahead of print]

Overweight and Weight Loss Statistics. Worldometers. Retrieved Mar 21, 2016 from: http://www.worldometers.info/weight-loss/

Pedersen, S.D., Kang, J. & Kline, G.A. (2007). Portion control plate for weight loss in obese patients with type 2 diabetes: a controlled clinical trial. *Arch Intern Med. (167)*12:1277-83.

Preis, S.R., Massaro, J.M., Robins, S.J., Hoffman, U., Vasan, R.S., Irlbeck, T., Meigs, J.B., Sutherland, P., D'Agonstino, R.B. Sr., O'Donnell, C.J. & Fox, C.S. (2010). Abdominal subcutaneous and visceral adipose tissue and insulin resistance in the Framingham heart study. *Obesity (Silver Spring). (18)*11:2191-8. doi:10.1038/0by.2010.59.

Regnier, S.M. & Sargis, R.M. (2014). Adipocytes under assault: environmental disruption of adipose physiology. *Biochim Biophys Acta. (1842)*3:520-33. doi:10.1016/j.bbadis.2013.05.028.

Ross, S.E., Flynn, J.I. & Pate, R.R. (2016). What is really causing the obesity epidemic? A review of reviews in children and adults. *J Sports Sci. (34)*12:1148-53. doi:10.1080/0264041 4.2015.1093650.

Seidell, J.C. (1998). Societal and personal costs of obesity. *Exp Clin Endocrinol Diabetes. (106 Suppl)* 2:7-9.

Shi, H. & Clegg, D.J. (2009). Sex differences in the regulation of body weight. *Physiol. Behav. (97)*: 199-204.

Shretha, N., Kukkonen-Harjula, K.T., Verbeek, J.H., Ijaz, S., Hermans V. & Bhaumik, S. (2016). Workplace interventions for reducing sitting at work. *Cochrane Database Syst Rev. (17)*3:CD010912. [Epub ahead of print]

Sluik, D., Atkinson, F.S., Brand-Miller, J.C., Fogelholm, M., Raben, A. & Feskens, E.J. (2016). Contributors to glycaemic index and glycaemic load in the Netherlands: the role of beer. *Br J Nutr. (115)*7:1218-25. doi:10.1017.S0007114516000052.

Soltani, S., Shirani, F., Chitsazi, M.J. & Salehi-Abargouei, A. (2016). The effect of dietary approaches to stop hypertension (DASH) diet on weight and body composition in adults: a systematic review and meta-analysis of randomized controlled trials. *Obes Rev.* doi:10.111/obr.12391.[Epub ahead of print]

Stein, A.C., Liao, C., Paski, S., Polonsky, T., Semrad, C.E. & Kupfer, S.S. (2015).Obesity and Cardiovascular Risk in Adults With Celiac Disease. *J Clin Gastroenterol.* 2015 Oct 6. [Epub ahead of print]

Tarantino, G., Citro, V. & Finelli, C. (2015). Hype or Reality: Should Patients with Metabolic Syndrome-related NAFLD be on the Hunter-Gatherer (Paleo) Diet to Decrease Morbidity? *J Gastrointestin Liver Dis. (24)*3:359-68. doi:10.15403/jgld.2014.1121.243.gta.

Tay, J., Luscombe-Marsh N.D., Thompson, C.H., Noakes, M., Buckley, J.D., Wittert, G.A., Yancy, W.S. & Brinkworth, G.D. (2015). Comparison of low- and high- carbohydrate diets for type 2 diabetes management: a randomized trial. *Am J Clin Nutr. (102)*4:780-90. doi:10.3945/ajcn.115.112581.

Thomas, D. & Elliott, E.J., (2009). Low glycemic index, or low glycemic load, diets for diabetes mellitus. *Cochrane Metabolic and Endocrine Disorders Group.* doi:10.1002/14651858.CD006296.pub2.

Thomas, D., Elliott, E.J. & Baur, L., (2007). Low glycaemic index or low glycaemic load diets for overweight and obesity. *Cochrane Metabolic and Endocrine Disorders Group.* doi:10.1002/14651858.CD005105.pub2

Tomei, S., Mamtani, R., & Al Ali R., et al. (2015).Obesity susceptibility loci in Qataris, a highly consanguineous Arabian population. *J Transl Med. (13)*119. doi: 10.1186/s12967-015-0459-3.

Tran, T.T., Yamamoto, Y., Gesta, S. & Kahn, C.R. (2008). Beneficial effects of subcutaneous fat transplantation on metabolism. *Cell Metab. (7)*:410-420.

Van Baak, M.A., van Mil E., Astrup, A.V., Finer, N., Van Gaal, L.F., Hilsted, J., Kopelman, P.G., Rossner, S., James, W.P. & Saris, W.H. (2003). Leisure-time activity is an important determinant of long-term weight maintenance after weight loss in the Sibutramine Trial on Obesity Reduction and Maintenance (STORM trial). *Am J Clin Nutr. (78)*:2:209-14.

Watanabe, Y., Saito, I., Henmi, I., Yoshimura, K., Maruyama, K., Yamauchi, K, Matsuo, T., Kato, T., Tanigawa, T., Kishida, T. & Asada, Y. (2014). Skipping Breakfast is Correlated with Obesity. *J Rural Med. (9)*2: 51-58. doi: 10.2185/jrm.2887.

Wax, E. (2014). Portion Size. *MedlinePlus, U.S. National Library of Medicine.* Retrieved from: https://www.nlm.nih.gov/medlineplus/ency/patientinstructions/000337.htm

World Health Organization (WHO) (2015). *Obesity and Overweight.* Fact sheet No 311. Retrieved from: http://www.who.int/mediacentre/factsheets/fs311/en/.

World Health Organization, (WHO) (Oct 2015). *Links between processed meat and colorectal cancer.* Retrieved from: http://www.who.int/mediacentre/news/statements/2015/processed-meat-cancer/en/

World Health Organization (WHO) (2003). *Controlling the global obesity epidemic.* Retrieved from: http://www.who.int/nutrition/topics/obesity/en/

World Health Organization (WHO) (1998). *IARC Monographs on the Evaluation of Carcinogenic Risks to Humans. Vol 44. Alcohol drinking. Summary of Data Reported and Evaluation.* Retrieved from: http://monographs.iarc.fr/ENG/Monographs/vol44/

Yapko, M. (2014). The Spirit of Hypnosis: Doing Hypnosis versus Being Hypnotic. *Am J Clin Hyp.* *(56)*: 234-248. Doi: 10.1080/00029157.2013.815605

Yiannikouris, F., Gupte, M., Putnam, K. & Cassis, L. (2010). Adipokines and blood pressure control. *Curr Opin Nephrol Hypertens.* *(19)*2:195-200. doi:10.1097/MNH.0b013e3283366cd0.

Zhang, W., Yu, Q., Siddiquie, B., Divakaran, A. & Sawhney, H. (2015). "Snap-n-Eat": Food Recognition and Nutrition Estimation on a Smartphone. *J Diabetes Sci Technol.* *(9)*3:525-33. doi:10.1177/1932296815582222.

ABOUT THE AUTHOR

The house you grow up in is simply your house. And things you did...were simply things you did.

Our broken cement driveway, laid in uneven slabs, led to a broken garage. I had never seen the garage doors up. Wood by the looks of it, they were stuffed up in the garage rafters. Just up there. That's where they were.

My garage didn't need doors. That's the way it was. The back window similarly had a hole, ever since I demonstrated the accuracy of my throwing arm. After we got our trailer, it was parked in that garage, along with garden tools, a few toys, our new coppertone duomatic bikes complete with banana seats and sissy bars, and a wasp's nest.

One of the things got in my mouth once. No, not a bike, and not a nest. I was poking around in the garage, looking for a ball or something. A wasp somehow got in my mouth. It didn't want to be in there and let me know.

Want to remember something? I remember that. Full colour, kodachrome. Kodafreakinghurt.

I remember the watch on my wrist. Grade 2 or 3. So I could get myself and my little brother home for lunch. Or dinner. Or bed. Because we were never home. That's the way it was, a different time, fifty years ago. It was ok. Back then.

We'd hear mom holler for lunch, and go home for fried baloney sandwiches. Or maybe that was my Dad's specialty...things get fuzzy. Who cooked them is fuzzy. The baloney sandwiches, non-fuzzy.

I remember his big feet, going up stairs. I have a vivid image in my memory. Dad's huge calves. So big. I wondered if I'd ever get so big. His big hands explained to me the pulleys on his drill press, showed how just taking apart something often fixed it. I put my feet exactly where his went, looking up, seeing his profile in the light from the side door...he left us, too early. Way too early.

My brother and I would have competitions jumping down those stairs. He usually won. Figured it was because of his red hair. Everyone knew redheads were crazy.

Had to beat him once, just once. I launched myself from the landing quite sure I could hit the bottom with both feet. I did, then lost my foothold and landed on my back, knocking all the wind out of me.

Thought I was going to die. Another kodapain moment.

Summers just zoomed. There were no organized sports back then, just our bikes, riding around, monopoly games with friends, lemonade, scrapes and bruises. One big one, still have the scar. Big, gaping knee laceration. We almost never saw a doctor, and not that time, either. Mom dressed it up.

We had pick up baseball games once or twice. But usually it was just running, chasing each other. Biking. Throwing wildly, smashing the odd window.

Times are different. They just are. No sense whining, and reminiscing, and saying what should and shouldn't be.

But that was, basically, an active childhood. Sure, black and white TV existed. My Favourite Martian, I Dream of Jeannie or Petticoat Junction. The Beverly Hillbillies. And the cartoons, of course. Saturday mornings my folks let us watch the cartoons, for hours. I think about two. With the cereal commercials. And McDonalds...

What else did we do when we weren't crashing around? Crafts. Mechano sets. Lego, electronic kits to wire.

Reading, actual books. For a while...

Then that was it. Helping with vacuuming, dusting, then out the door.

I actually remember my mother pushing us out the door. Not that we required that much of a push...

So that was it. The early days.

It's how life was lived.

Sort of infectious.

Back then.

But doesn't how we live life...always seem to catch on?

Did you enjoy this book? Looking for a next step?
Consider the course on Teachable based on this infor-
mation. Just look under Ron Ireland. It's called,
The Emergence Protocol: Adipose.

Pretty impressive, huh?

Visit Desmond on Instagram, at obrien.desmond.
Connect at ronireland.com.

CPSIA information can be obtained
at www.ICGtesting.com
Printed in the USA
LVOW12s0310240817
546160LV00005B/8/P